GLUTEN-FREE WISH LIST

GLUTEN-FREE WISH LIST

SWEET & SAVORY TREATS YOU'VE MISSED THE MOST

Jeanne Sauvage

Photographs by Eva Kolenko

CHRONICLE BOOKS

SAN FRANCISCO

Library of Congress Cataloging-in-Publication Data available.
ISBN 978-1-4521-3833-6

Manufactured in China

Designed by Alice Chau
Typesetting by DC Typography

Photographs by Eva Kolenko
Food styling by Lillian Kang
Prop styling by Glenn Jenkins

Bisquik is a registered trademark of General Mills, Inc.
Oreos are a registered trademark of Intercontinental Great
Brands LLC.

10 9 8 7 6 5 4 3 2 1

Chronicle Books LLC
680 Second Street
San Francisco, California 94107
www.chroniclebooks.com

ACKNOWLEDGMENTS

Thank you to everyone who made my wishes for this book come true.

To the terrific team at The Lisa Ekus Group: My tireless and amazing agent, Sally Ekus, for seeing the spark of an idea and encouraging me to go for it. To Lisa Ekus, for always being there. To Jaimee Constantine, for her good cheer and for keeping track of all the things!

My wonderful editor, Amy Treadwell, for having faith in me.

The team at Chronicle Books: Peter Perez, David Hawk, Doug Ogan, Alice Chau, Beth Steiner, Tera Killip, and Lesley Bruynesteyn.

To my amazing photographer, Eva Kolenko, and talented stylist, Lillian Kang. Thank you for bringing the recipes to beautiful life.

My recipe testers, who are worth their weight in gold. This book wouldn't be nearly as good as it is without your dedication, good cheer, and hard work (in no particular order): Becca Knox, Jo Treadwell, Sofia Reino, Kate Sawyer, Pam Fillin, Stephanie Colman, Rita Biggs, Lorraine Faubion, Ruth Frobe, Dai Polcari, TJ Lato, Kalliope Dimitrakopoulos, Laurie Robbins, Nikol Mitchell, Monica Kirby, Ivanna Wilianty, Lisa Mitchell, Jeanette Gitzel, Cheryl Samuels, Marie Jensen, Mary Wikle, Terri Toscani, Jo Allen, Carolyn Castagno, Carolyn Houghton, Joe Davidson, Dina Neneux, Joy Manoleros, Amy Fothergill, Sherri Carroll, Katie Dellermann, Karen Murphy, Karen Wilson, Janette Gross, Ruby Hylton, Wendy Harrison, Elena M. Stamm, Christine Goers-Barton, Asha Soares, Alice Shipman, Lynne Knopp, Celine Feagan, Elena Nilsson, Mariette Muijsken, Joni Jensen, Carol Kane, Shirley Gardner, Susan Buentello, Clarissa Fleps, Cathlean Sanada, Cheryl Sloane, Debby Vernon, Terrence Dempsey, Laurie Sanders, Deby Bauer, Marie Puffalt, Gail Grunschel, Debbie Anderson, Jean Bolivar, Linda Hartlaub, Erin Williams, Katherine Polhill, Debbie Ellison, Sharla Ashcraft, Julie Ward, Kathy Imbriani, Pat Ewing, Odile Wolf, Jennifer Carden.

My pal Abra Soule, who helped me to figure out how to organize the testing group.

My dear friend, comrade in arms, and cheerleader, Kim O'Donnel, for your emotional support for this book and always.

My friend Kim Ricketts, who left us too soon but is always in my thoughts. Your support and confidence in my work started me on the book-writing path. I miss you every day.

My mother- and father-in-law, Charlene and Mark Braun, who have served, since my first days of being diagnosed as gluten intolerant, as my baking guinea pigs and also as tireless supporters! I got lucky in the in-law lottery—I feel privileged to be your daughter!

My husband, Jeff, and my daughter, Eleanor, I couldn't have done this book without your unending support and patience and letting me take over every surface in our house with books and papers and baked items. I love you both as high as the sky and as deep as the ocean.

CONTENTS

THE GRANTING OF WISHES

When I was developing and writing my first book, *Gluten-Free Baking for the Holidays: 60 Recipes for Traditional Festive Treats*, I had the good fortune of being surrounded by several amazing women whom I considered my fairy godmothers. They supported and inspired me and were always there to let me know that I could do it and it would be fine. They were instrumental to my getting my wish to write a gluten-free baking book to help gluten-intolerant individuals navigate the baking-dense holiday season.

With this book, it's my turn to be a fairy godmother. I am thrilled to grant the wishes of readers who have written to me over the years asking for gluten-free recipes for their favorite treats. This is the book I've wanted to write for years. I know how hard it is to have a food intolerance and find some or most of your beloved foods suddenly off-limits. It can be devastating. Food is very personal, and it's often wrapped up with memories of childhood and sense of self. If you can't eat the foods linked to your fondest memories or family traditions, it feels like a part of you is missing. Also, it's just plain annoying not to be able to eat a cookie when you want one.

I went through a mourning process when I was first diagnosed with gluten intolerance. The world seemed to be filled with gluten, and I felt like I couldn't eat anything. Of course this wasn't true, but that's how I felt. I didn't get much guidance from my

doctor on how to eat after my diagnosis, and I spent that first year in a bit of a panic, unclear about what I could and couldn't eat. On top of that, I was devastated that baking, my favorite activity, might be off-limits. I spent days agonizing over the fact that not only could I not bake anymore, but I wouldn't be teaching my daughter how to make cookies or how to knead bread.

Eventually, I got out of my funk and made a decision to figure out how to eat again. I came to the conclusion that I had to bake. Baking is a fundamental passion of my life. Although I always thought of it as a hobby, it became clear that it was much more to me—it was a necessity. So I pulled myself together and started on what a friend of mine called "the road to deliciousness." I began to research and experiment with gluten-free baking, and I pored over every book on gluten-free baking that I could find, looking for recipes and techniques that would work for me. Even though all the books and recipes were fine, I realized that I wanted *my* favorite recipes, the ones I had been baking with from childhood and that I missed the most. In addition, I wasn't satisfied with the commercial gluten-free flour mixes I was finding. Some contained beans or other strong-tasting flours, which made my baked goods taste weird; some had too many whole grains, which made my baked items taste gritty; some contained flours that my friends couldn't eat; and others just didn't perform well. I wanted a mix that behaved and tasted as close to all-purpose wheat flour as it could, which is why I decided to create my own recipe. I spent several years of trial and error developing a recipe for a mix that eventually became Jeanne's Gluten-Free All-Purpose Flour (page 39), which is the base ingredient used in most of my baking recipes.

I also came to recognize that I had a second passion: sharing what I baked. I loved having freshly baked treats for myself and my family, but I also wanted to share with others what I baked. I wanted those treats to be accessible to all the different folks in my life, from those who could eat everything to those who had all sorts of food intolerances. As I started to share my new gluten-free treats, I became aware of other common foods that many people with other food sensitivities and allergies couldn't eat. This informed the development of my flour mix, leading me to create a mix that is allergen-free for most people. My flour mix doesn't contain beans, nuts, dairy, or nightshades—all of which are common allergens. In addition, I started seeking out substitutions for common ingredients like butter and eggs so I could create baked items everyone could enjoy.

As my education into the subject proceeded, I found myself learning what each ingredient contributed to the baking process, which allowed me to use each ingredient to its fullest potential. I figured out which ingredients were necessary for successful baking and which ingredients were not as important and could be modified. That lead me to what I consider my bottom line: Although I am flexible on ingredients, I am not flexible on taste or texture. I want to eat baked items that taste like their wheat counterparts. I consider myself a classic baker, so I use classic ingredients like fat and sugar and

starches, as well as classic techniques in order to create baked items that look and taste the way I expect them to.

There's a third component to my passion for baking: sharing knowledge. I am a teacher at heart and helping other people learn how to bake delicious gluten-free treats gives me joy. This is why I started my blog, Art of Gluten-Free Baking. It's why I teach classes, and it's why I write cookbooks. I want parents to be able to give their gluten-free child his or her favorite chocolate chip cookie. I want celiacs to feel welcome at dinner parties by offering great recipes that they can eat with pleasure. And I want every recipe I create to be enjoyed by everyone, whether they adhere to a gluten-free diet or not.

It's no accident that my favorite fairy tale is *Cinderella*—a story about going from despair to joy by wishes made real. Except instead of turning a pumpkin into a fabulous coach, we are turning gluten-free flours into irresistibly delicious pasta, pizza, cookies, cakes, breads, and pastries, and they won't turn back into pumpkins at midnight. All you have to do is turn the page to have all your wishes come true.

CHAPTER 1

HOW TO BAKE GLUTEN-FREE

COMBINING THE OLD AND THE NEW

My job developing delicious gluten-free recipes requires me to know how baking with wheat flour works and how to manipulate this knowledge to address the needs of baking and cooking without gluten. I've learned to be flexible and open to a new paradigm in the kitchen while keeping traditional techniques in sight.

Let's be honest, a lot of gluten-free baked goods aren't very tasty. There are countless recipes available that create flat, gritty, dense, hockey puck–like baked items. And every time the result of a yucky gluten-free recipe is eaten by someone and they hate it, it just reinforces the pervasive notion that gluten-free baked goods are disgusting. I'm here to dispel that notion with the light, flavorful, and—yes—delicious treats you'll find in this book.

I expect nothing short of perfection from my baking. Gluten-free baked items should be excellent baked items, period. They are not just "good for gluten-free," they are simply "good." We can achieve this standard because exceptional gluten-free baking uses the same ingredients—except for the type of flour—and techniques used by excellent wheat baking.

The primary differences between gluten-free baking and wheat baking are the use of a gluten-free flour mix (which includes a gluten-replacer) and, often, how the ingredients are manipulated. Once you find a good recipe, it's important to trust the recipe and to follow it, even though it might contain unusual amounts of common ingredients, different techniques, and textures and batters that look nothing like what you are used to seeing in wheat baking. For example, gluten-free bread dough is often wetter and much softer than wheat-bread dough, which can be confusing if you're expecting the dough to be stiff and easily malleable. When faced with these differences, just go with the flow. The end result will leave you pleasantly surprised, I promise.

WHEAT FLOUR: HOW IT WORKS

In the West, the most commonly used flour for baking is wheat flour, in large part because it contains the most gluten of all of the grains that contain gluten. The grains that contain gluten are all forms of wheat (durum, einkorn, emmer, farro, kamut, and spelt); rye (which includes triticale, a cross between wheat and rye); and barley.

There is an array of wheat flours used for baking and they contain varying amounts of gluten, depending on the purpose of the flour and the type of structure it is required to supply in the baked item. Conventional bread flour, made from hard, or high-protein, wheat, needs more structure and strength to work with yeast, so the gluten percentage is on the high side—13 to 14 percent. Pastry and cake flours are made from soft, or low-protein, wheat and are designed for pastries and cakes, which are more delicate and need less gluten in order to create tender baked items. Pastry flour contains 9 to 10 percent gluten and cake flour contains 7 percent to 9 percent gluten. In the middle is all-purpose flour (whether it's bleached or unbleached), which is the everyday baking flour most wheat-eating people use. It contains 10 to 12 percent gluten.

To understand why gluten is so important to baking, it's useful to know what it is and does. Gluten is a remarkable substance. It is a protein composite made up of two proteins, gliadin and glutenin, that work in tandem with each other. When water is added to these proteins and they are mixed together they tangle around each other, creating what we call "gluten." There are three primary jobs gluten performs in baking. First, it is a binder—it holds baked items together. Second, it provides structure by using its binding function to create a skeleton to which starches adhere. The starches then create a covering for leaveners to push against to create the loft of a baked item. And third, gluten has elasticity. It can be stretched and still hold together without breaking. Not only can it be stretched, it is also malleable, which means that it can be formed into shapes and hold them. Gluten also helps baked items retain moisture, which contributes to prolonging the shelf life of the baked item. The higher the gluten content, the better its shelf life. This is why commercially baked items are often made with a high-gluten flour.

In addition to gluten, wheat flour contains a high percentage of starch, about 70 percent, which plays a crucial role in the baking process. Starch is the often-ignored heavy hitter in baking. Starch works with gluten and ensures that baked goods (like your favorite scones or baguettes) hold their final form. Many gluten-free bakers are so focused on trying to replace or replicate protein that they forget that starch is another key structure-builder in baking. Without gluten, the starches have a hard time holding structure, and without starch, gluten has a hard time forming structure.

THE CRITERIA FOR A GLUTEN-FREE FLOUR MIX FOR EXCELLENT BAKING

No one gluten-free flour adequately substitutes for wheat flour in baking—a mix of different flours is necessary. When I developed my gluten-free flour mix for baking, I kept in mind all the functions that the elements of wheat flour serve in the baking process. A gluten-free flour mix has some pretty big shoes to fill.

A gluten-free flour mix that mimics all-purpose wheat flour needs to meet several criteria:

1. It must have the correct ratio of starches to proteins, with means that it contains mostly starches and a small amount of whole grains and proteins.

2. The alternative flours should be as finely ground as wheat flour so that the baked item is not gritty.

3. It needs to contain a gluten-replacer such as xanthan gum.

4. It should be fairly neutral in taste so that it doesn't interfere with the flavors of the final baked item. This means that your lemon cookies should taste like lemon instead of garbanzo beans.

GLUTEN REPLACERS

The key component of wheat flour that needs to be replicated in a gluten-free flour mix is gluten. There are three main gluten replacers currently in use: xanthan gum, guar gum, and ground seeds such as flax, chia, and psyllium. Each one is a polysaccharide, meaning that it absorbs and holds many times its own weight in moisture. They each serve as a binder, which helps with the structure-building requirement. Unfortunately, they don't all behave in the same way.

Xanthan gum behaves the most like gluten in baking. It's not perfect, but it has excellent binding and structure-building capabilities. And it is pretty good in terms of elasticity. It creates baked items that do not have a flavor or gumminess that can be attributed to the gum. And for most recipes, you only need to use about ¼ tsp of xanthan gum per 1 cup [145 g] of my flour mix. After 15 years of researching gluten-free baking, I've come to prefer xanthan gum for the type of gluten-free baking I do—baking items that mimic their wheat counterparts and taste the way I remember wheat-baked items taste.

Xanthan gum is the product of fermenting *Xanthomonas campestris*, a bacteria. The bacteria is introduced to a sugar solution—which can be made from wheat, corn, soy, dairy, cabbage, or beans—and is broken down during the fermentation process. The resulting xanthan gum is then dried into a powder. It is important to emphasize that the xanthan gum is a product of the process that uses *Xanthomonas campestris* and the sugar medium. It is not, by itself, either of these things—it is something new. This is one of the reasons why xanthan gum can be grown on something like wheat sugar and still be gluten-free. Sugar is not what people react to when they have a gluten sensitivity.

The part of the food people react to is the protein (gluten). Since there is no protein in sugar, there is no gluten in wheat sugar.

Guar gum, another gluten replacer, is made from the guar bean plant. It is pretty good at binding and structure building. But it is much less elastic than xanthan gum. The image that comes to mind when I use guar gum is that of old chewing gum—hard to chew and is not very elastic. Guar gum is fine in a pinch, but it's not my first choice. When I use it, I use about ¼ tsp per 1 cup [145 g] of my flour mix—the same ratio that I use when I use xanthan gum—but it never seems to be the correct ratio for every recipe. In a nutshell, guar gum requires more tweaking than I'm interested in doing.

At first glance, various combinations of ground psyllium, chia, and flax seeds seem to be the holy grail of gluten-replacers, although you have to use a lot (3 to 4 Tbsp in a single recipe). They are good at binding and effective at building structure. And, initially, they appear to be excellent in terms of elasticity. I've used the seeds as gluten-replacers in breads that can be kneaded (although kneading gluten-free bread isn't necessary because there is no gluten to develop) and shaped by hand, and the breads rise, bake, and look just like a wheat loaf. But where they fail is in the end product. First, the seeds can be tasted in the baked item (which isn't necessarily horrible, it's just not what I want). Also, there is a tone of gumminess in the texture, which I find unpleasant. Finally, after a day or two, the baked item separates into gummy chunks. The seeds produce baked items that look good but don't taste or feel the way I want them to. I don't use them as gluten-replacers, but I do use them as egg replacers, where I think they do a great job.

MEASURING INGREDIENTS: THE GREAT WEIGHT VS. VOLUME DEBATE

Here's the deal: I think it's fine to measure by volume (e.g., cups) if that's your preference. I've been measuring by volume for my entire baking career. And my baked items turn out superbly. I often measure by weight, too—that also works out beautifully. Therefore I can't, in good conscience, say that measuring by weight is the only way to measure in order to get the best results, because my experience tells me otherwise. I realize that this stance puts me in the minority of current baking wisdom. I know that bakers outside of the United States measure by weight, which is why I always include weight measurements in my books and on my blog. That said, I'm surrounded by excellent bakers who measure by volume, and I am happy to let them do what they've been doing.

I know baking is a more exacting process than cooking. You can't randomly add an extra pinch of baking powder or dash of flour to a muffin recipe the way you might add another pinch of dried chile peppers to a sauce—the muffins won't turn out well. But baking is not rocket science, and home baking in particular is not so exacting that you are doomed to failure if you are a bit off here and there with your measurements. Home baking has a fairly large margin for error. If you are off by a few grams when measuring the flour or sugar, your cake or cookies will still come out just fine. And that is the kind of difference you get in home baking—grams of error. When you measure by volume, the slight variation you get each time you measure the same ingredient with the same cup is a few grams. If you know weights, grams are tiny amounts.

My bottom line is that both methods work and are fine to use if you're a home baker as long as you follow good measuring practices. If you bake and you like how you measure and your recipes turn out well, you have my blessing to keep doing what you've been doing.

MEASURING FOR SUBSTITUTIONS

There are certain occasions when volume measurements are superior to weight measurements—when you're substituting for various ingredients. My experience is that baked goods turn out better when the substitution is done by volume rather than weight. This is because different items, even if they are similar, have different densities. And the volume (space) the ingredients fill seems to be more important than the weight they have. For example, different kinds of gluten-free flour have different densities and wildly different weights. So, when I substitute one gluten-free flour for another, or when I substitute my gluten-free flour mix for all-purpose wheat flour, the resulting baked item comes out much better if I do the substitution by volume rather than weight.

This holds true when people want to use a gluten-free flour mix in my recipes that is different from my mix. I recommend finding out what a cup of the substitute flour mix weighs, and to make the substitution in a way that matches the volume of my flour.

Another instance where it's important to substitute by volume rather than weight is when you're working with butter and other solid fats. A cup of butter, a cup of butter substitute, and a cup of vegetable shortening all have different weights. With these ingredients, substitute for the volume of the butter versus the weight of butter.

If you don't have United States measuring cups, I recommend you measure with a milliliter measuring cup—240 milliliters is equal to one U.S. cup. It's an unorthodox way to measure but it works so it can be used in a pinch.

GOOD MEASURING PRACTICES

HOW TO MEASURE BY VOLUME

For gluten-free flours and mixes, fluff the flour before measuring it—especially if it's been sitting for a while and the grains have settled. Shake the container or use a whisk to stir the flour a bit before you measure. I measure flours using the "scoop-and-sweep" method. I dip my measuring cup into the ingredient and scoop up a heaping cup of it. I tap the handle of the measuring cup on the side of the container to dislodge any starch that clings to the side of the cup (gluten-free flours tend to be lighter and more prone to static cling), and then I use a straight edge (usually the back of a knife or my kitchen ruler) to sweep off the mound and level it.

HOW TO MEASURE BY WEIGHT

Place the bowl the ingredients are to be measured into on the scale and turn on the scale. If the scale is measuring the weight of the bowl, press "tare" or "zero" to set the starting weight to zero. Pour the first ingredient, carefully and slowly, into the bowl until the scale indicates the weight needed. Press tare (or zero) again to set the scale back to zero. Now you're ready to measure the next ingredient the same way you did the first. Repeat this process for all of the ingredients meant for that bowl.

TEMPERATURE AS AN INGREDIENT

I feel that temperature is one of the most important ingredients in the baking process. The temperature for ingredients is given in the recipes (e.g., butter, cold; or eggs, at room temperature), but it's much more important than those small notes indicate. We're not always aware of it, but temperature comes into play during the baking process in the form of:

1. The ambient temperature of the kitchen

2. The temperature of each individual ingredient

3. The temperature of the bowls and pans

4. The temperature of the mixed batter or dough

5. The temperature of the oven

6. The temperature of the baked item

Quite often, when the temperature of ingredients, dough, or your oven are incorrect, it can result in a baked item that doesn't turn out the way we expect it to. At one time, bakers may have instinctively known this based on their experience. Nowadays, people new to baking often ignore the temperature recommendations, because they don't realize the importance of temperature. To rectify this, I've included directions for the proper temperature for the ingredients or dough in each recipe.

I highly recommend getting an instant-read thermometer if you plan to bake on a regular or even a semi-regular basis. It is one of the most-used tools in my kitchen.

KNOW YOUR OVEN

If you've used more than one oven over the course of your baking career, you know that every oven has its own personality and peculiarities. And, no matter how expensive or new an oven is, it can have quirks that need to be addressed in order to bake the best you can.

One of the biggest causes of baking failures is an oven that doesn't heat to the temperature it says it will. It doesn't matter if your oven cost thousands of dollars or if it is new, chances are it's probably not heating to the temperature you've set it at. Some people have their oven temperature calibrated on a regular basis to make sure that it's heating properly. But if you don't do this, an oven thermometer is an essential tool to have. I recommend that all bakers invest in an oven thermometer. They are cheap (I get mine at the local drugstore) and they can live in your oven. No fuss, no muss, and yet so helpful. In fact, I would go so far as to say that they are necessary. I have two in my oven (and I replace them every few years when they get too grungy to read), and I insist that all of my recipe testers get one, too.

Once you have an oven thermometer, it's helpful to do some tests to see how your oven is heating. First, place the oven thermometer in your oven and heat the oven to 350°F [180°C]. I would heat it for one hour to get a truly accurate reading. After an hour, check the thermometer and see what the temperature is. If the oven temperature

is not at 350°F [180°C], what temperature is it? Keep notes. If your oven heats to 325°F [170°C] when you set it to 350°F [180°C], then you know that you need to set the dial to 350°F [180°F] when you need it to heat to 325°F [170°C].

Second, set the oven to 375°F [190°C] and see what temperature it heats to after an hour. If it heats to 350°F [180°C], then you can make an educated guess that your oven runs 25°F [10°C] colder. Do one more test to see if this is indeed the situation. Heat the oven to 400°F [200°C]. Check the temperature after an hour. If it says 375°F [190°C], then you can be fairly sure that your oven is regularly heating 25°F [10°C] less than your control dial reads.

Alternatively, you can just put the thermometer in your oven, preheat the oven when you need to, and adjust the control dial until the thermometer indicates the temperature at which you need to bake. This method requires more fiddling for each baking session, but it gets the job done.

Regardless, you should check the oven temperature every time you bake—just to make sure the oven is still heating to the temperature you think it's heating to. If you have an old oven, you might have a situation where the oven heats to random temperatures every time.

Many ovens have hot spots and cool spots—areas that tend to be a different temperature than other areas. As a result, items that are positioned in the hot spots will bake more quickly than items in the cool spots, which may translate into (in extreme cases) burned cookies on one part of the baking sheet and underdone cookies on another part of the baking sheet.

You may already know your oven and how to work around the hot and cool spots. But if you don't, and you want to know where they are, use the following brilliant test from the fabulous Dorie Greenspan. She calls it the "litmus paper for your oven" on her blog, and it's done with unsweetened coconut flakes. Here's how it works: Preheat your oven to 350°F [180°C] (she doesn't specify what temperature to use, but this is a good general baking temperature). Spread a layer of unsweetened coconut flakes on a large rimmed baking sheet (the rim is necessary—using a flat baking sheet allows the flakes to spill onto the floor of your oven, creating a different problem) and bake for 2 to 5 minutes. Remove the baking sheet and see where the flakes are brown and where they are still white (or a lighter brown). The brown spots indicate hot spots on your oven. Do this twice—once on the middle rack and once on the bottom rack.

TIPS FOR SUCCESSFUL GLUTEN-FREE BAKING

Many nonbakers are taking up baking because the only way they can enjoy their favorite gluten-free treats is to make them themselves. And many experienced bakers are now baking with gluten-free ingredients, either for themselves or for friends or family members. This is excellent news! The more people are drawn to and enjoy baking, the more my heart flutters with joy. That said, baking is a combination of craft, science, and art—and that means in order to be good at it, you need to practice to gain experience.

I am not saying that you can't bake successfully without years of experience—far from it. I'm saying that there are things you learn each time you bake that inform your next baking session, making it better than the time before. I've been baking my whole life, I teach baking, I write about baking, and I'm still learning about baking. I've learned things from my past experiences, such as how a particular dough or batter behaves and how it should look when it's done baking, that a less experienced baker might not know without being told in a recipe. In this book, I give you tips and visual cues in each recipe so that you know how things should be working in each step. These, in turn, will help you build a body of knowledge that will allow you to become more proficient as you bake.

14 STEPS TO DELICIOUSNESS

Here is a list of tips I've developed to make your baking the most successful it can be—regardless of your experience level.

1. Read the entire recipe before starting. Consider it step 1 of each recipe. You want to be sure that you are prepared for everything the recipe calls for.

2. Gather all of the ingredients and equipment before starting the recipe. This way you are assured that you have

everything you need in the quantities you need. The French call this *mise en place* (literally, "putting in place").

3. Put an oven thermometer in your oven.

4. The first time you make a recipe, follow it exactly—especially if you are new to baking or new to gluten-free baking. Use the exact ingredients and baking pan called for, follow the steps, and bake at the temperature and for the time called for. You are almost guaranteed to fail if you start changing things from the get-go. Once you are comfortable with how a recipe works, then you can start experimenting with changing things.

5. Do not halve or double recipes (unless there are instructions given on how to do so). If you want to make less than the recipe yields, make the entire recipe and then freeze the extra according to the directions. If you want more than the recipe yields, make the recipe multiple times (this is what I do).

6. Use the pan shape and size called for. Pan size is important. For example, changing something as seemingly minor as using an 8-in [20-cm] round cake pan instead of the 9-in [23-cm] round cake pan called for will alter the baking time needed (a smaller pan needs a slightly longer baking time because the batter will be more densely distributed).

7. Understand that substitutions, even recommended substitutions, are not an exact replica of the ingredient originally called for. See page 28 for information on substitutions.

8. If you have little or no experience with baking, start with easier recipes (like cookies and bars) and work up to the harder recipes (like pastries). I've seen novice bakers tackle difficult recipes— like croissants—on their first attempt at baking. They are sorely disappointed when their results are less than stellar, and sometimes this causes them to give up altogether. If you were new to skiing you wouldn't go down the black diamond (advanced) run your first time on the mountain—you would go down the bunny slopes to get the feel of things and gradually work your way up to the more difficult runs.

9. Preheat the oven sufficiently. Most home ovens take at least 15 minutes to get to temperature—and often even longer for it to reach a high temperature (above 400°F [200°C]). Be patient—the time you let the oven preheat is time well spent.

10. Measure accurately and carefully. Pay attention while you're measuring. It doesn't matter if you are measuring by volume (using cups) or weight (using a scale), care is needed when you measure. Sloppy measuring often equals a poor baking outcome.

11. Place your baking pans on the middle rack of your oven unless the recipe states otherwise. Much of the time, you will be baking only one item at a time. If you are using two pans that are too big to fit on the middle rack, then use the middle and lower rack and switch the position of the pans halfway through baking. In addition, unless you have a convection oven, do not put pans on three racks if your oven has them—the upper and lower pans will block the heat from getting to the middle rack and the item there will not bake well.

12. Don't use expired products, (e.g., baking powder, yeast, or xanthan gum). These ingredients are no longer effective after a certain amount of time, hence their expiration date. Also, note that even flours have a use-by date. Old flour can

go rancid and taste unpleasant—usually metallic or musty.

13. Use an instant-read thermometer—it is a surprisingly helpful tool for new and experienced bakers alike. I became a convert to them a few years ago, and now I use one several times throughout the cooking and baking day. In particular, I use mine to test the doneness of bread—most gluten-free breads need to reach an interior temperature of about 205°F [96°C] before they are done. I also use it to check the temperature of water used in a yeasted recipe. And I hold it in the air to spot-check the temperature in different parts of my kitchen. In addition, I use it to check things like the doneness of my roast chicken or grilled hamburgers.

14. If you bake at high altitude (2,000 ft [610 m] or more above sea level), then you might need to make adjustments to the recipe, oven temperature, and baking time. See page 22 for more information on high-altitude baking.

HOW BAKED GOODS BECOME STALE

Home-baked items do not store well for very long unless you freeze them. This is natural—unlike commercially made baked goods, home-baked items do not contain artificial preservatives to keep them fresh for weeks. So, expect a shelf life of days as opposed to weeks for most home-baked items. Before you set about storing your baked goods, it's helpful to know how staling occurs.

Oddly, starch is the ingredient that causes baked items to go stale. Before being mixed and baked, starch molecules are tightly packed in an orderly manner inside the starch granules. When water and heat are added, gelatinization occurs. The starch molecules move around, become disorderly, and form new configurations, creating the structure and the crumb of baked items. (This is a greatly simplified version of what happens).

As soon as a baked item starts to cool, it begins to go stale. As the baked item cools, the starch molecules retrograde: They return to each other and the water that was absorbed during the baking process starts to be squeezed out of the molecules. What was a soft crumb directly after baking begins to become dry, and then hard and crumbly—this is "starch retrogradation," which is basically a fancy term for going stale.

The presence of certain other ingredients helps delay starch retrogradation, including sugars, proteins, and fats. This is why cookies and pastries tend to go stale at a slower rate than unenriched (unsweetened, nondairy, non-egg) bread.

Interestingly, refrigerating baked items accelerates starch retrogradation because it accelerates the cooling process. Contrary to what you might think, storing baked items in the refrigerator is not always effective. According to Harold McGee, noted food scientist, bread stored in the refrigerator goes stale up to six times faster than bread stored in a paper bag at room temperature. This is why you will rarely see instructions in this book for storing baked items in the refrigerator. Room temperature or freezing are the best temperatures for long-term storage. I've included storage recommendations for each recipe.

DEEP-FRYING PRIMER

Deep-frying intimidates a lot of people. But it's actually easy—as well as quite safe—if you just take a few simple precautions.

Use oil that is labeled "high-heat oil" or "high-smoke-point oil." These designations mean that the oil is suitable for deep-frying. Canola oil is a conventional choice, as is peanut oil. My favorite is rice bran oil. It can be difficult to find in grocery stores, but it's available online. Don't use low-heat oils like olive or walnut oil for deep-frying—these delicate oils will start to burn at the high temperatures required for deep-frying.

Also, use a heavy-bottomed pan that is at least 5 in [13 cm] deep for deep-frying. You need at least 3 in [7.5 cm] of oil to properly fry the foods in the deep-frying recipes in this book, so you'll need a pan that is at least twice as deep as the depth of oil called for in the recipe—the oil needs room to rise and bubble as the ingredients are placed in it.

My favorite pan for deep-frying is a 3-qt [2.8-L] heavy-bottomed saucepan. It is 7½ in [19 cm] in diameter and 5 in [13 cm] deep. It is large enough to hold a moderate amount of fried items so that they don't take a long time to fry, but not so big that it's difficult to regulate the oil temperature. Once you place the foods in the oil, the temperature will drop because the items are colder than the heated oil, so you'll likely need to increase the heat in order to bring the oil back to the appropriate temperature.

Keeping the oil temperature constant while you're frying is critical. All of the recipes for deep-frying in this book specify the oil temperature needed to fry each ingredient. Some ingredients are fried at lower temperatures, while others are fried at higher temperatures. It's very important to monitor the temperature of the oil and adjust the burner heat as needed to maintain the correct temperature. If the temperature of the oil stubbornly stays at a temperature lower than is required by the recipe, add some extra time to the frying process. If the oil heat stays higher, fry the items more quickly than called for in the recipe. I have found that big, wide, and/or heavier pans—

enameled cast-iron, in particular—are not good for deep-frying because they retain heat and it's hard to bring the oil back to the desired temperature.

Keep in mind that foods fried at the proper temperature do not absorb as much oil as you'd imagine. As I tested the recipes, I measured the oil level before and after each frying session. Each time the oil level barely dropped, meaning relatively little oil was absorbed by the fried items.

Depending on what foods you've fried in the oil, it can be reused. Let the oil cool completely in the pan to allow any stray pieces of food or flour to settle on the bottom of the pan. Place a fine-mesh strainer over the storage container and slowly pour the oil into the container. Seal the container with a lid and store the oil in the refrigerator for up to two weeks. Used oil goes rancid very quickly.

You should only reuse oil to fry the same or similar items that you fried the first time, because oil takes on some of the flavor of the foods you fry in it. Therefore, reusing oil that was originally used to fry fish to fry doughnuts will create doughnuts that have a fried-fish taste—which isn't very appealing unless you had your heart set on cod-flavored crullers. Some foods, such as fried chicken, leave behind so many particles in the oil that using the oil again isn't really feasible. The particles will burn in the oil when it's heated a second time.

DISPOSING OF USED OIL

First and foremost, do not pour used oil down a drain—it will clog the pipes and it is horrible for the environment. And don't pour it into a garbage can (this is illegal in many cities). Instead, let the oil cool completely (never dispose of hot or warm oil) and pour it back into the container it came in. Replace the cap, and put it in a garbage can. Or, mix the used oil with an absorbent material such as kitty litter, wrap up the litter, and then dispose of it in the trash. Ask a local restaurant if they would allow you to use their waste receptacle for cooking oil. My city, Seattle, has two biodiesel companies that will take used cooking oil. Try an Internet search to see if a similar option exists in your area.

BAKING AT HIGH ALTITUDE

What is considered high altitude? Most references say 3,000 ft [915 m] above sea level. That said, my recipe testers experienced baking challenges at altitudes lower than that. This makes sense to me. Water boils at a different temperature starting at about 2,000 ft [610 m] above sea level. And the air becomes much drier at about 2,500 ft [760 m] above sea level. I think it's safe to assume that 2,000 ft [610 m] and above should be considered "high altitude" when it comes to baking. And if you live above 1,000 ft [305 m], be alert for some quirks in your baking performance.

Because of the lighter air pressure and dry air found at high altitudes, you might need to make some alterations to baking recipes in order to get them to work well. Often high altitude can be a blessing for gluten-free baking because it literally takes the pressure off baked items. One of the challenges of gluten-free baking at sea level is getting the item being baked to rise to its full potential. This isn't a problem with cookies, but it is for cakes and yeasted items, which really get a boost from high-altitude baking.

On the other hand, high altitude can be too much of a good thing. Breads baked at high altitude have a tendency to rise higher and faster and will sometimes overflow the bowl and, later, the baking pan. Cakes may also rise too quickly and too high for the pan to sustain, causing them to rise and then deflate in the oven and turn out disappointingly flat. And the lack of humidity in the air causes some baked items to dry out more quickly, requiring additional liquid to be added to the recipe.

I live at sea level, so these recipes are developed for sea-level conditions. Some of my recipe testers baked at high altitude and helped me develop the following tips

for high-altitude baking. They are mostly guidelines, due to the vagaries that occur at each level. But they should help you make the necessary adjustments to the recipes in order for them to perform well.

The two types of recipes that tend to have the most problems at high altitude are cakes and yeasted items. Cookies and bars usually don't have rising problems, but dryness can be a problem for them starting at about 2,500 ft [760 m].

Common problems with baking at high altitude are:

- Cakes and yeasted items rise too high too quickly and then they fall and become disappointingly flat and dense.

- Cakes and yeasted items might stick to the pan more often.

- All types of recipes might not have enough liquid.

Adjustments to try for high-altitude baking (especially for breads and cakes) are:

- Do not beat the butter, sugar, and eggs as much as the recipe directs for cakes and muffins. Cut beating time in half (except for something like pâte à choux dough, which depends on beating the ingredients well).

- Reduce the amount of baking powder called for by ¼ tsp to ½ tsp.

- Reduce the amount of sugar called for by 1 Tbsp per 1 cup [200 g].

- Increase the amount of liquid called for by 1 to 4 Tbsp (this is especially important if you live in the high desert; experiment and see how the batter or dough looks).

- Increase the oven temperature by 25°F [10°C].

- Follow the directions for greasing and flouring pans.

- When making a sugar syrup, such as the filling for Stroopwafels (page 206), subtract 1°F from the final temperature for each 500 ft [155 m] above sea level.

These are just starting points. Depending on how high you live and what recipe you use, you will need to do some experimenting to see how the recipes behave.

INGREDIENTS

Good baking starts with good ingredients. I buy organic, fresh ingredients whenever possible, and if I'm using ingredients that expire I make sure they haven't reached their expiration date. Gluten-free ingredients can be expensive, but they are much less expensive than processed versions of gluten-free baked items, so I use the difference in cost to buy the best ingredients I can. Also, gluten-free folks often have other intolerances, which means they can't eat commercial versions of many foods. Even though all the recipes in this book are made with dairy, eggs, and nuts as needed, I've included substitution ideas for all of these things to help you bake to your needs.

One question that comes up routinely is where to find ingredients. I often buy ingredients online if I can't find them in my regular grocery or specialty stores. Most online vendors have reasonable shipping costs and delivery times, so I can usually get what I need when I need it.

It's important that you buy ingredients that are labeled "gluten-free." Sometimes it's hard to know if an ingredient is gluten-free if it's not labeled as such. Even if an ingredient is naturally gluten-free, it may have been processed on the same equipment or in the same area of a factory as ingredients containing gluten, making it subject to cross-contamination with gluten. For this reason, I don't recommend buying ingredients in packages that are not labeled "gluten-free."

In addition, I have seen many gluten-free flours in the bulk section of my natural-foods market next to or near ingredients containing gluten, which means there's a high probability of cross-contamination. Consequently, I don't recommend buying flours from bulk bins.

Following is a description of the building blocks for baking that will help you understand what each ingredient does and how it behaves.

BUTTER AND DAIRY PRODUCTS

Butter is the most widely used fat in baking. It tastes good and it creates baked items that have an appealing texture. I use unsalted butter for the recipes in this book, because I like to have control over the amount of salt in my recipes. If you like salted butter and prefer not to use unsalted butter, you may or may not need to reduce the amount of salt in a recipe by a small amount.

For some of the pastries in this book, I recommend using European butter. United States and Canadian regulations call for a minimum of 80 percent milk fat (or butterfat) in butter, with most companies producing butter with minimum of 80 percent milk fat. European regulations, on the other hand, call for a minimum of 82 percent milk fat in butter, and some European companies produce butter with up to 85 percent milk fat. Because of its higher fat content, European butter has less water, which makes it melt at a higher temperature (the more water, the lower the melting temperature). This is important for pastries that rely on butter to stay solid until they are further into the baking process. During the baking process, the solid butter melts between the layers of dough, which creates steam, which in turn creates a pocket between each dough layer. This is what gives pie crusts and laminated dough their flakiness. So, if possible, I highly recommend that you use European butter with at least 82 percent milk fat when it's called for in a recipe.

This leads us to one of the challenges that comes with using butter replacers. Most butter replacers have a higher water content than butter. This can be quite frustrating when using butter replacers in pastry recipes, because butter replacers tend to melt much earlier than needed for those recipes. To combat this, keep dough made with butter replacers colder than you would a batter or dough made with butter. In addition, consider using shortening instead of a butter replacer in a recipe for which the fat staying solid is essential, such as Pie Crust (page 246) and laminated doughs like Puff Pastry Dough (page 96), Croissants (page 147), and Master Danish Pastry Dough (page 154). These recipes perform much better with shortening than they do with butter replacers.

Milk and cream are used in baking recipes because they add body and smoothness to the resulting baked product. Often, you can get away with using water in the place of milk in many recipes, but the taste and feel of the baked item won't be as smooth. See page 28 for milk, cream, and other ingredient substitutions.

EGGS

After flour, eggs are the next most important structure-building ingredient in baking. If you remove both eggs and gluten from your baking, it will be difficult to get the baked item as light and fluffy as you'd like. Eggs also provide moisture to baked items. I typically recommend using extra-large eggs in my recipes. Extra-large eggs are the most uniform of all eggs, and the extra oomph provided by an extra-large egg is always helpful for gluten-free baking.

If you can't find or don't want to buy extra-large eggs, I recommend the following method: Crack as many eggs into a glass measuring cup as you need to reach ¼ cup [60 ml]. If you have a little bit more than ¼ cup [60 ml], beat the eggs well in the measuring cup and then pour out and discard the excess. For information on how to substitute for eggs, see page 29.

GLUTEN-FREE BEER

The recipes for Battered and Fried Fish (page 166) and Fried Onion Rings (page 160) both use gluten-free beer. Over the past few years, gluten-free beer has become easier to find. My local grocery store carries a few brands, as do my local organic co-op and stores like Trader Joe's.

GLUTEN-FREE FLOURS

I get a lot of comments about how expensive gluten-free flours are compared to wheat flour. There are many reasons for this. One of the primary reasons is that gluten-free flours are still considered specialty items and they aren't made in quantities that allow for lower pricing. Also, in the United States, wheat is a subsidized crop—the government pays farmers to grow it—which allows farmers to charge a lower price for their wheat, leading to a lower price for wheat flour at the grocery store. Also, processing gluten-free flours is more expensive than processing wheat flours because the processors have to have their ingredients, equipment, and buildings certified as gluten-free in order to be able to label their products as gluten-free.

My all-purpose flour mix is much less expensive than you might imagine. Buying four flours rather than one, plus xanthan gum, seems rather steep, but each bag of flour that goes into my mix makes several batches of the mix, making the cost fairly reasonable as far as gluten-free mixes go. This is one of the reasons I make the recipe available for people who want to prepare their own mix—it helps keep expenses down.

My Flour Mix

I developed my gluten-free flour mix over the course of several years. The more I baked gluten-free, the more I learned about how different flours and other ingredients behaved. In addition, when I started to bake for other people, I realized that many of them had other food intolerances in addition to gluten. So it was important to me to make my flour mix as allergen-free as possible. My mix doesn't contain corn products or nightshades (in the form of potato flour or starch). In addition, my daughter has a life-threatening allergy to peanuts, which comes with a sensitivity to soy, so my mix doesn't use soy flour (or any bean flours, for that matter—they have too strong of a taste and they go rancid quickly). Also, my husband has a sensitivity to almonds, so almond flour isn't in the mix. And I react to oats—the oats themselves, not just cross-contaminated oats—so there's no oat flour in the mix.

The end result is a mix that I call Jeanne's Gluten-Free All-Purpose Flour (page 39). It contains brown rice flour, white rice flour, sweet (white) rice flour (also known as glutinous rice flour), tapioca flour, plus a little bit of xanthan gum. Not only does this mix work very well in baking, it contains easy-to-find ingredients that you can combine yourself—which saves money.

Over the years, people have asked me for ideas on how to substitute for various flours in my mix. At first I was happy to figure out substitutes. As time went on, people began to use substitutes that were farther and farther away from the flours in my original mix. Their baked items weren't turning out as well as they would like, because the substitutes weren't behaving as well as the original ingredients. Then I heard from a reader who used substitutes for all the flours in the mix and wanted to know how to substitute for one of the substitutes. This was the final straw for me. My mix works well because of its ingredients. It wasn't developed haphazardly; it was the result of research and experimentation. While there are one or two commercial mixes that I can recommend (see Sources for Ingredients and Equipment, page 250) as substitutes for my mix, for the most part, I can no longer recommend in good conscience substitutes for the individual flours other than using potato starch (versus potato flour) as a substitute for tapioca starch. Other than that, I've found that using substitutes in the flour mix take the baker away from the excellent results that people have come to expect from recipes made using my flour mix.

If you do use substitutes for my flour mix in these recipes, it's best if you make the substitutions by volume versus by weight. See Measuring for Substitutions (page 14) for more information.

Sorghum Flour

There are a couple of recipes in this book, such as Animal Crackers (page 209) and Graham Crackers (page 210), that use sorghum flour (also known as sweet sorghum flour) in addition to my flour mix in order to give the recipe a more whole-grain taste. Also, Sourdough Starter (page 88) uses sorghum flour.

Tapioca Flour

In addition to using it in my flour mix, I use tapioca flour—also known as tapioca starch—to flour rolling surfaces and baking pans. In general, I don't use my flour mix for these jobs because it contains xanthan gum, which is a binder, so it makes things stick together. Tapioca flour is ideal for dusting because it is quite fine and doesn't add a gritty texture to the doughs being rolled or baked.

Some people report that they don't like the taste of certain brands of tapioca flour. I suspect that they are using tapioca flour that has gone bad. Tapioca flour is quite mild and really doesn't have much of a taste. But if it goes bad, it has an unpleasant metallic taste. So, if the tapioca flour you're using tastes metallic, it has gone bad and you should throw it out and get a new bag.

Teff Flour

Teff flour is made from a grain from Ethiopia that has gained popularity in the United States recently. Teff flour is the best flour with which to create a gluten-free sourdough starter (see page 88). My local organic grocery store carries it, but if you can't find it in your city or town, it can be ordered online (see Sources for Ingredients and Equipment, page 250).

LEAVENERS

Leaveners create the rise and the air pockets in baked items, which gives the baked goods their texture. The three primary leaveners in baking are baking soda, baking powder, and yeast. Steam also acts as a leavener in certain cakes and pastries.

Baking Powder

Single-acting baking powder is baking soda mixed with an acid (plus a starch to keep it dry). It was initially developed for use in recipes that didn't include an acid. Because it contains its own acid, it could work in any recipe. But single-acting baking powder doesn't solve the need for a leavener that

will work even after a batter has been mixed and let sit for some time.

Double-acting baking powder solves this problem. It contains two leaveners, one that is activated by the acid ingredient in the powder, and another that is activated by the heat of the oven. This allows the baker to mix up a dough or batter and let it rest for some amount of time before being baked without the dough or batter losing all of its leavening power. Double-acting baking powder is stronger than single-acting because of its double leavening actions. I recommend it for gluten-free baking, which needs all of the leavening it can get.

There is one issue to be aware of with certain kinds of double-acting baking powder. The second leavening acid that works in the oven is often sodium aluminum sulfate (SAS). The problem with SAS (in addition to it being aluminum) is that it has a distinctive and bitter metallic taste that is apparent in baked items and unpleasant for many people. This taste is especially noticeable in gluten-free baking because more baking powder is often needed. If you want to avoid risking an unpleasant taste turning up in your baked goods, look for a double-acting baking powder that is labeled "aluminum-free" (or that does not have SAS on the label).

A final note regarding baking powder: Starch is added to baking powder to keep the leaveners in it from reacting to moisture in the air after the container has been opened. In the United States and Canada, the starch is often corn. In the United Kingdom, the starch is often wheat. Be sure to read the label to make sure that the ingredients are gluten-free.

Baking soda

Also known as bicarbonate of soda, baking soda is simply sodium bicarbonate, a chemical that is activated by acid. When baking soda comes into contact with an acid in a liquid environment (e.g., dough or batter), it will fizz and bubble, creating carbon dioxide gas that pushes on the dough to create the rise and air pockets. Examples of acidic ingredients in baking that work with baking soda include buttermilk, brown sugar, lemon juice, vinegar, honey, unsweetened cocoa (except for the Dutch process kind, from which the acidity has been removed), molasses, and fruits. The limitation of baking soda is that it works immediately on contact with moisture and acid, so it is not a good leavener to use by itself in recipes that need to sit for a while after being mixed.

Yeast

A natural leavener that is most often used in bread, yeast is a living thing—a tiny fungus. When it eats food (starches and sugars) and drinks water, it expels gas, which produces a rise in baked goods. Since yeast is a living thing, it can and does replicate itself. At its optimal temperature, yeast doubles in about 90 minutes. This means that yeast functions like a little leavener factory, making its rising capabilities prodigious. You can also manipulate yeast to make it grow faster or slower depending on what you feed it (dough elements) and at what temperature.

Grocery stores typically carry several different versions of baking yeast, and it can be unclear which one to use because they are not all alike. Currently, there are three types of baking yeast in markets: fresh compressed yeast (which usually comes in cakes that are in the refrigerated section); active dry yeast; and instant yeast.

Fresh compressed yeast is often favored by artisanal and commercial bakers. It really is fresh, which means that it is viable for only a few days, which is why it is located in the refrigerated section of a grocery store.

Because it doesn't last very long, it's not a practical yeast to use in everyday baking.

Active dry yeast is what I grew up using. Indeed, I've always used it until recently. Active dry yeast has been dried, treated, and packaged to stay stable on the shelf. Active dry yeast seems to be the most widely available yeast in most grocery stores. It comes in jars, packets, and large bags. It can be stored at room temperature until opened, and then it needs to be stored in the refrigerator. Active dry yeast requires that you rehydrate it before using it—hence the instructions in baking recipes to "proof" the yeast, or prove that it works by activating it (placing it in warm water, stirring, and waiting until it bubbles).

A third kind of yeast—instant yeast—is what I prefer to use now. It, too, has been dried, treated, and packaged for shelf stability. The beauty of instant yeast is that it can be added to a recipe along with the dry ingredients. Instant yeast allows you to bypass the rehydrating step, which saves a little time. I use it for almost all of my yeasted recipes.

When you're buying instant yeast, be aware of the bewildering array of names manufacturers have given it: Bread Machine yeast, Rapid-Rise yeast, Quick-Rise yeast, and Perfect-Rise yeast. These are all instant yeasts. Also, I have found that different brands have different tastes that can affect the flavor of the resulting baked item. You may need to experiment to find one that you prefer. I prefer Red Star Quick Rise yeast.

Most commercial yeasts are gluten-free and they state that fact on the containers (albeit sometimes in very tiny print). As of this writing, there is one yeast, Red Star's Platinum Yeast, that *does* contain gluten. It contains dough conditioners and other additives, and some of those additives contain gluten. Always read the ingredient list on the package carefully.

Yeast comes in a variety of packaging, including packets, small jars, and bags. I recommend the jarred yeast, which is the easiest to measure from. The packages contain 2¼ tsp [7 g] of yeast, which some manufacturers call a "scant tablespoon." Since 1 Tbsp is the equivalent of 3 tsp, the packages are nowhere near 1 Tbsp, scant or not. Most of the recipes in this book call for amounts that do not correspond with the amounts in the packets, making the packets less practical here.

OIL

Several recipes in this book call for a neutral-tasting oil, either as an ingredient or for deep-frying. In these cases, I like to use rice bran oil. It has a very bland flavor, which doesn't interfere with the other flavors in the recipe; it is a high-smoke-point oil, meaning that it can be used at high temperatures for deep-frying without burning; and it is fairly hypoallergenic. If you don't want to use rice bran oil, canola oil is a good substitute. Store any oil you have in a cool dark place so that it doesn't go rancid. (Oils go rancid much more quickly than most people realize.)

RAW QUINOA FLAKES

Two recipes in this book, Oat-Free Granola (page 153) and Quinoa Flake Cookies (page 198), use raw quinoa flakes instead of rolled oats. A few years ago I discovered that I react to oats (as do many other gluten-intolerant or -sensitive people). I mean the oats themselves—not just oats that have been cross-contaminated with gluten. I learned that there is a prolamine in oats,

called avenin, that is similar to gliadin, the prolamine in gluten. Now I use quinoa flakes instead of oats in my recipes. One thing to keep in mind when you're buying quinoa flakes is to be sure you buy raw quinoa flakes and not the crispy quinoa breakfast flakes that are like cornflakes.

SUGAR

In addition to making baked items sweet, sugar acts with fats and eggs as a leavener by incorporating air bubbles into the batter while it's being mixed and beaten. It also serves as a preservative, allowing sweetened baked items to be stored longer than unsweetened items. It serves as a food for yeast, making yeast speed up a bit and work faster. And it attracts water, creating a fine crumb in cakes and muffins.

In this book, I use three primary types of sugar: granulated sugar, brown sugar (mostly dark brown sugar, which I like for its taste), and confectioners' (or powdered) sugar. For information on how to substitute for cane sugar, see facing page.

VANILLA EXTRACT

We used to think that alcohol made with a grain that contains gluten (such as wheat or rye) also contained gluten. This generated a belief that flavoring extracts, including vanilla, could potentially contain gluten because they contain alcohol. We now know that the gluten protein is too big to get through the distillation process, which means that flavoring extracts are gluten-free.

INGREDIENT SUBSTITUTIONS

If you're gluten-intolerant, chances are good that you have some other food intolerances as well. Depending on what foods

you can't eat, your intolerances can make gluten-free baking more challenging than it already is because you need to substitute for more than just ingredients containing gluten.

One thing to keep in mind with regard to substituting ingredients is that the farther away you get from the ingredient you're replacing, the less likely it is that the baked item will perform or taste the way the original does.

BUTTER

In nonpastry recipes, use any kind of butter replacer you like. It's best to use the stick form instead of the tub form if you can find it (the stick form has less water and performs a bit better than the tub form). Many butter substitutes are quite salty. If this is the case with the one you're using, reduce the salt in the recipe by ¼ tsp for each ½ cup [110 g] of butter replacer used.

To replace melted butter brushed on top of dough prior to baking, use vegetable oil.

To replace the butter in a laminated dough, use shortening instead of a butter replacer. Butter replacers tend to be too watery, and they melt too quickly to work well in laminated doughs. Note that shortening tends to have a radically different weight than the same amount of butter; therefore, you need to substitute by volume rather than by weight. Most shortening comes in a tub—this is fine because shortening contains no water.

BUTTERMILK

For every 1 cup [240 ml] of buttermilk, place 1 Tbsp of apple cider vinegar, white distilled vinegar, or lemon juice in a cup measure. Fill to the 1-cup [240-ml] mark with any dairy-free milk you like and whisk to combine. The milk might separate and curdle, but it will still work fine in recipes.

CANE SUGAR

The most common type of sugar available is cane sugar. This is what most forms of

sugar, including granulated sugar, brown sugar, and confectioners' sugar, are made from. If you can't or don't want to use cane sugar, use the following alternatives.

Beet granulated sugar is interchangeable with cane sugar and it comes in a variety of forms.

Coconut palm sugar comes in a variety of forms. It has a deeper and stronger flavor than cane granulated sugar, and it also tends to be lower on the glycemic index, which is nice for people who have health problems that are exacerbated by sugar.

Maple sugar is a nice sugar to use, but it tastes like maple, so keep that in mind. Experiment with it and see how you like it in your recipes.

CHEESE

Use your favorite dairy-free cheese.

CREAM

Canned coconut milk comes with a layer of cream at the top. I skim it off and substitute it for cream in recipes. It can even be whipped.

CREAM CHEESE

Use a dairy-free cream cheese of your choice.

EGGS

Eggs are one of the most difficult ingredients to substitute for successfully, because they provide so much structure and fluffiness to baked items. Most of the time, using a non-egg egg substitute will create a baked item that is a bit denser and rises flatter than one made with eggs.

Duck eggs

If you can tolerate duck eggs (and if you can find them), one duck egg can be substituted for one extra-large chicken egg. One duck egg usually measures out to a little over ¼ cup [60 ml], whereas one extra-large chicken egg measures out to be a little under ¼ cup [60 ml]. My local farmers' market has a vendor who carries duck eggs, and my local butcher carries duck eggs at certain times of the year.

Egg Yolks
Use 1 Tbsp of vegetable oil for each egg yolk.

Ground Flax Seeds Mixed with Hot Water
For 1 extra-large egg, place 1 Tbsp of ground flax seeds in a glass measuring cup. Pour hot water into the cup until you reach the ¼-cup [60-ml] mark, and whisk to combine. Let the mixture sit at room temperature, whisking often, for 20 minutes. This gives the flax seeds time to absorb the water and become a gel, and it gives the mixture time to cool. After 20 minutes, whisk again and use as you would an egg. If you are using it in a dough that needs to be cold (like pastry), chill the mixture before adding it to the dough. If you are using it in a yeasted item, also add an extra ½ tsp of aluminum-free double-acting baking powder for each egg called for in the recipe.

Ground flax seeds do not substitute well for eggs in meringue (whipped egg whites), pastry cream, pasta, gnocchi, ramen noodles, pâte à choux dough, funnel cakes, popovers, or an egg wash.

For an egg wash, substitute vegetable oil. It will add a sheen to the top but won't brown as an egg wash would.

ICE CREAM
Use any dairy-free ice cream you like.

MILK
Substitute a dairy-free milk of your choice. It's best to use a dairy-free milk that has some body instead of a watery one. I don't recommend using rice milk if you can find another choice you like.

SOUR CREAM (IN BAKED ITEMS)
Use your favorite unsweetened nondairy yogurt.

EQUIPMENT

BAKING PANS
The most important quality in a baking pan is that it be made out of metal. The exception to this is pie pans (discussed following). Baking pans made of other materials—like silicone or plastic—do not perform as well or as consistently as metal pans because they conduct heat in different ways. Glass and ceramic pans can work well, but their performance is uneven across the various brands, which is why I usually steer people away from them. I'm asked a lot of questions about failed baking endeavors, and the reason for the failure is often related to the type of pan used. In addition to metal, I recommend purchasing pans that are heavy-duty and that are made of aluminum-coated steel. Heavy-duty pans are a bit more expensive, but they perform well and will last a lifetime if you treat them well.

For the recipes in this book, you will need the following.

Half-Sheet Pans
Measuring 18 by 13 in [46 by 33 cm], these pans are a particular weakness of mine. My favorite type is a rimmed style with a textured bottom. The rim catches crumbs that might otherwise fall off onto the oven floor. And the textured bottom allows air-flow underneath the item(s) being baked,

promoting more even baking. I use them for baking and for cookie sheets. In addition to baking, half-sheet pans are useful for staging, rising, and cooling areas for various recipes. I recommend having two.

Loaf Pans

Loaf pans are essential for making sandwich bread. I recommend an 8½-by-4½-in [22-by-11-cm] pan (1-lb [455-g]) and a 9-by-5-in [23-by-12-cm] loaf pan (2-lb [900-g]).

Muffin Pans

Standard-size muffin pans come in either 6- or 12-portion sizes. I recommend getting one 12-portion and two 6-portion pans for the most flexibility.

Pie Pan

I prefer glass pie pans. They seem to work the best to create the flakiest pies. If you want a basic, do-it-all pie pan, I recommend a 9-in [23-cm] glass Pyrex pan—it's a workhorse. The one instance where I do recommend using a metal pie pan is when you need to freeze a pie crust for later use—a metal pie pan is the best for this.

Springform Pan

This is a round pan with a removable side. They usually range in diameter from 6 to 12 in [15 to 30 cm]. A 9-in [23-cm] springform pan is the perfect vessel for a basic cheesecake (see page 240).

Square Pan

Square baking pans are must-haves. There are so many recipes in the baking world that require them.

BAKING STONE

A baking stone absorbs and amplifies the heat in an oven and is used for baking bread and pizza. It can be used as the baking surface itself, or in tandem with a baking sheet. If you plan to make pizza and/or breads on a regular basis, a baking stone is worth

having. They come in a variety of shapes and sizes and are made out of ceramic or steel. The one I have is 14½ in [37 cm] in diameter and is ceramic.

BALLOON WHISK

There are so many uses for a balloon whisk. Every baker should have at least one, preferably made of stainless steel.

BENCH SCRAPER (OR BENCH CUTTER)

This is a recent addition to my kitchen and now that I have one, I love it. It's so handy for cutting and measuring dough (my scraper has a ruler on the scraper part) and for scraping dough pieces off working surfaces and rolling pins.

CANDY THERMOMETER

This is a must-have for deep-frying, because deep-fried recipes require that the oil be heated to a specific temperature in order to cook well—you'll need one of these to measure the temperature. It's best to get one that has an easy-to-read mark at least every 5 degrees.

CAST-IRON SKILLET

I love my cast-iron skillets. Once seasoned, a cast-iron skillet is virtually nonstick. I use a 12-in [30-cm] skillet to cook everything from English muffins (see page 134) to naan (see page 64). It can also function as a baking stone if you don't have the latter because it can withstand high temperatures.

COOKIE CUTTERS

I've been baking for a long time, so I have enough cookie cutters to stock a baking store. For basic dough-cutting needs, two sets are sufficient—a round set and a square set. Each set should have a range of sizes.

DOUGHNUT CUTTER

A doughnut cutter is one of those things you don't realize that you need until you need it. It only took a couple of times of cutting out doughnut dough with two cookie cutters for me to realize that a doughnut cutter would save time and effort. In addition, my doughnuts look a bit more even, which is nice.

ELECTRIC HAND MIXER

If you can't afford or don't want to buy a heavy-duty stand mixer, a hand mixer will work fine—especially if you're a casual or infrequent baker. The newer ones even come with dough hooks, which you will use when making the bread recipes in this book. I have both a stand mixer and a hand mixer. I find the hand mixer to be useful for smaller baking projects or for recipes that require two different things to be beaten or whipped at the same time.

HEAVY-DUTY STAND MIXER

Almost all of the recipes in this book use a heavy-duty stand mixer. I have a 5-qt [4.7-L] mixer that has whisk, paddle, and dough hook attachments. It has served me well for 15 years (and through two cookbooks) and counting. I think this is the optimal size for home baking needs. If you're purchasing a new mixer, I, like Goldilocks, recommend getting one that is not too big or too small. The ones I've used while teaching at cooking schools are often a bit too large to comfortably fit recipes meant for a home cook, while others are too small. I recommend getting one that is in the 4.5- to 5-qt [4- to 4.8-L] bowl capacity range. Any larger and your ingredients will rattle around in the large bowl. Any smaller and the batter in some recipes may jump out of the mixer during beating.

Also, to save money, you might want to consider purchasing a stand mixer that has been reconditioned, which means that it has been used, returned to the company, fixed, and then re-sold at a lower price. When you buy a reconditioned stand mixer, you are basically getting a new machine at a used-machine price.

INSTANT-READ THERMOMETER

Over the years I have come to rely on my instant-read thermometer. It does so much and it is a relatively inexpensive gadget. I use it to help me track temperatures throughout the baking process, including temperatures indicating when the interior of breads are done, how warm my "warm" water is, and the ambient temperature.

LAME

A *lame* (pronounced "lahm") is a bread-maker's tool that is basically a razor on a stick. It is used to make slashes in the tops of bread dough before being baked. It's a fun tool to have if you bake a lot of bread, but a sharp knife works well, too.

MEASURING SPOONS AND CUPS

A set of measuring cups and spoons is essential if you are going to measure by volume. I recommend getting good-quality metal versions. They are invaluable for measuring dry ingredients and small amounts of liquids like extracts and oils. I have two sets of each and I often use both of them during a single baking session. A standard set of American dry measuring cups should include ¼-cup [60-ml], ⅓-cup [80-ml], ½-cup [120-ml], and 1-cup [240-ml] scoops. It is important to get a set that corresponds to these cup/ml measurements. English or European dry measuring cups often have slightly different measures, with 1 cup equaling 250 ml—which is not accurate for the recipes in this book. I also recommend acquiring a glass 2-cup [480-ml] volume measure for liquids.

METAL TONGS

Also called clamshell tongs or locking tongs, these are excellent for baking as well as cooking. I use mine with any deep-fried recipe to pick up the items being fried, as well as for removing waffles from a waffle-cone iron, among other things. My favorite pair is 12 in [30 cm] in length.

OVEN THERMOMETER

An oven thermometer is one of the most important pieces of equipment for a baker. A lot of the baking failures reported by my readers are due to an incorrectly heated oven. Many ovens, no matter how fancy or new, do not heat to the temperature indicated on the control dial. For this reason, I recommend that every baker place an oven thermometer in their oven.

PARCHMENT PAPER

For most baking projects, I prefer to use parchment paper to line my baking sheets rather than greasing them or using a Silpat mat. A Silpat mat can sometimes change the time needed for baking or the texture of the baked item. And greasing a pan is messy and requires more cleanup. The parchment paper I use can be composted, which is a bonus.

PASTRY BAG AND TIPS

There are a few recipes in this book that call for piping out dough into shapes or piping fillings into pastries. If you've never used a pastry bag before, it can seem a bit daunting. There seem to be a zillion different bag and tip sizes and types; but they are easy to use. The basic idea is, the pastry bag holds the dough (or filling) to be piped, and the tip controls the shape and amount of dough that comes out of the bag.

Pastry bags come in a variety of materials: clear plastic, a flexible type of opaque plastic fabric, and parchment paper. I like

the plastic fabric bags. They are sturdy and can be washed and reused many times. My favorite is the Ateco 14-in [35-cm] bag—this seems to be a good basic size, not too small and not too large for most home-baking projects. Pastry bags usually come with a small hole at the bottom, which you may need to cut a bit to accommodate a coupler or a large tip. I generally have two bags—one that's cut for a coupler and one that's cut for large tips.

Tips are the little metal cones that go on the end of the pastry bag. They come in an endless variety of sizes and shapes. They usually have a number, which corresponds to the size and shape of the tip. I like Ateco tips—they are strong and hold up over the years. If you're using a small tip, then you usually need to use a coupler with it in order to keep it on the bag. A coupler is a two-piece gadget that fits on the small end of the bag and holds the tip in place.

To use a coupler, unscrew it to separate it into two parts and put the longer, threaded part of the coupler into the pastry bag and push it down until a portion of it sticks out of the end of the bag. Then place the pastry tip (usually metal) onto the end of the coupler that is sticking out of the bag. Screw on the ring of the coupler to hold the tip in place. You will be screwing it onto part of the bag as well.

If you're using a large tip, you don't need a coupler. You can just put the tip inside the bag and push it down through the small end of the bag so there is enough of the tip sticking out to create the shape of the dough being piped, but so that it doesn't push all the way out of the bag.

Filling a pastry bag can be awkward—it sometimes feels to me like I'm wrangling an octopus. The secret to doing it with the least fuss and muss is to place the bag (already fitted with the tip) in a tall drinking glass. Fold the open end of the bag up and over the lip of the glass. Then use a spoon or rubber spatula to fill the bag. When you've filled the bag about halfway, carefully pull the sides of the bag straight up. Holding the top of the bag in one hand, use your other hand to squeeze the dough down toward the small end where the tip is. Keep the tip end in the glass until a bit of the dough comes out—this way you won't accidentally squeeze dough all over the counter. Then twist the large, unfilled end of the bag several times to further push the dough down to the tip and to make sure the dough doesn't come out at the top. Hold the bag with one hand at the twisted end (to keep the end twisted and the dough from coming out of that end) and the other hand at the end with the tip.

PASTRY BRUSH

I use pastry brushes all the time for brushing oil into pans or bowls, brushing an egg wash on top of pastries, and brushing off excess flour on my rolling surface. I have three: a silicone brush that I use for brushing hot surfaces like preheated cast-iron skillets; a boar's-hair brush for brushing dry ingredients like flour off a dough that needs to be fried or baked; and another boar's-hair brush for brushing wet ingredients like an egg wash or melted butter onto the tops of buns.

PIZZA PEEL

A pizza peel is a shovel-like tool for sliding large and unwieldy items like pizza on and off a baking stone in an oven. If you plan to make a lot of pizza, a pizza peel is very useful.

PLASTIC DOUGH-RISING CONTAINERS

I have three 2-qt [2-L] containers and three 4-qt [3.8-L] containers that I use for letting yeasted dough sit, rest, and rise. Buy containers that are BPA-free.

PLASTIC WRAP

Plastic wrap is an excellent tool in the baking kitchen. I use it to cover doughs and batters before they are baked so they don't dry out, and to wrap doughs for storage in the refrigerator or freezer. Often, you can reuse a piece of plastic wrap because in many cases it doesn't really touch the batter or it doesn't come away with dough. As I tested recipes for this book, I used several pieces of plastic wrap over and over again to cover things.

In addition, rolling out dough between two pieces of plastic wrap is an excellent way to ease into the art of rolling out a pie crust. Gluten-free pie crust dough is more delicate than wheat-flour pie crust dough and it can be challenging to roll out if you're not used to it.

PORTION SCOOPS

I have to come to love portion scoops. They look like ice-cream scoops (in fact, an ice-cream scoop is just a big portion scoop) and they are extremely helpful for portioning out a specific amount of dough—like cookie or cream puff dough—over and over again. I recommend getting a 1-Tbsp scoop and a 1-tsp scoop.

ROLLING PINS

Every baker needs at least one heavy-duty rolling pin. I recommend that you get a good, solid, wooden rolling pin that is 18 to 19 in [46 to 48 cm] long. All of my rolling pins are made of wood, which in my experience is the best material for rolling pins. Nevertheless, there are many types of rolling pins on the market, so choose the one that works best for you. I also have a small Asian rolling pin that is 14 in [36 cm] long and ¾ in [2 cm] wide. Asian rolling pins are narrow and light, and they're handy for rolling out smaller amounts of dough, such as pasta, wonton wrappers, or smaller pieces of pastry, like cut croissant dough. In fact, I have many different shapes of rolling pins and I cycle in and out of which is my favorite at any given time.

SCALE

Many people prefer to measure ingredients by weight rather than by volume. A scale is useful for all sorts of other applications, including portioning out amounts of dough to be used in a recipe. I use mine almost every day—for both cooking and baking. I recommend getting one that measures in at least 1-gram increments.

TAPE MEASURE AND/OR RULER

These tools are invaluable for a baker. Many of the recipes in this book require you to roll a piece of dough to a certain length or width, and you'll need a clean measuring tool for the job. In addition to a long metal ruler, I use a retractable measuring tape that I got at a hardware store.

WAX PAPER

Rolling out cookies and flatbreads between two sheets of wax paper is an excellent way to manage what can be a challenging process. The wax paper holds the dough together, minimizes cracks, and also creates a less messy rolling situation because there's no flour flying around.

WIRE RACKS

Wire racks are must-haves for baking. They are useful not only for cooling baked items, but also for cooling deep-fried items, as well as for placing over a baking sheet to catch glaze dripping off doughnuts or pastries while the glaze sets. I recommend buying two large wire racks that are 18 by 10 in [46 by 25 cm].

WOODEN DOUGH-ROLLING BOARD

If you plan to make a lot of bread or pastry and you don't have continuous surface counters, I highly recommend that you invest in a good-quality wooden board for rolling dough. I have tile countertops, so I always need a separate surface on which to roll dough. I use a large, reversible, maple cutting board that is 20 by 15 by 1½ in [51 by 38 by 4 cm]. I consider it one of the best investments I've ever made for my kitchen. It's big enough to accommodate dough that needs to be rolled extra long (like laminated doughs), but not so big that it's awkward to use. It's heavy-duty and solid, and it's gorgeous. I have a small kitchen, so I just lean it against a wall when I'm not using it.

SPECIALTY EQUIPMENT

CHALLAH BAKING FORM

I was never fully satisfied with the texture of the braided challah recipes I developed, and my testers were equally as lukewarm on them. Then I discovered a challah baking form. It works like a loaf pan, but it imprints the shape of braiding on the top. This pan comes in two models: a braided straight loaf pan for weekly Sabbath challah, and a braided ring loaf pan for holiday challah.

CRÊPE PAN

I like the traditional French crêpe pans that are made of steel. You have to season them before you use them, but once you do, they are virtually nonstick.

DOUGHNUT PAN

Used for baked doughnut recipes. I have two—one for standard-size doughnuts and another for mini doughnuts.

FOOD PROCESSOR

I don't use a food processor very often. It is a good tool to have on hand if you make a lot of pies or pastries that require cold butter to be cut into them. But otherwise, I don't use it enough to recommend it as a must-have for a baker.

HAMBURGER BUN PAN AND HOT DOG BUN PAN

These two pans are essential for making gluten-free buns, because the dough is too loose to shape. These pans create buns that have the light and airy crumb that are necessary to good hamburger and hot dog buns.

POPOVER PAN

A popover pan is necessary if you like making popovers. I've found that muffin pans don't work quite as well as the specialized popover pans do.

POTATO RICER

This is an instrument that is used to mash cooked potatoes by forcing them through a disk with small holes in it. I like to use one for mashing potatoes for gnocchi and for *lefse* so there are no big chunks that will interfere with the shaping of the doughs.

WAFFLE-CONE IRON

I use a special waffle-cone iron to make waffle cones and stroopwafel cookies. It's a neat gadget to have—I love playing with it.

JEANNE'S GLUTEN-FREE ALL-PURPOSE FLOUR

MAKES 4½ CUPS [650 G]

Use this flour mix cup-for-cup for the flour in any recipe that calls for all-purpose flour (see Measuring for Substitutions on page 14). Because of density differences, I've found that it's best if you substitute by volume rather than by weight (even if you do all of your other measuring by weight). If you do not have American measuring cups, use a milliliter cup to measure the flour—240 ml is approximately equivalent to one U.S. cup (it's an unusual way to measure, but it will work). One cup of Jeanne's Gluten-Free All-Purpose Flour weighs 145 grams. The recipe can be multiplied as needed.

1¼ cups [170 g] brown rice flour
1¼ cups [200 g] white rice flour
1 cup [160 g] sweet (white) rice flour (glutinous rice flour)
1 cup [120 g] tapioca flour
Scant 2 tsp xanthan gum

In a large bowl, whisk together the brown rice flour, white rice flour, sweet rice flour, tapioca flour, and xanthan gum. Transfer to an airtight container.

Store in a cool, dark place for up to 4 weeks, in the refrigerator for up to 2 months, or in the freezer for up to 6 months.

GLUTEN-FREE SELF-RISING FLOUR

Despite the fact that I was born and raised in California, I have a strong affinity with the South and feel that I am a Southern girl at heart. Southerners love to use self-rising flour, especially in biscuits. Self-rising flour is just all-purpose flour to which a leavener (usually baking powder) and salt have been added. I developed this mix to be able to easily adapt Southern recipes that call for self-rising flour. This flour mix expires when the baking powder expires, so write the expiration date of the baking powder on the container you're using to store the self-rising flour. The recipe can be multiplied as needed. Use this mix for Simple and Easy Baking Powder Biscuits (page 55).

1 cup [145 g] Jeanne's Gluten-Free All-Purpose Flour (page 39)
1½ tsp aluminum-free double-acting baking powder
¼ tsp salt

In a small bowl, mix together the flour, baking powder, and salt until well blended. Transfer to an airtight container.

Store in a cool, dark place for up to 4 weeks, in the refrigerator for up to 2 months, or in the freezer for up to 6 months.

BAKING MIX

This baking mix is the perfect substitution for Bisquick in pancake and biscuit recipes and can be used measure for measure. The recipe can be multiplied as needed. Use it for Simple Streusel Coffee Cake (page 106).

1 cup [145 g] Jeanne's Gluten-Free All-Purpose Flour (page 39)

1½ tsp aluminum-free double-acting baking powder

¼ tsp baking soda

¼ tsp salt

1 tsp granulated sugar (optional; use for sweet recipes)

1 tsp cold vegetable shortening

In a small bowl, mix together the flour, baking powder, baking soda, salt, and sugar (if using). Using your fingers or a pastry cutter, rub or cut in the shortening until it's evenly distributed throughout the dry ingredients in pea-size pieces. Transfer to an airtight container.

Store in a cool, dark place or in the refrigerator for up to 1 month, or in the freezer for up to 3 months.

STARCH-FREE CONFECTIONERS' SUGAR

MAKES ABOUT 1¼ CUPS [200 G]

Commercial confectioners' sugar contains a starch—usually cornstarch—to keep the sugar from clumping, so gluten-intolerant people who are also corn-intolerant can't use commercial versions of confectioners' sugar, which puts a big cramp in their baking endeavors. Wholesome Sweeteners uses tapioca starch in their confectioners' sugar, but it's often difficult to find (see Sources for Ingredients and Equipment, page 250). This homemade version doesn't contain any starch. It's also handy when you run out of commercial confectioners' sugar during a baking session (which seems to happen to me more frequently than I would like!). The weight of a cup of homemade starch-free confectioners' sugar is not the same as that of commercial confectioners' sugar. Weights in the book correspond to commercial weights. Adjust accordingly if using homemade confectioners' sugar.

1 cup [200 g] granulated sugar

Place the sugar in the bowl of a food processor or blender. Cover the lid with a clean kitchen towel to prevent sugar dust from drifting out. Turn on the processor for 1 minute. After a minute, check the texture of the sugar—if it is still grainy, continue to pulse in 30-second increments until the sugar is powdery. Depending on the strength of your food processor or blender, the confectioners' sugar may retain a bit of graininess. Transfer to an airtight container.

Store indefinitely. The sugar may clump over time—if it does, just stir it with a fork to get rid of the clumps.

HOW TO TOAST NUTS

I am a huge fan of toasting nuts before using them in baking. Toasting releases the oils in nuts, bringing out their full flavor, which adds a depth of flavor to recipes. The following toasting times are guidelines. Pay close attention to the nuts while they are toasting to make sure they don't burn.

Preheat the oven to 300°F [150°C]. Line a large rimmed baking sheet with parchment paper.

Scatter the halved nuts over the baking sheet in one layer. With a metal spoon, carefully stir the nuts once or twice while they are roasting.

Pecan halves: 20 minutes
Walnut halves: 20 minutes

Let the nuts cool completely before chopping and using in a recipe. Store in an airtight container at room temperature for up to 1 week.

BAKED BAKING SODA

There are a few recipes in the baking and cooking world that require the use of a strong alkaline ingredient to create a certain texture and strength—pretzels (see page 69) and ramen noodles (see page 188) being the two most prominent. Traditionally, these recipes are made with alkalis that are strong enough to require gloves and careful treatment in a kitchen. Food-grade lye is typically used for pretzels, and a solution called *kansui* is typically used to create ramen noodles.

Instead of using lye or *kansui*, both of which are somewhat challenging to find and to use, there is another option: Baked baking soda. Baking the baking soda increases its alkaline nature, making it an excellent substitute.

A word of caution: While cooking with baked baking soda doesn't require the use of special gloves, it can be irritating to skin so care should be taken when using it.

1 cup [230 g] baking soda

1. Preheat the oven to 250°F [130°C]. Line a large baking sheet with aluminum foil.

2. Spread the baking soda on the prepared baking sheet in an even layer and bake for 1 hour. Remove from the oven and let cool completely. Transfer to an airtight container.

Store at room temperature indefinitely, as long as the baking soda doesn't get wet.

HOW TO BLANCH ALMONDS

If you can't find blanched (skinned) almonds at your local grocery store, they're easy to make. Blanched almonds are used in the recipe for Almond Paste (page 127).

Place the almonds in a small bowl and pour boiling water over them, barely covering them.

Let the almonds sit for 1 minute (no longer). Drain the water and rinse the almonds quickly under cold water. Drain them again.

Place two layers of paper towels on a work surface and turn out the almonds onto them.

Place another paper towel over the almonds and gently press down to dry them.

Take one almond and squeeze it between your thumb and forefinger. The skin should come off easily. If it doesn't, use a knife or your fingernail to scrape it off. Repeat for the remaining almonds.

Store in an airtight container in the refrigerator for up to 5 days, or in the freezer for up to 3 months.

CHAPTER 2

BREADS AND CRACKERS

I love baking bread. It's fun and relaxing, and I like that it requires me to slow down a bit. To be successful at making bread, you need patience—bread will not be rushed. This doesn't mean that bread takes a lot of active time to make, but it does require rest periods in order to allow the dough to rise and develop flavor. When you make bread, give it the time it needs and you will be rewarded with loaves that are superior to those you find in stores.

Those who are new to gluten-free baking are usually surprised at the consistency of some of the doughs, especially bread dough. Gluten-free bread dough is often quite soft, sticky, and loose. It doesn't seem possible that this dough can turn into a delicious loaf of bread. But it can and it does—beautifully—so trust the recipe and follow it carefully. Crackers are the flat, crunchy cousins to bread. They may or may not contain yeast. Like breads, they are used as a vehicle for butter, oil, dips, spreads, and cheeses. There's not much that crackers don't pair well with.

In this chapter I usually direct you to allow whatever you are baking to cool completely before serving it. This is because many doughs—bread doughs in particular—continue baking during the cooling process. A loaf of bread generally takes an hour or more to cool completely once it's removed from the oven. During this time, heat is still present and is still cooking the dough. In addition, steam is still inside the bread and it needs some time to be expelled naturally.

When it is cold in my kitchen, I often use my oven as a makeshift proofing box for my dough. I preheat my gas oven to 350°F [180°C] for 20 seconds, then I turn it off and place the covered bowl of dough inside. It's a warm but not hot place for the dough to rise.

SOURDOUGH LOAF

MAKES 1 LOAF

This recipe makes a pleasingly dense and chewy loaf. I love it toasted and slathered with butter and my favorite jam—there is a wonderful contrast between the sourness of the bread and the sweetness of the jam. This bread also makes excellent croutons (see page 85).

Vegetable oil for greasing
Tapioca flour for dusting
1 recipe Master Sourdough (page 87)
1 egg beaten with 1 Tbsp water, for egg wash, or olive oil (optional)

1. Grease an 8½-by-4½-in [22-by-11-cm] loaf pan with vegetable oil and dust it with tapioca flour.

2. Carefully turn out the dough into the prepared loaf pan. Lightly smooth the top and shape the edges of the dough with an oiled spatula so they touch all sides of the pan. Press on the dough as little as possible to preserve the rise.

3. Cover the dough lightly with plastic wrap and let rise in a warm, draft-free place for 2 hours.

4. If you are using a baking stone, place it on the middle rack of the oven. After the bread has been rising for 1½ hours, preheat the oven to 475°F [240°C] for 30 minutes.

5. Remove the plastic wrap from the loaf. Using a *lame* or a sharp knife, make a slash along the top of the loaf. This will allow it to rise without cracks appearing across the top.

6. Using a pastry brush, brush the top of the loaf lightly with the egg wash (if using).

7. Place the loaf pan in the oven (and on the baking stone, if using). Bake until the top is a golden brown (it will be somewhat difficult to tell how brown it is due to the dark color of the dough, but the edges will look brown) and an instant-read thermometer inserted into the middle of the bread reads at least 205°F [95°C], 50 minutes.

8. Let the bread cool in the pan for 5 minutes. Carefully turn out the bread onto a wire rack and let cool completely. Be patient—the bread is still baking during this time. If you cut it while it's warm, it will be gummy inside. The bread is best eaten the day it is baked.

Store in a paper bag at room temperature for up to 3 days, or tightly wrapped in plastic wrap in the freezer for up to 3 months. Defrost in the refrigerator for 24 hours before serving. If you like, refresh the bread in a 400°F [200°C] oven for about 10 minutes before serving.

SOURDOUGH BAGUETTES

MAKES 3 BAGUETTES

When I was studying theater in graduate school in New York City, I made a trip to the Bread and Puppet Theater headquarters in Vermont. They are one of the oldest nonprofit political theater companies in the United States. They were known for offering bread at their puppet shows, because their philosophy was that theater is "... like bread, ... a necessity." When I arrived, they had just left on tour (clearly I didn't plan that well), so I didn't get to see a show, but they did leave loaves of their bread out for anyone who wanted it. I took a baguette and left a note of thanks in return. I ate that bread throughout the remainder of my trip. There was something so special about that bread—it was brown and dense and flavorful. It seemed to embody the proverbial "staff of life." These baguettes are like the Bread and Puppet bread—delicious, dense, and quite flavorful. And like the Bread and Puppet bread, they feed body and soul.

Tapioca flour for dusting
1 recipe Master Sourdough (page 87)
1 egg beaten with 1 Tbsp water, for egg wash (optional)

1. Line a large baking sheet with parchment paper. Lightly dust a large work surface (at least 16 in [40 cm] long) with tapioca flour.

2. Turn out the dough onto the work surface. Carefully shape it into a roughly even dome. Using a tapioca-floured bench scraper or sharp knife, cut the dough into three equal wedges.

3. With lightly floured hands, take a wedge of dough and begin to shape it into a cylinder. Place the dough on the work surface and roll it into a cylinder that is about 16 by 2 in [40 by 5 cm]. Shape each end of the cylinder into a point to make the traditional baguette shape. Position the prepared baking sheet near the work surface. The cylinder will be a little floppy, so use both hands to pick it up and quickly transfer it to the baking sheet. Use your fingers to tidy the shape and smooth any parts that have fissures from moving.

4. Repeat the process with the remaining two wedges of dough, positioning them at least 2 in [5 cm] apart on the baking sheet.

5. Cover the dough lightly with plastic wrap and let rise in a warm, draft-free place for 2 hours.

6. If you are using a baking stone, place it on the middle rack of the oven. Place an 8-in [20-cm] square metal baking pan on the bottom rack. After the baguettes have been rising for 1 hour and 15 minutes, preheat the oven to 475°F [240°C] for 45 minutes.

7. Remove the plastic wrap from the baguettes. Using a *lame* or a sharp knife, make several shallow diagonal slashes down the length of the tops of each baguette. This will minimize the amount of cracking that occurs while they're baking and gives them their iconic look.

8. Using a pastry brush, brush each baguette lightly with the egg wash (if using).

CONTINUED >>

9. Fill a 2-cup [480-ml] glass measuring cup with ice cubes and pour in enough water to reach the 1-cup [240-ml] mark. Open the preheated oven and carefully pour the ice water into the hot baking pan. The water will create the steam that helps make a nice crust on the baguettes. Quickly close the door.

10. Wait 1 minute, and then place the baking sheet on the middle rack (on the baking stone, if using). Bake until an instant-read thermometer inserted into the middle of a baguette reads at least 205°F [95°C], about 35 minutes.

11. Transfer the baguettes to a wire rack to cool completely before cutting. Be patient—the baguettes are still baking during this time. If you cut them while they're warm, they will be gummy inside. Baguettes are best eaten the day they are baked.

Store in a paper bag at room temperature for up to 2 days, or tightly wrapped in plastic wrap in the freezer for up to 3 months. Defrost in the refrigerator for 24 hours before serving. If you like, refresh the baguettes in a 400°F [200°C] oven for about 10 minutes before serving.

SOFT BREADSTICKS

MAKES 16 BREADSTICKS

Soft and fluffy breadsticks are perfect for sopping up the last little bits of food on your dinner plate or for dipping into soup, spaghetti sauce, gravy, or olive oil.

Tapioca flour for dusting

1 recipe Master Bread Dough (page 92; add ½ tsp garlic powder with the dry ingredients if you like)

Olive oil or melted unsalted butter for brushing

1. Position racks in the middle and bottom of the oven and preheat to 450°F [230°C] for 45 minutes. Line two large baking sheets with parchment paper.

2. Dust a work surface with tapioca flour. Turn out the dough and shape it into a dome. Using a floured bench scraper or sharp knife, cut the dough into quarters by cutting the dome in half vertically and then again horizontally. Cut each piece into quarters. You should now have 16 wedges. Lightly dust your hands with tapioca flour. Using your hands, take a wedge of dough and shape it into a smooth ball. Place the ball on a corner of the work surface and repeat the process with the remaining wedges.

3. Dust the work surface and your hands again with tapioca flour. Place a ball of dough on the work surface and, using your hands, roll it into a cylinder that is about 6 in [16 cm] long by 1 in [2.5 cm] wide. Pinch and tidy the ends if they are shaggy.

4. Place the cylinder on a prepared baking sheet and repeat with the remaining balls of dough, dividing the cylinders between the baking sheets and placing them at least 1 in [2.5 cm] apart.

5. Using a pastry brush, lightly brush each stick with olive oil.

6. Place a baking sheet on each oven rack. Bake for 10 minutes, then switch the positions of the baking sheets and bake for another 10 minutes, or until the breadsticks are light brown and an instant-read thermometer inserted into the side of one reads at least 205°F [95°C].

7. Transfer the breadsticks to a wire rack. They may be served hot or cooled to room temperature. Breadsticks are best eaten the day they are baked.

Store in an airtight container at room temperature for up to 3 days, or in the freezer for up to 3 months.

HAMBURGER BUNS

MAKES 6 BUNS

The perfect hamburger bun is soft and fluffy yet strong enough to stand up to a burger with all the fixings. These buns fit the bill. They won't fall apart like other gluten-free buns tend to. This dough does not hold its shape well, so it's essential to use a hamburger bun pan (see Sources for Ingredients and Equipment, page 250).

Vegetable oil for greasing
Tapioca flour for dusting
1 recipe Master Bun Dough (page 93)
2 Tbsp unsalted butter, melted and cooled

1. Grease the cups of a hamburger bun pan with vegetable oil and dust it with tapioca flour.

2. Spoon the dough evenly into the cups of the pan. The dough will be extremely soft and loose. Use an oiled rubber spatula to smooth the tops.

3. Cover the pan loosely with plastic wrap and let the dough rise in a warm, draft-free place for 45 minutes. The dough should be puffy.

4. After the dough has been rising for 15 minutes, preheat the oven to 375°F [190°C].

5. Remove the plastic wrap. Using a pastry brush, brush the tops of the dough lightly with the melted butter.

6. Place the pan on the bottom rack of the oven. Bake until the tops of the buns are golden brown and an instant-read thermometer inserted into one of the buns reads at least 205°F [95°C], 30 to 35 minutes.

7. Let the buns cool in the pan for 5 minutes before turning them out onto a wire rack to cool completely, about 45 minutes. Be patient—the buns are still baking during this time. If you cut them while they're warm, they will be gummy inside.

8. When the buns have cooled, cut them in half horizontally. Hamburger buns are best eaten within 2 days of baking.

Store in a paper bag at room temperature for up to 2 days, or in an airtight container in the freezer for up to 3 months.

HOT DOG BUNS

MAKES 10 BUNS

These hot dog buns are made in a New England hot dog bun pan (see Sources for Ingredients and Equipment, page 250). Don't worry if you've not heard of this type of bun—this pan makes excellent buns. Instead of being oblong in shape, they are rectangular—almost like very thick pieces of bread. After baking, they are cut out along the indentations made by the pan, and then each one is cut in half to insert the hot dog. Using this pan allows us to use a very loose dough that makes buns that are soft and fluffy and yet strong enough to stand up to hot dogs and the toppings that are put on them. These buns are perfect baked or toasted and buttered before filled—which is how I grew up eating them.

Vegetable oil for greasing
Tapioca flour for dusting
1 recipe Master Bun Dough (page 93)

1. Grease a hot dog bun pan with vegetable oil and dust it with tapioca powder.

2. Turn out the dough into the prepared pan. The dough will be extremely soft and loose. Use an oiled rubber spatula to spread the dough throughout the pan and smooth the top. The dough is elastic, so it may be difficult to get it to stick in the corners—do the best you can.

3. Cover the pan loosely with plastic wrap and let the dough rise in a warm, draft-free place for 45 minutes.

4. After the dough has been rising for 15 minutes, preheat the oven to 400°F [200°C].

5. Remove the plastic wrap. Place the pan on the bottom rack in the oven. Bake until the tops of the buns are golden brown and an instant-read thermometer inserted into one of the buns reads at least 205°F [95°C], 30 minutes.

6. Let the buns cool in the pan for 5 minutes before turning them out onto a wire rack to cool completely, about 45 minutes. Be patient—the buns are still baking during this time. If you cut them while they're warm, they will be gummy inside.

7. Cut into the buns along the indentations—the buns will be rectangular. Then cut into each bun lengthwise but not quite all the way through (this will be where your hot dog will go). Hot dog buns are best eaten within 2 days of baking.

Store in a paper bag at room temperature for up to 2 days, or in an airtight container in the freezer for up to 3 months.

SIMPLE AND EASY BAKING POWDER BISCUITS

MAKES 8 BISCUITS

Here is another recipe that harkens back to the Southern heritage I wish I'd had. There are countless recipes for baking powder biscuits, and believe me, I've tried just about all of them. What makes this recipe special is that it's simple, fast, and easy—it requires no rolling out or biscuit cutters. You just form the dough and then cut the biscuits into squares with a knife. It produces gluten-free biscuits that are fat and fluffy and taste great with a slathering of butter, jam, or gravy. It's important to keep the ingredients cold in order to form the flaky layers, so work quickly as you mix and shape the dough.

2 cups [290 g] Gluten-Free Self-Rising Flour (page 40)

6 Tbsp [85 g] unsalted butter, cold and cut into 12 pieces

¾ cup [180 ml] buttermilk, cold

Tapioca flour for dusting

1. Preheat the oven to 450°F [230°C]. Line a large baking sheet with parchment paper.

2. Place the self-rising flour and butter in the bowl of a food processor. Pulse several times until the mixture looks like sand mixed with pebbles. With the machine running, slowly add the buttermilk through the feed tube. The mixture should come together quickly and will be quite stiff. If you don't have a food processor, place the self-rising flour and butter in a large bowl and use your fingers or a pastry cutter to rub the butter into the flour. Add the buttermilk and mix with a large wooden spoon until the mixture comes together.

3. Dust a work surface with tapioca flour. Turn out the dough onto the work surface and sprinkle it with tapioca flour. Using your hands, pat the dough into a 6½-by-4½-in [16.5-by-11-cm] rectangle that is 1 in [2.5 cm] thick. Using a large, sharp knife dusted with tapioca flour, cut the dough into eight squares with a straight up-and-down motion. Do not wiggle the knife or the sides of the squares will stick together and the biscuits won't rise as high. Place the squares of dough on the prepared baking sheet at least 1 in [2.5 cm] apart.

4. Bake until the tops of the biscuits are light brown, 20 minutes. Transfer the biscuits to a wire rack to cool. Eat them hot from the oven or at room temperature.

Store in an airtight container at room temperature for up to 2 days, or in the freezer for up to 2 months.

CHALLAH

This braided egg bread is served during the Jewish Sabbath. While there is some signifi-cance to the fact that it is braided (braiding is said to symbolize unity), it isn't required by religious law. This recipe results in an outstanding challah that is sweet and eggy with a tender crumb. The recipe calls for a pan with a molded bottom that gives the bread a braided appearance. There are two types of pans that this dough can be used with—a 15-in [38-cm] straight pan for the weekly Sabbath and a 13-in [32-cm] ring pan for Rosh Hashanah (see Sources for Ingre-dients and Equipment, page 250).

**Vegetable oil for brushing,
plus ¼ cup [60 ml]**

**4 cups [580 g] Jeanne's Gluten-Free
All-Purpose Flour (page 39)**

1½ tsp xanthan gum

**1 Tbsp aluminum-free double-acting
baking powder**

1 tsp salt

½ cup [100 g] granulated sugar

1 Tbsp instant yeast

1 tsp vinegar

4 extra-large eggs, at room temperature

**1½ cups [360 ml] warm water (about
95°F [35°C])**

1 cup [145 g] raisins (optional)

**1 tsp sesame seeds or poppy seeds
(optional)**

1. Position a rack at the bottom of the oven and preheat to 425°F [220°C]. Using a pastry brush, brush the challah pan with vegetable oil.

2. In a large bowl, mix together the flour, xan-than gum, baking powder, salt, sugar, and yeast.

3. In the bowl of a stand mixer, use a balloon whisk to mix the vegetable oil, vinegar, eggs, and water. Add the flour mixture and place the bowl into the stand mixer fitted with the paddle attachment. Beat on low speed to combine, then increase the speed to medium-high and beat for 4 minutes. Use an oiled rubber spatula to scrape down the sides if necessary. Remove the bowl from the mixer, add the raisins (if using), and stir to combine. The dough should be very soft—almost like cake batter.

4. Scrape the dough into the prepared pan and smooth the top with the oiled spatula. Lightly brush the top of the dough with vegetable oil, cover the pan with plastic wrap, and let the dough rise in a warm, draft-free place for 30 minutes. The dough should rise to just above the top of the pan.

5. Remove the plastic wrap, place the pan on the oven rack, and lower the oven temperature to 400°F [220°C]. Bake for 30 minutes.

CONTINUED >>

6. Line a large baking sheet with parchment paper. Remove the pan from the oven (leave the oven on) and carefully turn out the hot loaf onto the prepared baking sheet with the "braided" side facing up. Lightly sprinkle the top with the sesame seeds (if using). Place the baking sheet on the bottom rack in the oven and bake for another 15 minutes, or until an instant-read thermometer inserted into the middle of the loaf reads at least 205°F [95°C].

7. Place the loaf on a wire rack to cool completely for at least 1 hour. Be patient—the bread is still baking during this time. If you slice it while it's warm, it will be gummy inside. Challah is best eaten the day it is baked.

Store in a large paper bag at room temperature for up to 2 days, or tightly wrapped in plastic wrap in the freezer for up to 3 months. Before serving, defrost the bread by placing it in the refrigerator for 24 hours. After it is cut, store cut-side down on a cutting board for up to 2 days.

FOCACCIA

MAKES 1 FOCACCIA

Along with pizza, focaccia is Italy's version of a flatbread. What distinguishes it from pizza is that it is slathered with a large amount of olive oil that is then absorbed throughout the entirety of the dough, creating what amounts to an olive-oil bread. Focaccia is a very forgiving bread to make—you press it into a roughly rectangular shape and then dimple the dough to allow the oil to pool and be absorbed. Here, I've seasoned the focaccia with rosemary, which is one of the most common herbs used for this bread, but feel free to experiment with other herbs.

4 Tbsp olive oil

1 recipe Master Bread Dough (page 92), prepared through the first rise

2 tsp dried rosemary

1 tsp kosher salt

1. Preheat the oven to 425°F [230°C]. Oil a large baking sheet with 1 Tbsp of the olive oil.

2. Turn out the dough directly onto the prepared baking sheet. Dip the tips of your fingers in some of the olive oil. Gently push down the dough so it is flattened. Pour 1 Tbsp olive oil onto the flattened dough, smear it over the top of the dough, and then gently and firmly push out the dough into a roughly 15-by-10-by-½-in [38-by-25-by-1.25-cm] rectangle. Pour 2 Tbsp olive oil on the dough and smear it across the top. With your fingers, create deep divots across the top of the dough, making sure that you do not break through the bottom of the dough to touch the pan. Sprinkle the dough evenly with the rosemary and then the salt.

3. Cover the dough lightly with plastic wrap and let rise for about 30 minutes. It should be somewhat puffy by the end of the rising time.

4. Remove the plastic wrap and place the baking sheet in the oven. Bake until the top of the bread is golden brown, about 15 minutes.

5. Remove the focaccia from the oven and let cool on the baking sheet. Cut into pieces with a bread knife or tear off sections to serve as desired. Serve hot, warm, or at room temperature.

Store at room temperature in a plastic zip-top bag for up to 3 days.

LEFSE

MAKES 12 LEFSE

Lefse is a Norwegian flatbread that was originally made from flour and water and cooked until it was hard. The flatbread was stored in boxes or simply stacked on kitchen shelves. When someone wanted to eat one, they would sprinkle it with water (or place it between two wet kitchen towels) until the flatbread became soft and pliable. When potatoes came on the scene in Norway around the mid-1700s, they were mixed into lefse dough—which made the flatbread a bit softer and added flavor. Today, lefse are usually made during the holidays in very large rounds on special griddles, but you can make your own, smaller, version in a cast-iron skillet. If you want to make an authentic lefse, buy a special rolling pin, specifically for lefse, which is grooved and adds a pattern to the flatbread. (A regular rolling pin works just fine, too.) Use a ricer to mash the potatoes to make sure they're as smooth as possible when they're incorporated into the dough—lumps will make it hard to roll out the dough. Lefse are traditionally eaten buttered (and sometimes with jam) and folded in half or rolled into a hand-size portion.

This recipe uses russet potatoes, which are starchy baking potatoes. In the United Kingdom, King Edward, Rooster, and Maris Piper potatoes would be good choices. Waxy potatoes, such as Yukon gold, will not work for this recipe.

1 lb [455 g] starchy potatoes such as russet, peeled and quartered

¼ cup [55 g] unsalted butter, at room temperature

¼ cup [60 ml] heavy cream, at room temperature

½ tsp salt

1 cup [145 g] Jeanne's Gluten-Free All-Purpose Flour (page 39), plus more as needed

Tapioca flour for dusting

1. Place the potatoes in a heavy saucepan with water to cover by 1 in [2.5 cm]. Bring to a boil and boil until the potatoes are soft and can be easily pierced with a sharp knife. Drain.

2. Force the potatoes through a potato ricer into a large bowl (or mash thoroughly with a potato masher) while they are still hot. Immediately add the butter and cream and stir until the butter is melted and everything is well combined. Add the salt and stir to combine. Add the all-purpose flour and stir until completely combined. Use your hands to do the final mixing. The dough should be soft and just a bit tacky. If the dough is too sticky, add more all-purpose flour, 1 Tbsp at a time, until it is just tacky. Cover the bowl with plastic wrap and place in the refrigerator to cool completely.

3. Lightly dust a work surface with tapioca flour and turn out the dough onto the work surface. Shape the dough into a dome and cut it into 12 equal wedges with a sharp knife.

4. Using your hands, roll each piece of dough into a ball and place the balls on a corner of the work surface. Cover lightly with plastic wrap.

5. Preheat a 10- or 12-in [25- or 30-cm] cast-iron skillet over high heat until it is very hot but not smoking. The dough cooks quickly, so watch it carefully so that it doesn't burn. Have ready a large dinner plate and a clean kitchen towel.

6. Lefse should be rolled as thin as possible—roll each piece just before you cook it. As the pan is preheating, dust the work surface with tapioca flour. Using your palm, press a ball of dough into a fat disk. Sprinkle the top of the disk with tapioca flour. Roll the disk into a circle that is quite thin—less than ⅛ in [4 mm] thick and 6 to 7 in [15 to 18 cm] in diameter. The dough is sticky, so sprinkle the top with tapioca flour frequently to avoid having bits of dough stick to the rolling pin.

7. When you are sure the pan is hot, sprinkle the top of the dough circle with tapioca flour. Place a rolling pin (I like to use my narrow Asian rolling pin for this step) on the upper edge of the circle. Carefully and slowly roll the dough onto the rolling pin, making sure there is always flour between the pieces of dough that overlap. Once the dough is rolled, gently unroll it into the pan. (It may take one or two tries before you get the hang of it.) If the dough tears, don't worry about it. It will cook fine—it just won't look perfect.

8. Cook for 2½ to 3 minutes. The dough should bubble up in various places. The bottom should be speckled with brown spots. Watch the dough carefully so that it doesn't burn. Using metal tongs, turn over the flatbread and cook the other side until it is covered with brown spots—another 2½ to 3 minutes. Using tongs, transfer the lefse to the plate and cover with the clean kitchen towel.

9. As each lefse is cooking, roll out the next one. Place each cooked lefse on top of the one cooked before it and cover them with the kitchen towel. The towel will keep them warm and lightly steam them to keep them soft. Lefse are best eaten the day they are made.

Store in a zip-top bag at room temperature for up to 2 days, or in the freezer for up to 3 months.

FLOUR TORTILLAS

MAKES ABOUT 9 TORTILLAS

I have yet to find a commercial version of gluten-free flour tortillas that I like. They are often quite stiff and they tend to break into crumbles when you roll or fold them. This recipe makes soft and pliable tortillas, perfect for rolling around fillings for a sandwich or burrito. Or, you can melt cheese between two of them and make one of my daughter's favorite snacks—quesadillas. These are the tortilla of choice at our family taco nights—they stand up well to a variety of fillings, including cheese, rice, lettuce, and refried beans.

Tapioca flour for dusting

2 cups [290 g] Jeanne's Gluten-Free All-Purpose Flour (page 39)

1½ tsp salt

2 tsp aluminum-free double-acting baking powder

5 Tbsp [70 g] unsalted butter, cold and cut into 5 pieces

¾ cup [180 ml] warm water (about 95°F [35°C])

1. Have ready a dinner plate, a clean kitchen towel, and a large baking sheet lightly dusted with tapioca flour to hold the uncooked rolled tortillas.

2. Place the all-purpose flour, salt, and baking powder in the bowl of a food processor and pulse a few times to mix.

3. Add the butter and pulse until the mixture looks like wet sand. Add the water and process until a ball of dough forms. The dough will be soft and pillowy. If you don't have a food processor, place the all-purpose flour, salt, and baking

powder in a large bowl and mix with a spoon. Add the butter and use your fingers or a pastry cutter to rub the butter into the dry ingredients, creating a mixture that looks like sand mixed with pebbles of varying sizes. Add the water and mix with a fork until the dough starts to come together. Use your hands to shape the dough into a ball.

4. Wrap the dough tightly in plastic wrap and let sit at room temperature for 1 hour. This rest period will help distribute the water throughout the dough. (If you don't plan on using the dough the day you make it, you can refrigerate the wrapped dough for up to 24 hours and bring it to room temperature before you roll it out and cook the tortillas.) If the dough is too warm, it will be difficult to roll and transfer to the pan. If this happens, place the dough in the refrigerator for 15 minutes, then resume rolling the dough.

5. Dust a work surface with tapioca flour and turn out the dough onto it. Using your hands, gently shape the dough into a dome. Using a bench scraper or a sharp knife, cut the dough into three equal wedges. Then cut each of the wedges in thirds, giving you nine smaller wedges. Using floured hands, gently shape each wedge into a ball and place them on a corner of the work surface.

6. **To make tortillas using a tortilla press:** Dust the top and bottom of the press with tapioca flour. Sprinkle a work surface with tapioca flour. Place a ball of dough in the middle of the tortilla press and press firmly. Open the press and carefully transfer the disk of dough to the floured baking sheet. Sprinkle the surface of the disk with tapioca flour. The dough may stick to the

upper part of the press (it often does for me). Some of my testers have had luck lining the press with pieces of plastic wrap, but I find that dusting with tapioca flour is more reliable. If the dough does stick, carefully pry it off with the edge of a spatula. Repeat with the remaining balls of dough.

To make tortillas using a rolling pin: Roll out a ball of dough into a 7-in [18-cm] disk. It should be about ¼ in [6 mm] thick and no thinner. Place the disk on the floured baking sheet and sprinkle the surface with tapioca flour. Repeat with the remaining balls of dough.

7. Cut away any ragged edges using a sharp knife.

8. Preheat a well-seasoned cast-iron skillet over medium-high heat for about 5 minutes.

9. Carefully transfer a disk of dough to the heated skillet using a large metal spatula. This can be tricky to do without the dough breaking. If it does break, it is still fine—it just won't look perfect.

10. Cook until the surface of the tortilla is covered with puffed-up bubbles, about 1 minute. The bubbles on the bottom should be brown but not burned. Flip the tortilla and cook for about 1 minute longer.

11. With a metal spatula, transfer the tortilla to the dinner plate, hot-side up, and cover with the clean kitchen towel. Repeat the process with the rest of the disks of dough. Transfer each successive tortilla onto the tortilla stack, hot-side up, and cover with the kitchen towel. Serve warm. Tortillas are best eaten the day they are made.

Store in an airtight container at room temperature for up to 2 days, or in the freezer for up to 3 months. To refresh, microwave for a few seconds before serving.

NAAN

MAKES 6 NAAN

A traditional Indian flatbread, naan is similar to pita but contains yogurt or milk in the dough, giving it a slightly tangy taste. My family loves Indian food, and our local restaurant offers naan with green onions or garlic in the dough, which we think gives the bread a delightful flavor, so I've included both as options in this recipe.

2 cups [290 g] Jeanne's Gluten-Free All-Purpose Flour (page 39)

½ tsp xanthan gum

1 tsp salt

2 tsp granulated sugar

1 Tbsp aluminum-free double-acting baking powder

1 Tbsp instant yeast

¾ cup plus 2 Tbsp [210 ml] warm water (about 95°F [35°C])

3 Tbsp plain yogurt or buttermilk

2 Tbsp olive oil

2 Tbsp chopped green onions or 2 tsp minced garlic (optional)

Tapioca flour for dusting

2 Tbsp unsalted butter, melted

1. Line two large baking sheets with parchment paper. Have ready a dinner plate on which to place the baked naan, plus a clean kitchen towel to cover them.

2. In a small bowl, whisk together the all-purpose flour, xanthan gum, salt, sugar, baking powder, and yeast.

3. In the bowl of a stand mixer, whisk together the water, yogurt, olive oil, and green onions (if using).

4. Add the flour mixture to the water mixture and place the bowl into the stand mixer fitted with the dough hook. Beat on low speed to combine, then increase the speed to medium-high and beat for 4 minutes. Use an oiled spatula to scrape down the sides of the bowl, if necessary.

5. Turn out the dough into an oiled bowl, cover with plastic wrap, and let rise in a warm, draft-free place for at least 2 hours. The dough should puff up and be full of bubbles.

6. Dust a work surface with tapioca flour and turn out the dough onto it. Using your hands, gently shape the dough into a dome. Using a bench scraper or sharp knife, cut the dough into three equal wedges. Then cut each of the wedges in half, giving you six smaller wedges. Gently shape each wedge into a ball using floured hands and place them on a corner of the work surface.

7. Dust the work surface with tapioca flour again and place one ball of dough onto it. Sprinkle a little tapioca flour on top of the ball and, using the palm of your hand, press the ball into a disk. Using a rolling pin, roll out the dough into an oblong shape that is roughly 7 in [18 cm] long by 5 in [13 cm] wide and no thicker than ⅛ in [4 mm]. The key to getting the naan to puff up and bubble is for the dough to be thin. Transfer the rolled dough to a prepared baking sheet. Repeat the process with the remaining balls of dough.

8. Heat a well-seasoned cast-iron skillet over high heat until it is very hot but not smoking. Make sure you have a lid that is wide enough to fit the skillet.

9. Place a rolled piece of dough in the pan, taking care not to tear it (which will impede puffing). Cook until the dough is puffed up with bubbles, 1 to 2 minutes. Flip the dough with a metal spatula, cover the pan with the lid, and cook for another 1 to 2 minutes. One side will probably have brown marks where the bubbles cooked; the other side will not have much browning. Watch the naan carefully so that they do not burn.

10. Transfer the naan to the dinner plate. Use a pastry brush to brush it lightly with some of the melted butter and cover it with the kitchen towel. Repeat with the rest of the rolled dough, placing each cooked naan on top of the one cooked before it and covering them with the kitchen towel. This serves to steam the naan lightly and keep them supple. (If the dough starts to stick to the pan when cooking, lightly brush the pan with a high-heat-tolerant vegetable oil like rice bran oil and continue cooking.) Naan is best eaten the day it is made.

Store in an airtight container at room temperature for up to 3 days, or layered with wax paper in an airtight container in the freezer for up to 3 months.

PITA BREAD

Pita bread seems to go with everything. It pairs well with dips, especially hummus, and it's a perfect travel and picnic food—just pack a few in a lunch box or picnic hamper with a variety of fillings and everyone can make their own pocket sandwiches. I proof the dough for at least 20 minutes, and then I flour the baking surface before using a very hot oven.

3 cups [435 g] Jeanne's Gluten-Free All-Purpose Flour (page 39)

1 tsp xanthan gum

2 tsp salt

1 Tbsp aluminum-free double-acting baking powder

1 Tbsp plus 1 tsp instant yeast

2 Tbsp olive oil, plus more for greasing

1 tsp vinegar

1½ cups [360 ml] warm water (about 95°F [35°C])

Tapioca flour for dusting

1. In a medium bowl, mix together the all-purpose flour, xanthan gum, salt, baking powder, and yeast with a spoon. In the bowl of a stand mixer, lightly whisk together the olive oil, vinegar, and water with a fork. Place the bowl into the stand mixer fitted with the dough hook, add the flour mixture, and beat on low speed until just combined, then increase the speed to medium-high and beat for 4 minutes.

2. Scrape the dough into an oiled bowl, cover with plastic wrap, and let rise for at least 1 hour, or up to 24 hours. If the dough is to rest for longer than about 4 hours, place it in the refrigerator.

If the dough has been refrigerated, let it sit for 1 hour at room temperature before using.

3. An hour before you're ready to bake the pitas, place a baking stone or cast-iron skillet on the bottom rack of the oven and preheat to 475°F [240°C]. A hot oven and baking surface are imperative for the pita to puff properly.

4. Line two large baking sheets with parchment paper and dust each lightly with tapioca flour. Have ready a dinner plate on which to place the baked pitas, plus a clean kitchen towel to cover them.

5. Lightly dust a work surface with tapioca flour. Remove the plastic wrap and turn out the dough onto the work surface. Using a knife or bench scraper, cut the dough into eight equal pieces. Lightly flour your hands and roll each piece of dough into a ball.

6. Take one of the balls and roll it lightly around the work surface with the palm of your hand to create a smooth surface on the dough. Lightly dust the work surface with tapioca flour again. With the palm of your hand, press the ball into a disk. Lightly sprinkle the top of the disk with tapioca flour and use a rolling pin to roll the disk out to about ⅛ in [4 mm] thick. Add more tapioca flour as needed to the work surface to keep the dough from sticking. Place the finished round on one of the prepared baking sheets. Repeat with the rest of the balls of dough, arranging them at least 1 in [2.5 cm] apart on the prepared baking sheets. Cover the rounds of dough with plastic wrap so they don't dry out.

7. Allow the rounds to proof, or sit, for at least 20 minutes before baking.

CONTINUED >>

8. Pick up a round of dough, making sure that the bottom has a little tapioca flour on it. If it doesn't, sprinkle some tapioca flour on the spot where it sits and set the round on top of the flour. Pick it up again, taking care not to tear the dough. Place the round directly on the hot baking stone or cast-iron skillet, floured-side down, and quickly close the oven door.

9. Bake until the round is puffed but not brown, about 4 minutes. (If the pita hasn't puffed after 4 minutes, it won't puff. Remove the unpuffed pita from the oven, place it on the plate, and cover with the clean kitchen towel. It is still fine to eat.) My baking stone can comfortably accommodate only one round of dough at a time. If your baking surface can accommodate more than one round at a time, bake several at once.

10. Give the oven about a minute to get back up to temperature and repeat the process with the remaining rounds of dough. Place each baked pita on top of the one that was baked before and cover with the clean kitchen towel to keep the pitas warm (covering them also helps maintain their softness). Pitas are best eaten within 24 hours of baking.

Store wrapped in parchment paper (while they're still warm) and placed in a large zip-top bag at room temperature (this will keep them soft) for up to 2 days, or layer with wax paper in a zip-top bag in the freezer for up to 3 months. Rewarm by heating them in a microwave oven for a few seconds.

SOFT PRETZELS

My fellow gluten-intolerant gal pal Jill says she misses soft pretzels the most. I developed this recipe with her in mind. It meets all the requirements for a soft pretzel—chewy on the outside, soft on the inside, with a complex malty flavor and a pleasing mahogany brown crust. The pretzels' depth of flavor comes from using a starter in the dough instead of yeast straight from the package. The extra step means you'll need to start this recipe the day before you actually make the pretzels, but it is well worth it for the flavor the starter imparts (indeed, my family has been known to devour an entire batch over the course of a single day). Try them with the Honey-Mustard Dipping Sauce (page 73) and a gluten-free beer to wash them down.

STARTER

⅔ cup [160 ml] warm water (about 95°F [35°C])

Small pinch of instant yeast

1 cup [145 g] Jeanne's Gluten-Free All-Purpose Flour (page 39)

4 cups [580 g] Jeanne's Gluten-Free All-Purpose Flour (page 39)

¾ tsp xanthan gum

1 tsp instant yeast

2 tsp salt

1 Tbsp dark brown sugar

1 cup [240 ml] cold gluten-free beer (a Pilsner is a good choice)

¼ cup [60 ml] warm water (about 95°F [35°C])

1 tsp apple cider vinegar

3 Tbsp unsalted butter, cubed and at room temperature

Tapioca flour for dusting

SOAKING SOLUTION

2 cups [480 ml] boiling water

¼ cup [50 g] Baked Baking Soda (page 43)

Coarse or flaked salt for sprinkling (optional)

3 Tbsp unsalted butter, melted

CONTINUED >>

1. **TO MAKE THE STARTER:** Place the water into a plastic, glass, ceramic, or nonreactive metal container. Sprinkle the yeast on the surface of the water and stir to dissolve. Add the all-purpose flour and mix thoroughly with your fingers or a spoon. The mixture will be stiff but should be smooth with no clumps of flour. Cover the container with plastic wrap and let rise at room temperature for 12 to 16 hours. The mixture will puff up.

2. After the starter has risen for at least 12 hours, mix together the all-purpose flour, xanthan gum, yeast, salt, and brown sugar in the bowl of a stand mixer using a spoon. Add the starter, beer, water, vinegar, and butter and place the bowl into the mixer fitted with the dough hook. Beat on low speed for a few seconds to combine the ingredients, then increase the speed to medium-high and beat for 4 minutes. Stop the mixer twice and scrape down the sides with an oiled rubber spatula. The dough will be very stiff and sticky.

3. Using an oiled rubber spatula, scrape the dough into a lightly oiled bowl, cover with plastic wrap, and let rise in a warm, draft-free place for 2 hours. The dough should be puffy by the end of the rising time.

4. Position racks in the middle and bottom of the oven and preheat to 500°F [260°C]. Line two large baking sheets with parchment paper.

5. Using a sharp knife, cut the dough into twelve equal pieces, place them on a corner of the work surface, and cover with plastic wrap. Dust your palms very lightly with tapioca flour, pick up one piece of dough, and shape it into a ball. The flour on your hands should be enough to stop the dough from sticking to the work surface. If you find that the dough is sticking, dust the work surface with a tiny amount of tapioca flour. Gently roll the ball of dough on the work surface with your palm to smooth out the surface of the dough.

6. Roll the ball of dough into a rope that is about 7 in [18 cm] long. Using both hands, roll the two end-thirds of the rope thinner, to make the total length of the rope about 14 in [36 cm]. The middle of the rope will be thicker than each end.

7. To make the iconic pretzel shape, bring the two thin ends up on either side so that the rope forms a U shape (the thicker part of the dough will be at the bottom of the U). Bring both ends to the middle and gently wrap them around each other twice. Bring the wrapped ends down toward the bottom of the U and press each of the ends onto opposite sides of the lower part of the U (see diagram). You should now have

a circle with a twist in the middle. Using your fingers, gently tug down the lower sides of the circle. Transfer the shaped dough to one of the prepared baking sheets and cover lightly with a kitchen towel to keep the dough from drying out. Repeat with the remaining pieces of dough, spacing them at least 1 in [2.5 cm] apart on the baking sheets.

8. Set aside the baking sheets, covered with the kitchen towel.

9. **TO MAKE THE SOAKING SOLUTION:** Pour the boiling water into an 8-in [20-cm] square baking pan. Sift the baked baking soda into the water and whisk to dissolve (the baking soda may not dissolve completely—this is fine). Let the water cool to about 95°F [35°C].

10. Carefully place the pretzels in the soaking solution, three at a time, and let sit for 2 minutes. Spoon the solution over the top of the pretzels to make sure each pretzel is entirely covered. Using a fork, gently lift each pretzel a bit to make sure they're not sticking to the bottom of the pan. Let sit for another 2 minutes. Using a slotted metal spatula, carefully remove each pretzel from the solution, holding it over the pan for a few seconds to drain. Place each pretzel on a prepared baking sheet. Repeat with the remaining pretzels, working in batches of three.

11. If you like, sprinkle each pretzel lightly with coarse salt (use less than you think you need— a little goes a long way).

12. Place a baking sheet on each oven rack and lower the oven temperature to 450°F [230°C]. Bake for 12 minutes, switch the position of the baking sheets, and bake for another 12 minutes. The pretzels should be dark mahogany brown when done.

13. Remove the pretzels from the oven and brush with the melted butter while they're hot— use all the butter. Transfer the pretzels to wire racks to cool completely.

Store in a paper bag at room temperature for up to 12 hours. Wrapped in plastic wrap, they will keep for another 24 hours. You can also wrap them tightly with plastic wrap and place in the freezer for up to 3 months.

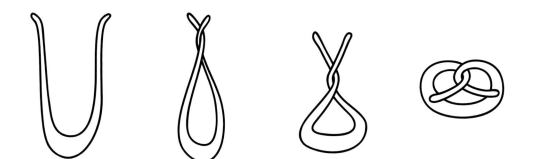

SOFT PRETZEL BITES

MAKES 48 PRETZEL BITES

These are soft pretzels in a handy bite-size shape—convenient as a snack or to serve at a party.

1 recipe Soft Pretzels dough (see page 69), made through the rising instruction

Tapioca flour for dusting

SOAKING SOLUTION

2 cups [480 ml] boiling water

¼ cup [50 g] Baked Baking Soda (page 43)

Coarse or flaked salt for sprinkling (optional)

3 Tbsp unsalted butter, melted

1. Position racks in the middle and bottom of the oven and preheat to 500°F [260°C]. Line two large baking sheets with parchment paper.

2. Using a sharp knife, cut the dough into twelve equal pieces, place them on a corner of the work surface, and cover with plastic wrap. Dust your palms very lightly with tapioca flour, pick up one piece of dough, and shape it into a ball. The flour on your hands should be enough to stop the dough from sticking to the work surface. If you find that the dough is sticking, dust the work surface with a tiny amount of tapioca flour. Gently roll the ball of dough on the work surface with your palm to smooth out the surface of the dough.

3. Roll the ball of dough into an evenly sized rope that is about 6 in [15 cm] long. Using a bench scraper or a sharp knife, cut the rope into four equal pieces. Roll each piece into a ball and place them on one of the prepared baking sheets. Cover with a kitchen towel. Repeat with the remaining dough. You should have twenty-four pieces per baking sheet.

4. Set aside the baking sheets, covered with the kitchen towel.

5. **TO MAKE THE SOAKING SOLUTION:** Pour the boiling water into an 8-in [20-cm] square baking pan. Sift the baked baking soda into the water and whisk to dissolve (the baking soda may not dissolve completely—this is fine). Let the water cool to about 95°F [35°C].

6. Carefully place twelve pieces of dough in the soaking solution and let sit for 2 minutes. Spoon the solution over the top of the pretzel bites to make sure they are completely covered. Using a fork, gently lift each pretzel bite to make sure it's not sticking to the bottom of the pan. Let sit for another 2 minutes. Using a slotted metal spatula, carefully remove the pretzel bites from the solution, holding them over the pan for a few seconds to drain. Place the pretzel bites on a prepared baking sheet. Repeat with the remaining pieces, working in batches of twelve.

7. If you like, sprinkle the pretzel bites lightly with coarse salt (use less than you think you need—a little goes a long way).

8. Place a baking sheet on each oven rack and lower the oven temperature to 450°F [230°C]. Bake for 9 minutes, switch the position of the baking sheets, and bake for another 9 to 11 minutes. The bites should be dark mahogany brown when done.

9. Remove the pretzel bites from the oven and brush with the melted butter while they're hot—use all the butter. Transfer the pretzel bites to wire racks to cool completely.

Store in a paper bag at room temperature for up to 12 hours. Wrapped in plastic wrap, they will keep for another 24 hours. You can also wrap them tightly with plastic wrap and place in the freezer for up to 3 months.

HONEY-MUSTARD DIPPING SAUCE

MAKES A LITTLE MORE THAN ½ CUP [120 ML]

This sweet and slightly spicy dipping sauce pairs perfectly with the saltiness of the pretzels. The recipe can be multiplied as needed.

¼ cup [65 g] Dijon or brown mustard
¼ cup [60 ml] mayonnaise
2 Tbsp honey
⅛ tsp cayenne pepper

In a small bowl, whisk together the mustard, mayonnaise, honey, and cayenne until well combined.

Store in an airtight container in the refrigerator for up to 5 days. Do not freeze.

GOUGÈRES

Gougères are French cheese puffs made from a classic pâte à choux dough. I love making these for cocktail parties—they are easy to prepare, the recipe yields enough for a large group, and they are a crowd-pleaser because they are so delicious. We like to eat them as an afternoon snack, too. Gruyère is the traditional cheese choice but any variety that grates well is fine.

1¼ cups [90 g] lightly packed grated cheese
½ to 1 tsp dry mustard powder (optional)
1 recipe Pâte à Choux Dough (page 248), leave the dough in the mixer

1. In a small bowl, toss the grated cheese with the mustard powder (if using).

2. Add the cheese to the dough and beat for another 20 seconds to combine.

3. Position racks in the middle and bottom of the oven and preheat to 425°F [220°C]. Line two large rimmed baking sheets with parchment paper.

4. Drop the dough by the heaping tablespoon (or use a pastry bag fitted with a large round tip to pipe 1-Tbsp portions) onto the prepared baking sheets, leaving at least 1 in [2.5 cm] between each portion. Tidy the dough with a fingertip dipped in water, lightly pressing down on any sharp points on the dough.

5. Place the baking sheets on the middle and bottom racks of the oven. Bake for 20 minutes, switch the positions of the baking sheets, and bake until the gougères are lightly browned, 8 to 10 minutes more.

6. Using a spatula, transfer the gougères to a wire rack to cool completely. Gougères are best eaten the day they are made.

Store at room temperature in an open container for up to 24 hours (a closed container will cause them to become wilted and soggy), or in an airtight container in the freezer for up to 3 months. To defrost, place the container in the refrigerator overnight. Then, transfer the gougères to a baking sheet and refresh in a 375°F [190°C] oven for about 5 minutes.

KNISHES

MAKES 8 DUMPLINGS

Knishes are Eastern European Jewish dumplings. I was introduced to knishes when I attended graduate school in New York City—they were often served at parties and buffets. I immediately loved them, and I adored the fact that they came with a variety of fillings, giving everyone options from which to choose. The most well-known filling for knishes is mashed potatoes with onions, the recipe for which I've included here. Of course, you can experiment with your own fillings.

FILLING

1½ lb [680 g] starchy potatoes such as russet, peeled and quartered

2 Tbsp vegetable oil

1 small yellow onion, diced

2 tsp dried parsley or 2 Tbsp chopped fresh parsley

½ tsp salt

Freshly ground black pepper

DOUGH

1½ cups [215 g] Jeanne's Gluten-Free All-Purpose Flour (page 39)

1½ tsp aluminum-free double-acting baking powder

1 tsp salt

Dash of freshly ground black pepper

2 extra-large eggs, at room temperature

2 Tbsp vegetable oil

2 Tbsp water, plus more as needed

Tapioca flour for dusting

1 egg beaten with 1 Tbsp water, for egg wash

1. **TO MAKE THE FILLING:** Place the potatoes in a large, heavy-bottomed pot and cover with water by 1 in [2.5 cm]. Bring to a boil and cook the potatoes until they are tender and can be easily pierced with a sharp knife, about 15 minutes. Drain and place in a large bowl to cool.

2. Heat the vegetable oil in a heavy skillet over medium heat. Add the onion and cook, stirring frequently, until it is brown and caramelized, about 30 minutes. Watch carefully so that the onion doesn't burn. Scrape the caramelized onion into the bowl with the potatoes and mash them together with a potato masher until fairly smooth. Add the parsley, salt, and a few grinds of pepper and stir until well combined. Place the bowl in the refrigerator to cool.

3. **TO MAKE THE DOUGH:** Place the all-purpose flour, baking powder, salt, and pepper in the bowl of a food processor and pulse several times to mix. Add the eggs, vegetable oil, and water and process until the dough comes together in a rough ball. Using your hands, scoop out a bit of the dough and press it together. If the dough is shaggy and not quite sticking together, add a bit more water, 1 tsp at a time, and pulse after each addition. Repeat the scooping-and-pressing test until the dough stays together.

4. Remove the dough from the processor, wrap it in plastic wrap, and let it rest for at least 30 minutes at room temperature.

5. Center a rack in the oven and preheat to 375°F [190°C]. Line a large baking sheet with parchment paper.

6. Dust a work surface lightly with tapioca flour. Unwrap the dough and place it on the work surface. Cut the dough into eight equal pieces with a sharp knife.

7. Using your hands, roll each piece of dough into a ball. Place the balls in a corner of the work surface and cover lightly with plastic wrap.

8. Place a ball of dough on the work surface and sprinkle the top with tapioca flour. Press down on the ball with your palm to create a fat disk. Using a rolling pin, roll the disk into a circle that is 5 to 6 in [13 to 15 cm] in diameter.

9. Remove the filling from the refrigerator. Place 3 Tbsp of filling in the center of the circle of dough. Carefully pick up the circle and place it in the palm of one hand and slowly bring your fingers toward your palm. This will bring the dough together around the filling like a drawstring purse. Use the fingers of your other hand to gently and slowly squeeze the top edges of the dough together. There may be an excess of dough at the top once the dough is pinched together; if there is, gently pinch it off and discard. Once the dough is pinched together, gently and firmly press the top of the pinched dough down toward the filling. You should now have a nice dumpling. Place it on a prepared baking sheet, pinched-side down so that the smooth part of the dumpling is facing up. Repeat the process with the remaining dough and filling. You should have eight dumplings.

10. Use a pastry brush to brush the tops of each knish with the egg wash. Bake until the knishes are light brown, about 20 minutes.

Store in an airtight container in the refrigerator for up to 2 days, or in the freezer for up to 2 months.

GRISSINI

MAKES 32 GRISSINI

These are the thin, crisp, Italian breadsticks that you see in restaurants, often displayed like a bouquet of flowers in a cup at your table. They are wonderful for a quick snack on their own, and even better dipped in olive oil, hummus, or your favorite dip.

Tapioca flour for dusting
1 recipe Master Bread Dough (page 92)

1. Position racks in the middle and bottom of the oven and preheat to 450°F [230°C] for 45 minutes. Line two large baking sheets with parchment paper.

2. Dust a work surface with tapioca flour. Turn out the dough onto the work surface and shape it into a dome. The dough will be oily from the container, so you probably won't need to dust your hands with flour, but check how sticky it is and flour your hands as needed. Using a floured bench scraper or sharp knife, cut the dough into quarters. Then cut each quarter into four wedges. You should now have sixteen wedges. Lightly dust your hands with tapioca flour. Using your hands, take one wedge of dough and divide it in half. Roll each half into a ball and place it on a corner of the work surface. Repeat the process with the remaining wedges. You should have 32 balls of dough.

3. Dust the work surface and your hands again. Using your hands, shape a ball of dough into a log. Place the log on the work surface and roll it into a rope that is about 12 in [30 cm] long. If there's too much tapioca flour on the work surface it will be challenging to roll the dough this thin—the tapioca flour causes it to slide around. You'll find the sweet spot where you have just enough tapioca flour to make sure the dough doesn't stick but not so much that it will interfere with rolling out the dough. Don't worry if the dough is a little misshapen. Handmade grissini will naturally be imperfect—it's part of their rustic charm.

4. Position one of the prepared baking sheets next to the work surface and, using both hands, carefully and quickly transfer the rope of dough to the baking sheet. The dough will be very loose and may be tricky to move, but it should hold its shape during a quick transfer. If the dough breaks, use your fingers to repair it.

5. Repeat the rolling and transferring process with the rest of the dough, dividing the ropes between the two baking sheets and leaving at least ½ in [12 mm] between each rope.

6. Place one baking sheet on the middle rack and the other on the lower rack of the oven. Bake for 10 minutes, switch the position of the baking sheets, and bake for another 10 minutes, until the grissini are medium brown. Transfer the grissini to a wire rack and let cool completely; they will crisp as they cool. Grissini are best eaten the day they are made.

Store in a paper bag at room temperature for up to 3 days.

PUFF PASTRY CHEESE STICKS

MAKES 24 CHEESE STICKS

Crunchy, delicate cheese sticks are a wonderful (and easy) way to become acquainted with puff pastry dough.

Tapioca flour for dusting

1 recipe Puff Pastry Dough (page 96), chilled to about 60°F [15°C] (warmer dough may stick to the rolling surface)

1 egg beaten with 1 Tbsp water, for egg wash

½ cup [35 g] finely grated Cheddar cheese

Coarse salt for sprinkling (optional)

1. Preheat the oven to 425°F [220°C]. Line two large baking sheets with parchment paper.

2. Sprinkle tapioca flour onto a work surface and rolling pin.

3. On the floured work surface, roll out the dough into a rectangle that is ⅛ in [4 mm] thick and about 24 in [60 cm] long and 8 in [20 cm] wide. Measure the length of the dough and cut it in half. You should now have two halves that are roughly 12 in [30 cm] long and 8 in [20 cm] wide.

4. Use a pastry brush to brush both halves of the dough with the egg wash (reserve some of the egg wash for later). Be careful that it doesn't drip down the sides of the dough—this will hinder the rising action. Sprinkle one of the halves with the grated cheese.

5. Lay the other half of the dough the on top of the half with the cheese, egg wash–side down.

6. Gently, but firmly, roll once across the top of the dough with a rolling pin to force out any air pockets. Continue to roll out the dough until it is about ⅛ in [4 mm] thick.

7. With a sharp knife, cut off the raggedy ends of the dough and discard. You should now have a neat rectangle.

8. Carefully brush the top of the dough with more egg wash (don't let it drip down the sides) and sprinkle lightly with coarse salt (if using).

9. Orient the dough so that the short ends are at the top and bottom. Using a ruler, mark the dough in ½-in [12-mm] increments along the left side of the dough. At each mark, cut the dough into strips with a sharp knife. You should now have 24 thin dough rectangles that are roughly 8 in [20 cm] long.

10. Carefully twist each strip two or three times, taking care not to twist too tightly. Place each strip on a prepared baking sheet, about ½ in [12 mm] apart. Anchor the strips by gently pressing each end onto the parchment paper.

11. Bake until the cheese sticks are light golden brown, 10 to 14 minutes. Transfer to a wire rack to cool completely. Cheese sticks are best eaten the day they are made.

Store in a paper bag at room temperature for up to 2 days. Do not freeze.

MATZO (MATZAH) CRACKERS

MAKES 4 LARGE CRACKERS

Symbolizing the dough that the Israelites didn't have time to leaven in their haste to flee Egypt, matzo is a crackerlike flatbread that is an integral part of the Jewish celebration of Passover. Because it is unleavened and made with simple ingredients, it is sometimes called "poor man's bread" and serves as a reminder to be humble. This recipe is not appropriate for Orthodox celebrations—gluten-free grains are not allowed because they aren't part of the authentic five species of grains designated as *chametz*, which were thought to be the grains used by the original Israelites who fled Egypt. They are just fine for non-Orthodox celebrations.

3¼ cups [470 g] Jeanne's Gluten-Free All-Purpose Flour (page 39)
1¼ cups [300 ml] water
Tapioca flour for dusting

1. Place a baking stone or well-seasoned cast-iron skillet on the middle rack of the oven and preheat to 475°F [240°C].

2. In a large bowl, mix the all-purpose flour and water with a spoon until just combined. Use your hands to finish mixing. The dough should be firm and tacky but not too sticky. (Add a bit more flour or water, if needed, to achieve the right texture.)

3. Dust a work surface with tapioca flour. Form the dough into a large ball, place it on the work surface, and shape it into a dome. Using a bench scraper or sharp knife, cut the dough into four equal wedges. Flour your hands and shape each wedge into a ball.

4. Cover the work surface with a large piece of parchment paper and dust the paper with tapioca flour. Place one of the balls of dough on the floured parchment paper and sprinkle the top of the dough lightly with a bit more tapioca flour.

5. Roll out the dough as thin as you can. It should look a bit transparent in places. With a fork, dock the dough by piercing it all over. Docking the dough will inhibit it from puffing, which gives the matzo its signature flatness.

6. Trim the parchment paper around the rolled-out dough so that it is only about 1 in [2.5 cm] bigger than the size of the dough all around.

7. Place the parchment paper with the rolled-out dough on the baking stone in the oven. After 3 minutes, grasp the cracker with long metal tongs and pull the parchment paper out from underneath the cracker with your other hand (the paper usually isn't too hot for your hands to touch) and discard it. Bake the cracker for another 3 minutes. Using the tongs, flip the cracker and bake for another 2 minutes, until the edges become a bit brown.

8. Transfer the cracker to a wire rack to cool and repeat the process with the remaining three wedges of dough. Serve the crackers with the docked side up. Matzo are best eaten the day they are made.

Store in an airtight container at room temperature for up to 2 days, or in the freezer for up to 6 months.

OYSTER CRACKERS

MAKES ABOUT 160 CRACKERS

Typically served with New England clam chowder, these round or octagonal crackers are often called "water crackers" because, back in the day, a predecessor was designed to accompany sailors on long voyages. The word "cracker" was coined because they make a crackling noise while baking. Sprinkle them on top of your favorite soup, stew, or chowder (of course), but they are a great little snack on their own, too.

1 cup [145 g] Jeanne's Gluten-Free All-Purpose Flour (page 39)

1 tsp salt

1 Tbsp granulated sugar

2 tsp aluminum-free double-acting baking powder

3 Tbsp unsalted butter, cold and cut into 6 pieces

¼ cup [60 ml] ice water

1. In a medium bowl, mix the flour, salt, sugar, and baking powder to combine. Add the butter and rub it into the dough with your fingers. It should look like a mixture of flakes, pebbles, and boulders.

2. Add the ice water and mix with a fork until combined. Use your hands to bring the dough together into a ball. It will be shaggy and just barely hold together.

3. Using your hands, shape the dough into a disk and wrap it in plastic wrap. Place the dough in the refrigerator for 1 hour to rest and chill.

4. After an hour, position racks in the middle and bottom of the oven and preheat to 400°F [200°C]. Line two large rimmed baking sheets with parchment paper.

5. Unwrap the dough and place it between two large sheets of wax paper. Roll out the dough until it is ⅛ in [4 mm] thick. Using a small round cookie cutter (I use the smallest round cutter I have: ¾ in [2 cm]), cut out as many circles as you can. Using a metal spatula, transfer the cut dough to a prepared baking sheet, leaving ½ in [12 mm] between each circle. Reroll the scraps and repeat the process until the baking sheets are filled. If the dough starts to get too warm to roll and cut without sticking, put the dough between wax paper and return it to the refrigerator for about 15 minutes to firm.

6. Place one baking sheet on the middle rack and the other on the lower rack of the oven. Bake for 5 minutes, switch the positions of the sheets, and bake for another 5 minutes, until the bottoms of the crackers are light brown. Transfer the crackers to a wire rack to cool; they will crisp as they cool. Crackers are best eaten the day they are baked.

Store in an airtight container at room temperature for up to 2 days, or in the freezer for up to 6 months.

SAVORY CRACKERS YOUR WAY

MAKES ABOUT 40 CRACKERS

My family goes through a lot of crackers. We eat them with cheese, with dips, or as take-along snacks. So you can imagine how important it was for me to develop a gluten-free variety. I always bring a batch of my own crackers to restaurants and parties just in case a gluten-free option isn't available. I like to switch up the flavors of my crackers, so this recipe suggests a few options for adding dried herbs or spices.

1 cup [145 g] Jeanne's Gluten-Free All-Purpose Flour (page 39)

1 tsp salt

1 Tbsp granulated sugar

2 tsp aluminum-free double-acting baking powder

1 tsp dried herbs such as thyme, basil, parsley, or oregano; garlic powder or onion powder; or a spice such as cumin or freshly cracked black pepper

3 Tbsp unsalted butter, cold and cut into 6 pieces

¼ cup [60 ml] milk

1. In a medium bowl, mix together the flour, salt, sugar, baking powder, and herbs. Add the butter and blend it in with your fingers. It should look like a mixture of flakes, pebbles, and boulders.

2. Add the milk and mix with a fork. Use your hands to bring the dough together. It will be shaggy and just barely hold together.

3. Using your hands, shape the dough into a disk and wrap it in plastic wrap. Place the dough in the refrigerator for 1 hour to rest and chill.

4. Position racks in the middle and bottom of the oven and preheat to 400°F [200°C]. Line two large rimmed baking sheets with parchment paper.

5. Unwrap the dough and place it between two large sheets of wax paper. Roll out the dough until it is ⅛ in [4 mm] thick. Using a 1½-in [4-cm] round cookie cutter, cut out as many circles as you can. Using the tines of a fork, prick each circle three times down the center. Using a metal spatula, transfer the circles to a prepared baking sheet, leaving 1 in [2.5 cm] between each circle. Reroll the scraps of dough and repeat the process until the baking sheets are filled.

6. Place one baking sheet on the middle rack and the other on the lower rack of the oven. Bake for 6 minutes, switch the sheet positions, and bake for another 6 to 9 minutes, until the bottoms of the crackers are light brown. Transfer the crackers to a wire rack to cool; they will crisp as they cool. Crackers are best eaten the day they are baked.

Store in an airtight container at room temperature for up to 2 days, or in the freezer for up to 6 months.

CROUTONS

When I teach, some cooking schools ask me to provide a meal at the end of the class. But when I'm teaching a bread-making class, there isn't much to make an actual meal, so I sometimes offer a salad topped with croutons from the bread we made in the class. It's a practical way to show the students how versatile the bread we just made is, and it's an unexpected treat for them. If you're gluten-intolerant, you've probably experienced the disappointment of ordering a salad at a restaurant only to see it arrive topped with delicious-looking croutons that you can't eat. And, not only that, you have to send the salad back and have them make a new one. So, it's a pleasure to see the joy on their faces when they realize they can have croutons on salad once more. I often season my croutons with salt, pepper, or minced garlic.

Any kind of gluten-free bread, any amount, cut or torn into roughly ½-in [12-mm] cubes

Olive oil

Seasonings such as salt, black pepper, minced fresh garlic (optional)

1. Preheat the oven to 400°F [200°C]. Line a large rimmed baking sheet with parchment paper.

2. Place the bread cubes in a large bowl. Drizzle olive oil over the bread and stir with a spoon until the cubes are lightly coated—don't soak them. Add the seasonings (if using) and stir to combine. Use a light hand when applying the seasonings—a little goes a long way.

3. Spread the bread cubes onto the prepared baking sheet and bake until the croutons are slightly brown and crisp, 15 to 20 minutes. Let the croutons cool completely on the baking sheet before using them. Croutons are best eaten the day they are made—I don't recommend storing them.

BREAD CRUMBS

Homemade bread crumbs are so easy to make, I don't really see the need to buy them. Whenever we have gluten-free bread in the house, I use the heels and any leftover slices to make bread crumbs and store them in the freezer so that they're always on hand. Make sure your bread is a little stale but not rock hard, otherwise your food processor will have trouble grinding it into crumbs.

Gluten-free bread, any kind, in any amount, cut into ½-in [12-mm] pieces

1. Preheat the oven to 300°F [150°C].

2. Place the pieces of bread on a large ungreased rimmed baking sheet in a single layer. Bake for 20 minutes, flip the pieces with a spatula, and bake for an additional 20 minutes. The finished bread should be crisp enough to snap when you break it in two. Test one piece for crispness. If it doesn't snap, return the pieces to the oven for a few minutes more.

3. Place the bread in a food processor or blender and process until the bread crumbs have an even, fine texture.

Store in a zip-top bag in the freezer for up to 6 months. You don't need to let the bread crumbs thaw before using.

MASTER SOURDOUGH

Once you have a healthy sourdough starter you can begin making bread with it! This dough is just right to make the Sourdough Loaf (page 46) or the Sourdough Baguettes (page 47).

Vegetable oil for greasing

2½ cups [360 g] Jeanne's Gluten-Free All-Purpose Flour (page 39)

½ tsp xanthan gum

1 Tbsp aluminum-free double-acting baking powder

1 Tbsp granulated sugar

1 tsp salt

2 cups [480 ml] well-stirred and active Sourdough Starter (page 88)

1 Tbsp unsalted butter, at room temperature

½ cup [120 ml] warm milk (about 95°F [35°C])

1. Grease a large bowl or a plastic dough container with vegetable oil and set aside.

2. In the bowl of a stand mixer fitted with the dough hook, mix the flour, xanthan gum, baking powder, sugar, salt, and starter on low speed. Add the butter and milk and beat on low speed to combine, then increase the speed to medium and beat for 5 minutes. Once or twice during the process, stop the machine and scrape down the sides of the bowl with an oiled rubber spatula.

3. With an oiled rubber spatula, scrape the dough into the prepared bowl. Cover with plastic wrap or a secure lid and let the dough rise in a warm, draft-free place for at least 12 hours, or up to 24 hours (this is convenient to do overnight). Once the dough has risen, it should be full of bubbles. At this point, follow the desired recipe to finish and bake the dough.

SOURDOUGH STARTER

Sourdough starter, whether it's gluten-full or gluten-free, is made from flour and water. Yeast and bacteria are naturally present in varying amounts on different flours, including gluten-free flours. Other elements like grapes or cabbage or pineapple are sometimes added to jump-start the wild yeast, but they aren't necessary under the right conditions. Some gluten-free flours are better at creating and feeding a starter than others. I've found teff flour to be the one that contains enough natural yeast to reliably create a starter in a few days under the correct conditions. Teff, (sweet) sorghum, and brown rice flours are the best for maintaining a gluten-free starter. Take into account that tap water in most industrialized countries is typically treated with a chemical to purify it, usually chlorine, chloramine, or ozone. There is anecdotal evidence that chlorine and ozone are fine for a starter to live in, but that chloramine will kill the starter. If your tap water contains chloramine, use filtered water for the starter. And no matter what, if you are using tap water and your starter is having trouble getting going, start again and use filtered water to see if that helps. A healthy starter should be ready to bake in 4 to 5 days.

2¼ cups [315 g] teff flour, plus more for maintaining the starter

2¼ cups [530 ml] water (filtered, if chloramine is present)

Sorghum flour and/or brown rice flour (or a mixture of these) for maintaining the starter (optional)

1. Place ¼ cup [35 g] of the teff flour and ¼ cup [60 ml] of the water in a 1-qt [1-L] canning jar and screw on the lid. Shake well to mix the flour and water. Loosen the lid so gas can escape and place the jar in a warm, draft-free place. The optimal temperature range for the starter is 70° to 80°F [21° to 27°C]. If the temperature is warmer, the starter will probably accelerate its growth. Any cooler and the starter will grow more slowly.

2. Leave it alone—do not shake or stir it—for 48 hours. After about 24 hours you should see some bubbling in the mixture. At 48 hours, the bubbling should be more noticeable—you may hear gas escaping from the lid. This means your starter has begun!

3. Once the starter is actively bubbling, remove the lid and stir it well. Add ¼ cup [35 g] teff flour and ¼ cup [60 ml] water. Stir well and replace the lid but don't screw it on—just place it on top of the jar to allow gas to escape as needed.

4. Let the starter sit for 8 to 12 hours, stir the mixture well, add ¼ cup [35 g] teff flour and ¼ cup [60 ml] water, and stir again. Set the lid lightly on the jar again so air can get in and out but bugs and dust cannot.

5. Let the starter sit for another 8 to 12 hours, then transfer it to a larger container (at least 2 qt [2 L] and made of plastic, glass, ceramic, or nonreactive metal). I use a 2-qt [2-L] glass jar or a plastic container (I like the containers made by Cambro). Stir the starter and add ½ cup [70 g] teff flour and ½ cup [120 ml] water. Stir it well and set the lid lightly on the container or cover it lightly with a dish towel.

6. Wait another 8 to 12 hours, stir the starter well, and add the remaining 1 cup [140 g] teff flour and 1 cup [240 ml] water. Stir well and cover lightly with the lid or a dish towel.

7. At this point, you can feed your starter any of the following flours: teff, (sweet) sorghum, or brown rice (although brown rice seems to require more frequent feedings). If the starter begins to throw off liquid at the top—known as hooch—or starts to separate in an obvious way, or if it smells extremely sour (versus mildly sour, like yogurt), then the starter needs to be fed.

8. After 8 to 12 hours more, you should have about 4 cups [960 ml] of starter. Stir it well and then pour off and discard about half the starter. Don't worry about being precise. The more starter you have in a container, the more you will need to feed it. The general rule is to feed the starter with a mixture that is equal parts flour and water with a total volume that is equal to the volume of the starter in the container. For example, if you have 2 cups [480 ml] of starter, then you'd feed it 1 cup [140 g] flour and 1 cup [240 ml] water.

9. Your starter should be ready to use 12 hours after this feeding.

10. From here on, you should feed and water the starter every 8 to 12 hours. At each feeding, stir the starter well and then pour off and discard about half the starter before feeding it. Remember to cover the container lightly to keep out bugs and dust.

A well-fed and -watered starter is full of happy yeast that will perform at peak performance. If you forget feedings, the yeast will weaken and won't work as well in baking. And, it will become extremely sour due to acid buildup. If the starter becomes too weak (as evidenced by a lot of hooch on top), or if mold starts to grow on it, it's best to throw it out and start over.

If you don't plan on baking with the starter anytime soon and you get tired of feeding and watering it, you can preserve it in a semi-dormant state in the refrigerator. Feed it every 3 days or so to keep it healthy. You must take it out of the refrigerator and resume regular feedings for at least 2 days before using it in a recipe to reactivate the yeast in the starter.

SOURDOUGH STARTER PRIMER

Sourdough bread is made with a fermented starter, which in turn is made from wild yeast, flour, and water. The yeast ferments the mixture by eating the sugars in the flour and turning them into alcohol and carbon dioxide gas. The gas serves as a leavener and helps the bread rise. Lactic-acid bacteria works with the yeast to create an environment that allows the yeast to grow and develop without being invaded by mold. What distinguishes sourdough starter from commercial yeast and makes it "sour" is that it evolves over time.

Sourdough starter is also called a *levain* (pronounced "le-vahn"—it's also known as a pre-ferment, or the chef, among other names). The "sour" in sourdough is a pleasing, tangy flavor developed over time using the levain. The more mature the levain—the longer it's been cultivated—the more intense the sour flavors will be in the bread. Many sourdough breads made with young levains have no discernable sour taste at all.

KEEP THE STARTER HEALTHY

A healthy starter needs to be carefully maintained. If you have too much starter and you don't feed or water it enough, it can die. So, pouring off excess starter is part of the process. Yeast grows at a phenomenal rate—at optimal conditions, it will double every 90 minutes. The more yeast you have, the more food you will need to feed the starter for it to thrive. A large container of sourdough starter that isn't maintained properly will become overwhelmed in its own waste—alcohol—which is known as *hooch* in sourdough parlance. If there is a small amount of hooch, you can mix it back into the starter and create a more sour flavor, but if there is too much hooch, the yeast will be overwhelmed and the starter will weaken. Too much hooch means that the yeast is weaker, and that means it has less leavening power. So, the more sour the bread, the more dense it will probably be.

Because yeast and bacteria are living things, temperature is important to their growth. The optimal temperature for sourdough starter is 70° to 80°F [21° to 27°C]. In this range, the yeast and lactic-acid bacteria will be happily and healthily humming along. If the temperature rises any higher, the yeast will start to grow faster and will need to be fed and watered more often—resulting in increased hooch and the need for even more feeding and watering. If the temperature drops lower than this range, the yeast will slow down and, at around 50°F [10°C], go dormant.

The healthier the starter, the more able it is to fight off unwanted organisms that want to live in it. Lactic-acid bacteria actually create an antibiotic called cycloheximide that kills the less desirable organisms that might try to grow in a starter—without killing the yeast. So, if the lactic-acid bacteria are happy and being nurtured well, the starter will remain free of bad things like mold.

PLAY WITH FLAVORS BY USING DIFFERENT FLOURS

Different flours create different flavors in a starter. Start with flours made from whole grains like teff or (sweet) sorghum, which I've found are reliable and flavorful. Other whole-grain flours are fine, too—experiment with them to see how they affect the taste and smell of the bread.

LONG-TERM CARE OF THE STARTER

You can keep a starter going indefinitely by taking good care of it, or you can use it all up and make a new starter when you need one. I sometimes go for weeks or months without making sourdough bread, so I find it easier to use all the starter at once (or compost whatever I don't use) and then make a new starter a few days before I want to make bread again. Do what works best for you and your schedule.

MASTER BREAD DOUGH

This is a versatile dough that makes a good, basic white bread. It is the base dough for Calzones (page 168), Focaccia (page 59), Deep-Dish Pizza (page 170), Soft Breadsticks (page 50), and Grissini (page 79).

3 cups [435 g] Jeanne's Gluten-Free All-Purpose Flour (page 39)

1¼ tsp xanthan gum

1 Tbsp aluminum-free double-acting baking powder

1 tsp salt

¼ cup [50 g] granulated sugar

1 Tbsp plus 1 tsp instant yeast

¼ cup [60 ml] vegetable oil

1 tsp vinegar

2 extra-large eggs, at room temperature

1 cup [240 ml] warm water (about 95°F [35°C])

1. In a medium bowl, mix together the flour, xanthan gum, baking powder, salt, sugar, and yeast.

2. In the bowl of a stand mixer, add the vegetable oil, vinegar, eggs, and water and beat slightly with a fork. Add the flour mixture, place the bowl into the stand mixer fitted with the dough hook, and beat on low speed to combine. Increase the speed to medium-high and beat for 4 minutes. Use an oiled rubber spatula to scrape down the sides of the bowl during mixing if necessary.

3. Using an oiled spatula, scrape the dough into a large oiled bowl or container. Cover the bowl with plastic wrap or a lid and let the dough rise in a warm, draft-free place for at least 1 hour. The dough should double in size and be full of holes.

4. If you plan to store the dough longer than 4 hours, place it in the refrigerator for up to 48 hours. When you are ready to use the dough, remove it from the refrigerator and let it sit at room temperature for about 30 minutes.

MASTER BUN DOUGH

Hamburger buns and hot dog buns are lighter, softer, and more delicate than sliced bread, yet they are expected to hold up to the many fillings that we put in them. This dough does that superbly. It creates buns that are fluffy and soft, with a hint of sweetness, but that are stronger than they look and feel and able to stand up to any fillings you place in them.

3 cups [435 g] Jeanne's Gluten-Free All-Purpose Flour (page 39)

1¼ tsp xanthan gum

1 Tbsp aluminum-free double-acting baking powder

1 tsp salt

¼ cup [50 g] granulated sugar

1 Tbsp plus 1 tsp instant yeast

¼ cup [60 ml] vegetable oil

1 tsp vinegar

3 extra-large eggs, at room temperature

1¼ cups [300 ml] warm water (about 95°F [35°C])

1. In a medium bowl, mix together the flour, xanthan gum, baking powder, salt, sugar, and yeast.

2. In the bowl of a stand mixer, add the vegetable oil, vinegar, eggs, and water and beat slightly with a fork. Add the flour mixture, place the bowl into the stand mixer fitted with the dough hook, and beat on low speed to combine. Increase the speed to medium-high and beat for 4 minutes. Use an oiled rubber spatula to scrape down sides of the bowl during mixing if necessary.

3. Using an oiled spatula, scrape the dough into a large oiled bowl or container. Cover the bowl with plastic wrap or a lid and let the dough rise in a warm, draft-free place for at least 1 hour. The dough should double in size and be full of holes.

4. If you plan to store the dough longer than 4 hours, place it in the refrigerator for up to 48 hours. When you are ready to use the dough, remove it from the refrigerator and let it sit at room temperature for about 30 minutes.

LAMINATED DOUGH PRIMER

The key to making flaky pastries like croissants and Danish pastries is using a laminated dough. Working with a laminated dough requires patience, attention to detail, and skill, all of which are gained via lots of practice. Laminated doughs are sensitive to temperature changes, so the baker also needs to pay careful attention to the temperature of the dough throughout the process.

An advanced technique, laminating dough is a process where butter that has been plasticized, or pounded repeatedly until it reaches a consistency that bends rather than breaks, is sealed in a packet of dough that's then repeatedly folded and rolled to make multiple layers. The packet of dough is folded in thirds like a letter, turned 90 degrees, rolled, folded in thirds like a letter again, turned 90 degrees, rolled, and so on, for a certain number of turns. Turning and folding the dough creates hundreds of thin sheets of butter stacked between hundreds of thin sheets of dough. While baking, the layers of butter melting between the layers of dough creates steam—the secret that creates each flaky layer. The technique is labor-intensive, but the results are amazing: a flaky buttery pastry unlike any other.

There are two different techniques for folding the dough: the single, or wallet, fold and the double, or book, fold.

A single fold looks like this:

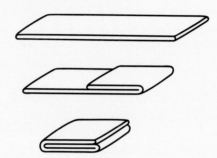

A double fold looks like this:

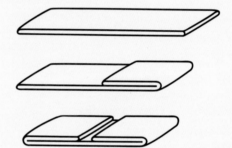

TYPES OF LAMINATED DOUGH

There are three types of laminated doughs: puff pastry dough, croissant dough, and Danish dough. The simplest to make is puff pastry dough, which uses just flour, water, and butter. Add yeast to those ingredients and you can make croissant dough. Making croissants using gluten-free ingredients is difficult. The challenge is to preserve the nice pliability that yeast adds to the dough without letting the strength of the yeast's leavening power weaken the not-so-elastic gluten-free dough. Danish dough is the most complex laminated dough—it uses eggs in addition to yeast. And yet, Danish dough is the most forgiving of the three. The eggs add an elasticity that isn't present in the gluten-free croissant or puff pastry dough, so it's more shapeable.

LAMINATED DOUGHS AND THE HOME BAKER

The recipes for these doughs tend to be long, but I assure you, they are completely manageable for the home baker. In fact, I used to make croissants in college for brunches with pals, unaware that they were supposed to be hard to make. I found a recipe, followed it, and was successful. I had no idea that croissants were considered complex for home cooks, so it didn't occur to me to be afraid to try making them. So, put your fear behind you, carefully follow the recipe, and you'll do just fine. Keep in mind that laminated doughs will not be rushed. Patience is required as you repeat the turning and folding, rolling, resting, and cutting several times.

Of all of the recipes in this book, laminated doughs are the most sensitive to temperature and need to be made in a narrow temperature range in order to succeed. If the dough is too cold, it won't roll well and will break. If the dough is too warm, the butter starts to melt into the dough, and you will lose the layers you have worked so hard to create. The ideal dough temperature for rolling and folding is between 60° and 65°F [16° and 18°C], with 60°F [16°C] being perfect. An instant-read thermometer is a great tool to help you make sure your dough is at the right temperature. Of course, a kitchen with an ambient temperature that is much higher than this range will create more challenging conditions in which to make a laminated dough.

If you are a new baker, I encourage you to develop your baking skills with simpler doughs before you attempt laminated doughs. Making laminated doughs with wheat flour is already pretty challenging, and making them with gluten-free flour substitutions doesn't make it any easier. Once you have a better sense of how the other gluten-free doughs work, you will be able to tackle laminated doughs with confidence.

PUFF PASTRY DOUGH

Having a supply of puff pastry in the freezer is very convenient. Many so-called "quick" pie or tart recipes start with the words, "Take a sheet of frozen puff pastry dough." Since there aren't any commercial gluten-free versions available (at least as of this writing), I developed my own. One of the easiest recipes to make with it is Puff Pastry Cheese Sticks (page 80). Before you begin, read the Laminated Dough Primer (page 94). You'll encounter three French terms in this recipe: *détrempe*, which refers to the water-flour dough; *beurrage*, which is the package of butter that you'll create; and *pâton*, the dough that is a laminated combination of the *détrempe* and *beurrage*.

It is important to prepare the dough in a cool environment. A kitchen that is 60° to 67°F [15° to 19°C] is ideal. A kitchen that is too warm will make preparing the dough more difficult, because the butter will melt in the dough. If you are making the dough on a day that is supposed to be very warm, start early in the morning and cool it in the refrigerator as often as needed.

DÉTREMPE

2 cups [290 g] Jeanne's Gluten-Free All-Purpose Flour (page 39)

1½ tsp salt

½ cup plus 2 Tbsp [150 ml] water, plus more as needed

BEURRAGE

1 cup [230 g] unsalted European butter (with at least 82% milk fat), cold

Tapioca flour for dusting

1. **TO MAKE THE *DÉTREMPE*:** Mix together the all-purpose flour and salt in a large bowl. Add the water and stir until the dough comes together in a rough ball. The dough should hold together well, but it shouldn't be wet and sticky. Add another 1 Tbsp water if the dough seems dry. Use your hands to form the dough into a smooth ball, wrap it in a clean, damp kitchen towel, and place it in the refrigerator.

2. **TO MAKE THE *BEURRAGE*:** Cut two pieces of parchment paper to about 12 in [30 cm] long by 13 in [33 cm] wide. Measure and draw a 4-in [10-cm] square on one side of one of the pieces of parchment paper.

3. Place the unmarked piece of parchment paper on a work surface. From here on, you should work as quickly as possible so that the butter doesn't become too warm. Remove the butter from the refrigerator and place it in the middle of the piece of parchment paper. Cover the butter with the parchment paper with the square drawn on it, penciled-side up (not touching the butter), centering the middle of the square over the butter. You are now going to plasticize the butter, or pound on it until it develops a consistency that bends rather than breaks when it is cold.

4. Using a heavy rolling pin, pound the butter until it spreads to about 1 in [2.5 cm] outside the lines of the square. Lift up the parchment paper and, using a bench scraper, cut off a bit of each side of the mound to straighten the sides and ensure that the butter block is still smaller than the drawn square. Use a knife to scrape the trimmed pieces of butter off the bench scraper onto the top of the butter block (never touch the

butter with your fingers because your body heat will warm it up). Replace the parchment paper and pound the butter some more until it spreads to about 1 in [2.5 cm] outside the lines of the square. Trim the sides again with the bench scraper and scrape the trimmed pieces onto the top of the block of butter with the knife. Repeat this process a few times to make sure the butter is properly plasticized.

5. To test for plasticity, move the parchment paper with the butter block to the edge of the counter so that half the block is hanging over the edge. Use your hand to gently press the butter down a bit over the edge. The butter should bend rather than break.

6. Make sure the block of butter is at least 1 in [2.5 cm] inside the square on all sides before you proceed to the next step.

7. Fold both pieces of parchment paper down along the lines of the penciled square (do your best with the bottom piece of parchment paper), tucking the paper under the block of butter. Place the parchment packet on the work surface, still with the square on top. Using a rolling pin, carefully roll out the butter so that it fills the entire square (be sure to fill out the corners). Try to make the butter as even as you can inside the packet. Place the packet on a flat surface in the refrigerator to cool.

8. Dust the work surface thoroughly with tapioca flour.

9. To prepare a *pâton*, remove the *détrempe* from the refrigerator and unwrap it. Place the dough on the work surface and roll out four flaps, about 5 in [13 cm] long, from the center of the ball to make a cross shape, leaving a roughly 4-in [10-cm] square of thick dough in the center. Roll each flap to the same thickness as the other flaps. The square of dough in the center should be thicker than the flaps.

10. Remove the *beurrage* from the refrigerator, unwrap the top piece of parchment paper, place the *beurrage* butter-side down in the center of the *détrempe*, and remove the second piece of parchment. Carefully fold the flaps of dough over the *beurrage*, one at a time. The top will look like the back of an envelope. The dough may break at the folds. If it does, press the breaks back together carefully with your fingers. Press together any gaps at the corners—the butter should be completely encased in dough so that it doesn't leak out.

11. Using the rolling pin, press diagonally (do not roll) across the dough from corner to corner, and again from the other corner to corner to make an *X*, then roll once across the top gently but firmly. This will help stabilize the butter so that it doesn't slide around inside the dough. Turn the *pâton* over so that the side with the flaps is on the bottom.

12. Wrap the *pâton* well in plastic wrap and place it in the refrigerator for 30 minutes to cool down.

13. Next, you'll turn and fold the *pâton* six times. First, dust the work surface and rolling pin with tapioca flour. Remove the *pâton* from the refrigerator and carefully roll it out into a long rectangle, about ½ in [12 mm] thick and 18 in [45 cm] long by about 8 in [20 cm] wide. As you roll out the dough, it will probably tear along the sides. Use your fingers and the rolling pin to repair the tears. The dough will look mottled and streaky. The streaks will diminish as you make each turn. Make more repairs to the edges of the *pâton* to make sure it looks like a neat rectangle.

14. Fold the rectangle of dough the same way you'd fold a letter into thirds before putting it in an envelope. Starting with a narrow end of the rectangle, fold about one-third of it over the dough. Then take the other narrow end and fold it over the dough.

CONTINUED >>

15. Repair and tidy the *patón*. Using the rolling pin, press diagonally across the dough from corner to corner, and again from the other corner to corner to make an *X*, then roll once across the top gently but firmly to stabilize the dough. Repair any tears as needed. You've now made one turn. Use the pad of your finger (and not your fingernail) to make an indentation in one of the corners of the *patón*. This indicates that you have done one fold and turn. This will help you keep track of how many turns you've completed. It's a good system to follow—especially if you need to put the dough into the fridge to cool down—you will be able to see how many folds you've made by looking at the number of indentations.

16. Using a pastry brush, brush off the flour that has accumulated on the bottom of the dough. Wrap the *patón* tightly in plastic wrap and refrigerate it for 20 minutes.

17. Dust the work surface and rolling pin with more tapioca flour. Remove the *patón* from the refrigerator, unwrap it, and place it on the work surface. Position the *patón* 90 degrees from the way it was facing during the previous fold. The folded edges should be at left and right. Repeat the rolling and folding process you followed while making the first turn, taking care to repair the edges as you go along. Mark the *patón* with two indentations to indicate that you've now made two turns. Wrap the *patón* tightly in plastic wrap and refrigerate it for 20 minutes. Repeat the process four more times, for a total of six turns, each time setting the *patón* in front of you at a 90-degree angle from the previous turn. After the first two turns, you might find that the dough is cold enough for you to do two turns per session before placing the dough in the refrigerator to cool. I usually do two turns at a time to complete the last four turns. Gauge your dough to see if it's cold enough—if it's too warm, it will stick to the rolling surface.

18. After the sixth and final turn, the dough should no longer be streaky. Repair the *patón* one final time to make it look as neat as possible. It should measure approximately 8-by-5-by-1-in [20-by-13-by-2.5-cm], which is roughly equivalent to the amount you get in a package of commercial (wheat) frozen puff pastry. Wrap the *patón* tightly in plastic wrap and refrigerate for 1 hour.

19. When you're ready to bake, you may need to rest the *patón* on the counter for 10 minutes or so to bring it to rolling temperature. If the dough starts to break or crack while you're rolling it, it's too cold and you should let it warm up a bit.

Store in the refrigerator for up to 2 days. After 2 days, the dough starts to lose its puffing ability, although the pastry will still be flaky.

If the dough has been in the refrigerator for longer than 2 hours, set it out on the counter for 30 to 60 minutes to warm up a bit. How long it needs to sit will depend on the temperature of your kitchen.

Puff pastry dough freezes beautifully. To freeze the dough, dust a work surface thoroughly with tapioca flour. Roll the dough into a rectangle until it is about ¼ in [6 mm] thick. Using a very sharp knife and making a straight up-and-down cut, trim off the raggedy edges. (If you like, stack the trimmed-off pieces, roll them out, wrap them in plastic wrap, and freeze them separately to use when you need smaller sheets of puff pastry.) Place the rectangle of dough on a large baking sheet and freeze it for 10 minutes, then wrap the dough tightly in several layers of plastic wrap and freeze for up to 3 months. (I usually cut the dough in half and wrap each half separately before storing them in the freezer.)

To use the frozen puff pastry dough, unwrap it and let it warm on the counter until it reaches about 60°F [15°C]. Do not use the dough if it's frozen—cutting it will crimp the edges and limit the rising.

TIPS FOR USING PUFF PASTRY

1. Cut the dough with a very sharp knife or shaped cutter, and don't use a back-and-forth or twisting motion while cutting the dough. Push straight down with the knife. The more you squish or crimp the edges, the less it will puff because the layers will be stuck together at the cut point.

2. Do not reroll the pastry dough. If you reroll it, it will not puff. It will still be flaky, but not as flaky as before.

3. If you are using flat pieces (like rectangles or strips), place the pieces of dough on the baking sheet upside down. This will help the pastry puff.

4. When you're using an egg wash on the top, be sure that it doesn't drip down the sides—this will seal the layers and limit the rise.

5. To enjoy its full flaky effect, let the baked puff pastry cool before eating it.

6. Keep in mind that gluten-free puff pastry doesn't puff quite as dramatically as wheat-flour puff pastry, but it will still be flaky and delicious!

BREADS AND CRACKERS

CHAPTER 3

MUFFINS, PANCAKES, DANISH, AND OTHER BREAKFAST TREATS

They say that breakfast is the most important meal of the day for the body. I would also argue that breakfast can be the most satisfying meal of the day for the soul. This is probably because I am a baker, but it's also because I am a hanger-outer. There is nothing I like better than to wake up and bake on a weekend morning and then linger into the afternoon with my family and friends over coffee, tea, and freshly baked goods. Scones, muffins, pastries, doughnuts, you name it—I love to bake them all and they all lend themselves to sitting and nibbling and chatting and relaxing.

BASIC MUFFINS

When my daughter was younger, muffins were one of my favorite things to bake for her and her friends. What I appreciate about muffins is that they can be customized in almost endless ways. My favorite additions are toasted nuts or fruit (or both) for an afternoon snack, or chocolate chips for a special after-dinner treat. As it turns out, even though my daughter and her pals are now teenagers, they still love a muffin for a snack. I encourage you to create your own muffin flavors. I've made some suggestions below to get you started.

2½ cups [360 g] Jeanne's Gluten-Free All-Purpose Flour (page 39)

2½ tsp aluminum-free double-acting baking powder

1 tsp salt

2 extra-large eggs

1 cup [200 g] granulated sugar, plus ⅓ cup [65 g] (optional)

¼ cup [55 g] unsalted butter, melted and cooled a bit

¼ cup [60 ml] neutral-flavored vegetable oil

1½ tsp pure vanilla extract

1 cup [240 ml] buttermilk

Optional mix-ins: Add one or more of each (for a total of 1 cup): 1 cup [120 g] dried fruit, such as currants, raisins, or cranberries; or 1 cup [110 g] fresh berries or chopped fruit; or 1 cup [120 g] chopped nuts; or 1 cup [170 g] chocolate chips

1. Preheat the oven to 425°F [220°C]. Prepare a 12-cup muffin pan with paper liners (or butter the cups).

2. In a small bowl, mix together the flour, baking powder, and salt.

3. In the bowl of a stand mixer fitted with the paddle attachment, beat the eggs on medium-high speed until light and airy, about 2 minutes. Add the 1 cup [200 g] sugar and beat on medium-high until light and fluffy, about 3 minutes. Turn the speed to low, slowly add the melted butter and vegetable oil, and beat until combined. Turn the speed to medium-high and beat for another 2 minutes. Add the vanilla and beat until combined.

4. Add the flour mixture alternately with the buttermilk in small batches, beginning and ending with the flour mixture. Add the mix-ins (if using).

5. Divide the batter evenly among the prepared muffin cups. If you like, sprinkle a bit of the remaining sugar on top of each muffin.

6. Bake until the tops are golden brown, about 20 minutes. Let the muffins cool in the pans for 5 minutes, then carefully turn them out onto a wire rack to cool completely.

Store in an airtight container at room temperature for up to 3 days, or in the freezer for up to 3 months.

BASIC SCONES

MAKES 15 TO 16 SCONES

I'm a devoted Anglophile and scones have always captured my imagination. Whenever I travel to England or Canada, I never pass up an opportunity to sit down to afternoon tea complete with scones and clotted cream. I'm so delighted that afternoon tea has become more popular in the United States. Making scones at home is a beloved family tradition, which started when my husband and I were first married and I would make them for breakfast on lazy weekends. When we became parents, my husband took on responsibility for making scones, and he now bakes them for special occasions like Mother's Day and birthdays.

3¼ cups [470 g] Jeanne's Gluten-Free All-Purpose Flour (page 39)

2 Tbsp aluminum-free double-acting baking powder

½ tsp salt

½ cup [100 g] granulated sugar

½ cup [110 g] unsalted butter, cold and cut into 16 pieces

2 extra-large eggs, lightly beaten

¾ cup [180 ml] buttermilk

1 cup [120 g] dried fruit, such as currants, raisins, or cranberries; or 1 cup [120 g] chopped nuts; or 1 cup [170 g] chocolate chips (optional)

1 tsp lemon, lime, or orange zest (optional)

Tapioca flour for dusting

1 egg beaten with 1 Tbsp water, for egg wash

1. In a large bowl, whisk together the all-purpose flour, baking powder, salt, and sugar. Add the butter and, with your fingers, rub the butter and dry ingredients together until the mixture looks like sand mixed with pebbles of varying sizes. Do this step quickly to avoid melting the butter.

2. Add the eggs and buttermilk and mix with a fork until the ingredients come together in a rough ball. Add the dried fruit (if using) and lemon zest (if using) and mix until well combined. The dough will be stiff, so you may need to use your hands.

3. Shape the dough into a fat disk, wrap well in plastic wrap, and place it in the refrigerator for 1 hour to rest.

4. Preheat the oven to 375°F [190°C]. Line two large baking sheets with parchment paper.

5. Remove the dough from the refrigerator and unwrap it, keeping the plastic wrap underneath it. Place another piece of plastic wrap on top of the dough. Using your hands, pat the dough until it's 1 in [2.5 cm] thick. Using a 2-in [5-cm] round cookie cutter, cut out as many circles as you can, dipping the cutter in tapioca flour before each cut. To ensure that the scones rise as high as possible, do not twist the cutter while you're cutting the dough—twisting the cutter will seal the edges of the scones, hindering their rise.

MUFFINS, PANCAKES, DANISH, AND OTHER BREAKFAST TREATS

CONTINUED >>

6. Place the scones on the prepared baking sheets at least 1 in [2.5 cm] apart. Carefully brush the top of each scone with the egg wash, taking care that the wash doesn't drip down the sides of the scone (this will also hinder their rise).

7. Bake one sheet of scones at a time until the tops of the scones have risen and are very light brown, 20 to 25 minutes.

8. Remove from the oven and carefully transfer to a wire rack to cool.

Store in an airtight container at room temperature for up to 3 days, or in the freezer for up to 3 months.

SIMPLE STREUSEL COFFEE CAKE

MAKES 1 (8-IN [20-CM]) SQUARE CAKE

When I was in college, I found a streusel coffee cake baking mix that was inexpensive, easy to make, and delicious. I made it once a week and ate it every day for breakfast. It allowed me to bake a little bit each week even though I was a ridiculously busy theater major with rehearsals that ran late each night and classes early each morning. Baking gave me a sense of comfort in those early days when college was new and a bit scary—no matter what, I could sit down with a slice of (semi) homemade coffee cake and start my day. This simple gluten-free version replicates the coffee cake of my early adulthood. It's sure to hit the spot for a morning treat. It's got a tender and moist crumb with a crunchy streusel topping. The streusel is quite sweet, so I've provided a range for the amount of sugar to use—you can decide how sweet to make your cake.

Tapioca flour for dusting

STREUSEL
⅓ cup [55 g] Baking Mix (page 41)
⅓ cup [65 g] packed dark brown sugar
½ tsp ground cinnamon
2 Tbsp unsalted butter, at room temperature

BATTER
2 extra-large eggs, at room temperature
⅔ cup [160 ml] milk, at room temperature
2 cups [340 g] Baking Mix (page 41)
2 to 4 Tbsp granulated sugar

1. Preheat the oven to 375°F [190°C]. Butter an 8-in [20-cm] square pan and dust with tapioca flour.

2. **TO MAKE THE STREUSEL:** In a small bowl, mix together the baking mix, brown sugar, and cinnamon. Add the butter and use the back of a spoon to incorporate the butter into the mix. Set aside.

3. **TO MAKE THE BATTER:** In a large bowl, whisk together the eggs and milk until foamy. Add the baking mix and granulated sugar and whisk until combined.

4. Scrape the batter into the prepared pan, making sure the mixture reaches into the corners. Smooth the top the best you can with a spatula. Sprinkle the streusel evenly over the top of the batter.

5. Bake until a tester inserted into the middle of the cake comes out clean, 25 minutes. Let the cake cool in the pan on a wire rack. Serve warm or at room temperature.

Store, covered, at room temperature for up to 3 days. Do not freeze.

SOURDOUGH PANCAKES AND WAFFLES

MAKES ABOUT 32 SMALL PANCAKES OR 8 WAFFLES

The sourness of these pancakes and waffles serve as an excellent foil to butter and maple syrup. My husband and I love them—they are a sophisticated change of pace from conventional pancakes and waffles, and the batter is easy to prepare either the morning you plan to eat them or the night before.

2 cups [480 ml] Sourdough Starter (page 88)

2 cups [480 ml] milk

2 cups [290 g] Jeanne's Gluten-Free All-Purpose Flour (page 39)

1 tsp salt

1 tsp baking soda

1 tsp aluminum-free double-acting baking powder

3 Tbsp granulated sugar (optional)

2 Tbsp neutral-flavored vegetable oil

2 extra-large eggs

1. In a large bowl, use a spoon to stir the starter, milk, and 1 cup [145 g] of the flour until combined. The mixture should be lumpy. Cover with plastic wrap and place in the refrigerator for at least 2 hours, or overnight.

2. When you are ready to make the pancakes or waffles, add the remaining flour and the salt, baking soda, baking powder, sugar (if using), vegetable oil, and eggs and stir well until the mixture is combined but still has some lumps.

3. **To make pancakes:** Preheat a cast-iron skillet or griddle until it's hot enough that a few drops of water scattered on it sizzle and pop. Working in batches of two or three (depending on the size of your pan), use a ladle or measuring cup to pour ¼ cup [60 ml] of batter per pancake in the pan or on the griddle, leaving room between each. Cook until bubbles form on the tops of the pancakes and start to pop. Use a metal spatula to check if the bottoms are golden brown. Flip the pancakes and cook for about 2 minutes more, or until the second sides are golden brown. Repeat with the remaining batter.

To make waffles: Heat a waffle maker according to the manufacturer's instructions. Even if your waffle maker is nonstick and seasoned, the batter may stick, so lightly oil it before making each waffle. Cook the waffles according to the manufacturer's instructions.

4. Pancakes and waffles are best eaten the day they are made.

Store in an airtight container, with a piece of wax paper layered between each, in the freezer for up to 3 months.

RAISED PANCAKES AND WAFFLES

MAKES ABOUT 20 SMALL PANCAKES OR 5 WAFFLES

One of the wonderful things about making a yeasted batter is that you mix it the night before and let it rise overnight while you sleep. In the morning, all you have to do is cook the pancakes or waffles. This batter makes pancakes and waffles that are crispy on the outside and pillowy on the inside. Serve with butter and maple syrup, fresh berries, or whipped cream and jam. They are my husband's favorite breakfast treat. He would eat them every day if he could!

2 cups [290 g] Jeanne's Gluten-Free All-Purpose Flour (page 39)

½ tsp xanthan gum

1 Tbsp granulated sugar

2 tsp aluminum-free double-acting baking powder

1 tsp salt

2 tsp instant yeast

1 tsp pure vanilla extract

3 Tbsp unsalted butter, melted and cooled

2 cups [480 ml] milk

2 extra-large eggs

1. In a large bowl, whisk together the flour, xanthan gum, sugar, baking powder, salt, and yeast. Add the vanilla, butter, milk, and eggs and whisk until well combined. There will still be small lumps of flour in the batter—this is okay. Cover with plastic wrap and place in the refrigerator for 12 to 24 hours.

2. **To make pancakes:** Preheat a cast-iron skillet or griddle until it's hot enough that a few drops of water scattered on it sizzle and pop. Working in batches of two or three (depending on the size of your pan), use a ladle or measuring cup to pour ¼ cup [60 ml] of batter per pancake in the pan or on the griddle, leaving room between each. Cook until bubbles form on the tops of the pancakes and start to pop. Use a metal spatula to check if the bottoms are golden brown. Flip the pancakes and cook for about 2 minutes more, or until the second sides are golden brown. Repeat with the remaining batter.

To make waffles: Heat a waffle maker according to the manufacturer's instructions and use the amount of batter recommended for your waffle maker. In my waffle maker this batter requires almost twice the cooking time as regular batter. You'll need to experiment to see how the batter cooks in your waffle maker. The outside of the waffles should be crisp and golden brown.

3. Pancakes and waffles are best eaten the day they are made.

Store in an airtight container, with a piece of wax paper layered between each, in the freezer for up to 3 months.

CRÊPES

MAKES 10 CRÊPES

Crêpes have a reputation for being fussy, but I find them as easy to make as pancakes—which is basically what they are. When my daughter was younger and life with a toddler seemed overwhelming and hard, we often had crêpes for dinner—rolled or folded with a variety of fillings. One of our favorite combinations was goat cheese, sautéed greens, and mushrooms (our daughter has always been a mushroom fan—she called them toadstools as a little one). Just about any filling that you can think of can be rolled into a crêpe, including grated cheese, sautéed vegetables, or ground meat. Dessert crêpes are equally as flexible—just choose a favorite sweet or semisweet filling. We like to spread Sweetened Cream Cheese Filling for Pastries (page 133) on them and roll them up. This recipe will work for both sweet and savory dishes. It contains some confectioners' sugar—I've always liked a little sweetness in savory crêpe dishes. If you prefer not to use sugar, substitute my all-purpose flour mix for the same quantity of confectioners' sugar. Crêpes can be made in any type of heavy-bottomed skillet, but a crêpe pan is a helpful piece of equipment to have if you make them a lot because it's lighter, making it easier to lift the pan to swirl the batter into shape.

¾ cup [105 g] Jeanne's Gluten-Free All-Purpose Flour (page 39)

½ tsp salt

1 tsp aluminum-free double-acting baking powder

2 Tbsp confectioners' sugar

2 extra-large eggs

½ cup [120 ml] milk

½ cup [120 ml] water

½ tsp pure vanilla extract or lemon or orange zest (optional)

Vegetable oil for brushing

1. In a medium bowl, mix together the flour, salt, baking powder, and confectioners' sugar.

2. In another medium bowl, whisk the eggs until lightly beaten. Add the milk, water, and vanilla (if using) and whisk to combine.

3. Add the egg mixture to the flour mixture and whisk for about 40 strokes. The batter should be fairly smooth but with small lumps of flour. The consistency will resemble heavy cream.

4. Cover the bowl with plastic wrap and place in the refrigerator for at least 1 hour, or up to 24 hours, before using.

5. When you are ready to cook the crêpes, have ready a dinner plate and a clean kitchen towel.

6. Heat a crêpe pan or heavy-bottomed skillet over medium-high heat until hot. Brush the pan lightly with vegetable oil.

7. Using a ladle or measuring cup, pour ¼ cup [60 ml] of batter in the middle of the pan and quickly tilt and rotate the pan (use a pot holder if the handle is hot) to spread the batter into a thin, even layer. Place the pan on the heat and cook for about 50 seconds. Using a long offset spatula, lift the crêpe and peek underneath to check for doneness. The bottom should be light brown and the top should be full of holes.

8. Carefully slide the offset spatula under the crêpe and make sure that it's not sticking to the pan, then quickly flip the crêpe onto the uncooked side.

9. Cook for about 40 seconds. Use the spatula to pick up and flip the crêpe top-side down onto the dinner plate. Cover the crêpe with the kitchen towel to keep it warm.

10. Let the pan reheat for several seconds, brush it again with oil, and repeat with the remaining batter. When each crêpe is finished, flip it top-side down onto the crêpe that was cooked before it and cover with the kitchen towel. Crêpes are best eaten the day they are made.

Store in a zip-top bag in the freezer for up to 3 months.

BAKED DOUGHNUTS

MAKES 24 MINI DOUGHNUTS OR 12 REGULAR DOUGHNUTS

The batter for this recipe is liquid enough that you will need to use a doughnut pan for the best results. These doughnuts are more springy and muffinlike than their fried brethren, but they have a classic doughnut flavor and are just as delicious. I've also given a chocolate variation—either is scrumptious with a dusting of confectioners' sugar or dipped in a chocolate, coffee, maple, or vanilla glaze.

2 cups [290 g] Jeanne's Gluten-Free All-Purpose Flour (page 39)

2 tsp aluminum-free double-acting baking powder

½ tsp baking soda

½ tsp salt

2 extra-large eggs, at room temperature

½ cup [100 g] granulated sugar

¼ cup [55 g] unsalted butter, melted and cooled

2 tsp pure vanilla extract

1 cup [240 ml] buttermilk, at room temperature

Confectioners' sugar for dusting (optional)

Doughnut Glaze (facing page; optional)

1. Preheat the oven to 425°F [220°C]. Butter two doughnut pans.

2. In a small bowl, mix together the flour, baking powder, baking soda, and salt.

3. In a large bowl, whisk the eggs until foamy. Add the granulated sugar and whisk until foamy. Add the butter and whisk until well combined. Add the vanilla and whisk until combined.

4. Add the flour mixture alternately with the buttermilk in small batches, beginning and ending with the flour, and mix with a spoon to combine.

5. Using a pastry bag fitted with a large round tip, pipe the batter into the doughnut pans. You can also spoon the dough into the doughnut pans, but the doughnuts will be uneven.

6. Bake for 8 minutes, or until a tester inserted into the middle of one of the doughnuts comes out clean. Turn out the doughnuts onto a wire rack to cool completely.

7. If you like, sift confectioners' sugar over the doughnuts just before serving (the sugar will be absorbed into the doughnuts if they're stored). Or, dip the top of each doughnut in the glaze, allowing any excess glaze to drip back into the bowl. Place each glazed doughnut on a wire rack to let the glaze set. Glazed doughnuts become soggy when stored, so only glaze as many as you will serve immediately.

Store plain doughnuts in an airtight container at room temperature for up to 3 days, or in the freezer for up to 3 months.

VARIATION

CHOCOLATE DOUGHNUTS: Replace ½ cup [70 g] of the flour with ½ cup [50 g] unsweetened cocoa powder and proceed as directed.

DOUGHNUT GLAZE

EACH RECIPE MAKES ENOUGH GLAZE FOR 24 DOUGHNUTS AND DOUGHNUT HOLES

MAPLE GLAZE

¼ cup [60 ml] heavy cream

1 Tbsp pure vanilla extract

2 tsp maple flavoring

2 cups [240 g] confectioners' sugar, sifted

In a medium bowl, whisk together the cream and vanilla. Add the maple flavoring and whisk to combine. Whisk in the confectioners' sugar until smooth. Use immediately.

COFFEE GLAZE

¼ cup [60 ml] heavy cream

1 Tbsp pure vanilla extract

2 tsp powdered instant coffee granules (caffeinated or decaffeinated)

2 cups [240 g] confectioners' sugar, sifted

In a medium bowl, whisk together the cream and vanilla. Add the instant coffee and whisk to combine. Whisk in the confectioners' sugar until smooth. Use immediately.

CHOCOLATE GLAZE

½ cup [110 g] unsalted butter

⅔ cup [110 g] semisweet chocolate chips or chopped semisweet chocolate

1½ tsp pure vanilla extract

2 cups [240 g] confectioners' sugar, sifted

1 to 4 Tbsp hot water

In a small, heavy-bottomed saucepan over medium-low heat, melt the butter and chocolate together and whisk to combine. Remove from the heat. Whisk in the vanilla and confectioners' sugar. Whisk in 1 Tbsp hot water until the glaze is smooth and slightly runny. If the glaze is too thick, whisk in more hot water 1 Tbsp at a time until it is at the desired consistency. Use immediately.

VANILLA GLAZE

2 cups [240 g] confectioners' sugar, sifted

½ tsp honey

⅛ tsp salt

½ tsp pure vanilla extract

¼ cup [60 ml] hot water, plus more as needed

Put the confectioners' sugar, honey, salt, and vanilla in a medium bowl. Add the hot water and whisk until combined. The glaze should be pourable but not too thick. If it's too thick, add more water, 1 tsp at a time, until it reaches the desired consistency. Use immediately.

MUFFINS, PANCAKES, DANISH, AND OTHER BREAKFAST TREATS

RAISED DOUGHNUTS

Raised doughnuts are the softer, fluffier cousins of the more humble and sturdy Cake Doughnuts (page 116). They are pillowy and cloudlike. They can be dipped in a variety of glazes. Before making this recipe, read the Deep-Frying Primer (page 20).

2½ cups [360 g] Jeanne's Gluten-Free All-Purpose Flour (page 39)

½ tsp xanthan gum

1 tsp salt

1 Tbsp aluminum-free double-acting baking powder

¾ cup [150 g] granulated sugar

2 Tbsp instant yeast

1 Tbsp unsalted butter, melted and cooled slightly

1 extra-large egg, at room temperature

1 tsp apple cider vinegar

¾ cup [180 ml] warm water (about 95°F [35°C])

Tapioca flour for dusting

Vegetable oil for frying

Doughnut Glaze (page 113)

1. In the bowl of a stand mixer fitted with the paddle attachment, mix together the all-purpose flour, xanthan gum, salt, baking powder, sugar, and yeast. Add the butter, egg, vinegar, and water and beat on medium speed for 5 minutes. The mixture will be soft and sticky—somewhat like a cake batter.

2. Cover the bowl with plastic wrap and let the dough rise in a warm, draft-free place for 1 hour. The dough should be noticeably puffy at the end of the hour.

3. Dust a work surface thoroughly with tapioca flour. Place more tapioca flour in a bowl large enough to accommodate a doughnut cutter. Line a large baking sheet with parchment paper.

4. Turn out the dough onto the work surface. The dough will be extremely soft and loose. Sprinkle the top of the dough with tapioca flour. Gently roll out the dough to ½ in [12 mm] thick. Dip the doughnut cutter in the tapioca flour and cut out as many doughnuts as possible, dipping the cutter into the tapioca flour before cutting each doughnut. The dough will probably stick to the cutter. To remove it, shake the cutter hard into your other hand; a few energetic shakes should do the trick. Brush any extra tapioca flour off the doughnuts with a pastry brush and place them on the prepared baking sheet.

5. Gather the scraps of dough and brush off any excess tapioca flour with the pastry brush. Using both hands, squeeze the scraps gently but firmly into a ball.

6. Dust the work surface with more tapioca flour, sprinkle tapioca flour on top of the dough, and repeat the rolling and cutting process until you have used all the dough. Cover the doughnuts and doughnut holes with plastic wrap and let rise in a warm, draft-free place for 1 hour.

7. Pour 3 in [7.5 cm] of vegetable oil into a heavy-bottomed saucepan fitted with a candy thermometer and heat the oil to 325°F [165°C]. Line a large baking sheet with paper towels and place a wire rack on the sheet.

8. When the oil has reached temperature, place as many doughnuts into the oil as will fit in the pan without crowding. Keep the remaining doughnuts covered with plastic wrap. When the doughnuts rise to the surface, let them fry for 30 seconds. Turn the doughnuts and fry for 30 seconds longer. Turn the doughnuts again and fry for another 20 seconds. The doughnuts should be golden brown (but not too dark). Using metal tongs or a slotted spoon, remove each doughnut from the oil, allow the excess oil to drip back into the pan, and transfer to the wire rack to cool completely.

9. Monitor the oil temperature and raise or lower the burner temperature to maintain 325°F [165°C]. Repeat with the remaining doughnuts.

10. Pile the doughnut holes onto a slotted spoon and gently slip them all into the oil (or as many as will fit in the pan without crowding). When the doughnut holes rise to the surface, let them fry for about 90 seconds, turning frequently. Using the slotted spoon, remove the doughnut holes from the oil, allow the excess oil to drip back into the pan, and transfer to the wire rack to cool completely.

11. Dip the top of each doughnut in the glaze, allowing the excess glaze to drip back into the bowl. Place each glazed doughnut on the wire rack to let the glaze set. Glazed doughnuts become soggy when stored, so only glaze as many as you will serve immediately. Doughnuts are best eaten the day they are fried.

Store plain doughnuts in an airtight container at room temperature for up to 3 days, or in the freezer for up to 3 months.

MUFFINS, PANCAKES, DANISH, AND OTHER BREAKFAST TREATS

CAKE DOUGHNUTS

Even though Raised Doughnuts (page 114) get all the attention, non-yeasted cake doughnuts are the ones I often crave. There is something so comforting about cake doughnuts—the crumb is denser and more filling, and cake doughnuts tend to have a depth of flavor that I like. This gluten-free version is easy to make, accommodates a variety of glazes, and holds up well to dunking in your coffee or tea. Read the Deep-Frying Primer on page 20 for technique tips before making these.

2¼ cups [325 g] Jeanne's Gluten-Free All-Purpose Flour (page 39)

2 tsp aluminum-free double-acting baking powder

1 tsp salt

½ tsp freshly ground nutmeg

½ cup [100 g] granulated sugar

2 Tbsp unsalted butter, at room temperature

1 extra-large egg

⅔ cup [160 ml] sour cream, at room temperature

Tapioca flour for dusting

Vegetable oil for frying

1 cup [120 g] confectioners' sugar (optional)

Cinnamon-Sugar for Doughnuts and Pastries (recipe follows; optional)

Doughnut Glaze (page 113; optional)

1. In a medium bowl, mix together the all-purpose flour, baking powder, salt, and nutmeg.

2. In the bowl of a stand mixer fitted with the paddle attachment, beat the granulated sugar and butter on medium speed for 1 minute more. Add the egg and beat for 1 minute more. The mixture should look smooth and yellow.

3. Add the flour mixture alternately with the sour cream in small batches, beginning and ending with the flour mixture, and beat to combine. The dough will be very stiff.

4. Scrape the dough into a bowl and cover with plastic wrap. Refrigerate for at least 1 hour, or up to 24 hours.

5. Dust a work surface thoroughly with tapioca flour. Place more tapioca flour in a bowl large enough to accommodate a doughnut cutter. Line a large baking sheet with parchment paper.

6. Turn out the dough onto the work surface and dust with tapioca flour. Gently roll out the dough to ½ in [12 mm] thick. Dip the doughnut cutter in the tapioca flour and cut out as many doughnuts as possible, dipping the cutter into the tapioca flour before cutting each doughnut. The dough will probably stick to the cutter. To remove it, shake the cutter hard into your other hand; a few energetic shakes should do the trick. Brush any extra tapioca flour off the doughnuts with a pastry brush and place them on the prepared baking sheet.

7. Gather the scraps of dough and brush off any excess tapioca flour with the pastry brush. Using both hands, squeeze the scraps gently but firmly into a ball.

8. Dust the work surface with more tapioca flour, sprinkle tapioca flour on top of the ball of dough, and repeat the rolling and cutting process until you have used all the dough. Cover the doughnuts and doughnut holes with plastic wrap so they don't dry out.

9. Pour 3 in [7.5 cm] of vegetable oil into a heavy-bottomed saucepan fitted with a candy thermometer and heat the oil to 325°F [165°C]. Line a large baking sheet with paper towels and place a wire rack on the sheet.

10. When the oil has reached temperature, place as many doughnuts in the oil as will fit in the pan without crowding. Keep the remaining doughnuts covered with plastic wrap. When the doughnuts rise to the surface, let them fry for 15 seconds. Turn the doughnuts and fry for 75 seconds longer. Turn the doughnuts again and fry for another 75 seconds. The doughnuts should be golden brown (but not too dark). Using metal tongs or a slotted spoon, remove each doughnut from the oil, allow the excess oil to drip back into the pan, and transfer to the wire rack to cool completely.

11. Monitor the oil temperature and raise or lower the burner temperature to maintain 325°F [165°C]. Repeat with the remaining doughnuts.

12. Pile the doughnut holes onto a slotted spoon and gently slip them all into the oil (or as many as will fit in the pan without crowding). When the doughnut holes rise to the surface, let them fry for about 90 seconds, turning frequently. Using the slotted spoon, remove the doughnut holes from the oil, allow the excess oil to drip back into the pan, and transfer to the wire rack to cool completely.

13. If you like, sift the confectioners' sugar over the doughnuts, or roll the doughnuts in cinnamon-sugar, just before serving (the sugar will start to melt into the doughnuts after about an hour).

14. Or, dip the top of each doughnut in the glaze, allowing any excess glaze to drip back into the bowl. Place each glazed doughnut on the wire rack to let the glaze set. Glazed dough-nuts become soggy when stored, so only glaze as many as you will serve immediately. Dough-nuts are best eaten the day they are fried.

Store plain doughnuts in an airtight container at room temperature for up to 3 days, or in the freezer for up to 3 months.

CINNAMON-SUGAR FOR DOUGHNUTS AND PASTRIES

MAKES ¼ CUP [50 G]

Use this simple mixture to top Churros (page 223) as well as cake doughnuts.

¼ cup [50 g] granulated sugar
¼ tsp ground cinnamon

In a small bowl, mix together the sugar and cinnamon.

Store in an airtight container at room temperature indefinitely.

OLD-FASHIONED DOUGHNUTS

MAKES 10 TO 12 DOUGHNUTS AND DOUGHNUT HOLES

If asked to choose my favorite doughnut, I would have to pick old-fashioned doughnuts. They are fried longer than other doughnuts, which causes the dough to crack and form delicious ridges and crunchy pockets that trap extra glaze. The conventional glaze for these doughnuts is vanilla. I've adapted the following recipe from one created by Top Pot Doughnuts, the popular Seattle dough-nut makers. Before making this recipe, read the Deep-Frying Primer (page 20).

2¼ cups [325 g] Jeanne's Gluten-Free All-Purpose Flour (page 39)

1 Tbsp aluminum-free double-acting baking powder

1 tsp salt

¾ tsp freshly ground nutmeg

½ cup [100 g] granulated sugar

2 Tbsp unsalted butter, softened

2 egg yolks

⅔ cup [160 ml] sour cream

Tapioca flour for dusting

Vegetable oil for frying

Vanilla Glaze (see page 113)

1. In a medium bowl, mix together the all-purpose flour, baking powder, salt, and nutmeg.

2. In the bowl of a stand mixer fitted with the paddle attachment, beat the sugar and butter on medium speed for 1 minute. Add the egg yolks and beat for 1 minute more. The mixture should look smooth and yellow.

3. Add the flour mixture alternately with the sour cream in small batches, beginning and ending with the flour mixture, and beat to combine. The dough will be very stiff.

4. Scrape the dough into a bowl and cover with plastic wrap. Refrigerate for at least 1 hour, or up to 24 hours.

5. Dust a work surface thoroughly with tapioca flour. Place more tapioca flour in a bowl large enough to accommodate a doughnut cutter. Line a large baking sheet with parchment paper.

6. Turn out the dough onto the work surface and dust with tapioca flour. Gently roll out the dough to ½ in [12 mm] thick. Dip the doughnut cutter in the tapioca flour and cut out as many doughnuts as possible, dipping the cutter into the tapioca flour before cutting each doughnut. The dough will probably stick to the cutter. To remove it, shake the cutter hard into your other hand; a few energetic shakes should do the trick. Brush any extra tapioca flour off the doughnuts with a pastry brush and place them on the prepared baking sheet.

7. Gather the scraps of dough and brush off any excess tapioca flour with the pastry brush. Using both hands, squeeze the scraps gently but firmly into a ball.

CONTINUED >>

8. Dust the work surface with more tapioca flour, sprinkle tapioca flour on top of the dough, and repeat the rolling and cutting process until you have used all the dough.

9. If you want the iconic ridge around the top that old-fashioned doughnuts are known for, use a sharp knife to make a cut ⅛ in [4 mm] deep around the top of the doughnuts. The cut will open up while the doughnuts are frying and create the crunchy ridge. Cover the doughnuts and doughnut holes with plastic wrap so they don't dry out.

10. Pour 3 in [7.5 cm] of vegetable oil into a heavy-bottomed saucepan fitted with a candy thermometer and heat the oil to 325°F [165°C]. Line a large baking sheet with paper towels and place a wire rack on the sheet.

11. When the oil has reached temperature, place as many doughnuts into the oil as will fit in the pan without crowding. Keep the remaining doughnuts covered with plastic wrap. When the doughnuts rise to the surface, let them fry for 15 seconds. Turn the doughnuts and fry for 90 seconds longer. Turn the doughnuts again and fry for another 90 seconds. The doughnuts should be dark golden brown. Using metal tongs or a slotted spoon, remove each doughnut from the oil, allow the excess oil to drip back into the pan, and transfer to the wire rack to cool completely.

12. Monitor the oil temperature and raise or lower the burner temperature to maintain 325°F [165°C]. Repeat with the remaining doughnuts.

13. Pile the doughnut holes onto a slotted spoon and gently slip them all into the oil (or as many as will fit into the pan without crowding). When the doughnut holes rise to the surface, let them fry for about 90 seconds, turning frequently. Using the slotted spoon, remove the doughnut holes from the oil, allow the excess oil to drip back into the pan, and transfer to the wire rack to cool completely.

14. Dip the top of each doughnut in the glaze, allowing any excess glaze to drip back into the bowl. Place each glazed doughnut on the wire rack to let the glaze set. Glazed doughnuts become soggy when stored, so only glaze as many as you will serve immediately. Doughnuts are best eaten the day they are fried.

Store plain doughnuts in an airtight container at room temperature for up to 3 days, or in the freezer for up to 3 months.

FRENCH CRULLERS

MAKES 24 CRULLERS

French crullers are an elegant version of a doughnut. They are made from pâte à choux dough, which cooks up puffy and lighter than air. French crullers have a fluted ring shape that is created by piping out the dough using a pastry bag fitted with a star tip. In fact, the word *cruller* comes from the Dutch word *krullen*, which means "to curl." These delicate and addictive pastries are much easier to make than they look, and they are good with just about any glaze in this book. Before making this recipe, read the Deep-Frying Primer (page 20).

1 recipe Pâte à Choux Dough (page 248)
Vegetable oil for frying
Doughnut Glaze (page 113)

1. Line two large baking sheets with parchment paper.

2. Using half of the pâte à choux dough, fill a pastry bag fitted with a ⅜-in [1-cm] (I use an Ateco #824) star tip. Pipe twelve rings 2½ in [6 cm] in diameter 1 in [2.5 cm] apart onto a prepared baking sheet. Refill the pastry bag and pipe another 12 rings onto the second prepared baking sheet. Use a pair of scissors to cut the parchment paper around each cruller. You will place the rings of dough and the parchment paper they're attached to into the oil, which will help this very loose dough keep its shape.

3. Pour 3 in [7.5 cm] of vegetable oil into a heavy-bottomed saucepan fitted with a candy thermometer and heat the oil to 375°F [190°F]. Line a large baking sheet with a double layer of paper towels and place a wire rack on the sheet.

4. Once the oil has reached temperature, place as many crullers (with their attached parchment papers) into the oil as will fit into the pan without crowding. After about 30 seconds, remove the pieces of parchment paper by peeling it off the rings of dough with metal tongs and discard. (I keep a plate next to the stove to hold the used parchment pieces as they come out of the oil.) Fry the crullers, turning them every minute or so, until they're golden brown, 5 to 7 minutes. Using metal tongs or a slotted spoon, transfer the crullers to the wire rack to cool completely.

5. Monitor the oil temperature and raise or lower the burner temperature to maintain 375°F [190°C]. Repeat with the remaining crullers.

6. Dip the top of each cruller in the glaze, allowing any excess glaze to drip back into the bowl. Place each glazed cruller on the wire rack to let the glaze set. Crullers are best eaten the day they are glazed.

Store plain crullers in a paper bag at room temperature for up to 3 days. Reheat in a 350°F [180°C] oven for about 10 minutes before serving. Do not freeze.

MUFFINS, PANCAKES, DANISH, AND OTHER BREAKFAST TREATS

CONTINUED >>

VARIATION

BAKED CRULLERS: You can also bake crullers, although they will have firmer crusts than the fried version. Preheat the oven to 425°F [230°C]. Line a baking sheet with parchment paper and pipe the crullers onto the paper at least 2 in [5 cm] apart. Bake for 10 minutes, then lower the oven temperature to 350°F [180°C] and bake for another 20 to 25 minutes, or until the crullers are deep golden brown. Remove from the oven and transfer to a wire rack to cool completely. Glaze as directed.

BEIGNETS

Beignets are basically fried cream puffs, which means that they are beyond decadent. Although they share a name with the famous New Orleans fried treat, the New Orleans beignets are closer in kinship to a raised doughnut than to cream puffs. They are delicious with mounds of confectioners' sugar on top. Before making this recipe, read the Deep-Frying Primer (page 20).

Vegetable oil for frying
1 recipe Pâte à Choux Dough (page 248)
½ cup [60 g] confectioners' sugar (optional)

1. Pour 3 in [7.5 cm] of vegetable oil into a heavy-bottomed saucepan fitted with a candy thermometer and heat the oil to 375°F [190°C]. Line a large baking sheet with a double layer of paper towels and place a wire rack on the sheet.

2. When the oil has reached temperature, drop as many 1-tsp-size balls of dough into the oil as will fit into the pan without crowding. Fry the beignets until golden brown, 5 to 7 minutes. They should turn by themselves in the oil, but if they don't, turn them occasionally so that all sides fry. Transfer the cooked beignets to the wire rack to cool completely.

3. Monitor the oil temperature and raise or lower the burner temperature to maintain 375°F [190°C]. Repeat with the remaining beignets.

4. If you like, sift confectioners' sugar over the beignets just before serving (the sugar will start to melt into the beignets after about an hour). Beignets are best eaten the day they are fried.

Store plain beignets in a paper bag at room temperature for up to 3 days. Do not freeze.

BEAR CLAWS

I love making these delicious and whimsical pastries. They are a much easier process than anyone realizes. While reading Beatrice Ojakangas's invaluable cookbook *The Great Scandinavian Baking Book,* I was intrigued to discover that what we Americans call "bear claws," the Danes call "cockscombs"— which makes sense! They are also sometimes called "scrubbing brushes."

Whatever their name, they're a scrumptious addition to any baker's repertoire.

Tapioca flour for dusting
1 recipe Master Danish Pastry Dough (page 154)
1 recipe Almond Paste (recipe follows), cold
1 egg beaten with 1 Tbsp water, for egg wash (optional)
Almond slices for decorating (optional)
1 recipe Simple Glaze for Pastries (recipe follows)

1. Line a large baking sheet with parchment paper. Dust a work surface lightly but thoroughly with tapioca flour.

2. Place the dough, with the folded edges at the top and bottom (with a long side facing you), on the work surface. Using a sharp knife, cut the dough down the middle. Rewrap half the dough in plastic wrap and return it to the refrigerator while you're rolling and shaping the other half.

3. Turn the dough so the cut edge is facing you. Carefully roll out the dough until it is about 13 in [33 cm] long by about 9 in [23 cm] wide and ¼ in [6 mm] thick. Tidy the edges by cutting off about ½ in [12 mm] on all sides. You should now have a rectangle that is approximately 12 in [30 cm] long and 8 in [20 cm] wide.

4. Cut the dough into six squares, each about 4 in [10 cm] square, by measuring 4 in [10 cm] across the width of the dough and cutting the dough in half from top to bottom. Then measure 4-in [10-cm] increments down the vertical side of the dough, making two cuts horizontally from side to side in the dough. Stack the squares on top of one another so they retain their coolness.

5. Lightly dust the work surface with tapioca flour again. Roll out a square of dough, flattening it a bit. Roll 1 Tbsp of almond paste between your palms into a log that is 3 in [7.5 cm] long. Place it horizontally on the dough just above the middle. Use a finger dipped in water to moisten the lower edge of the square. Gently fold the top edge of the dough over the almond paste to the moistened edge and press down along the bottom edge to seal the two sides of the dough together. Use a finger to gently press the dough snugly around the almond paste log. Make four cuts, each about ½ in [12 mm] long, evenly spaced along the bottom edge of the dough. Gently pull apart both sides of the outer bottom edges of the dough to open up the cuts slightly and create the bear claw's five fingers. Place the finished bear claw on the prepared baking sheet.

6. Repeat the process with the remaining squares of dough and place on the prepared baking sheet at least 1 in [2.5 cm] apart.

7. Cover with plastic wrap and let sit at room temperature for 30 minutes to proof. If the temperature in your kitchen is above 70°F [21°C], monitor the pastries. If they become sweaty or look like they are coming apart, place the baking

CONTINUED >>

sheet in the refrigerator for the remaining proofing time.

8. While the bear claws are proofing, preheat the oven to 450°F [230°C].

9. Remove the plastic wrap. Lightly brush each bear claw with the egg wash (if using). If you like, sprinkle the almonds over the pastries or place an almond slice on each finger to simulate a claw, pressing down lightly to make sure it sticks to the dough.

10. Place the baking sheet in the oven and lower the oven temperature to 425°F [220°C]. Bake until the bear claws are golden brown, 20 to 25 minutes.

11. Transfer the bear claws to a wire rack to cool completely. Repeat the process with the remaining dough.

12. Once the pastries have cooled, place a large baking sheet under the wire rack and use a fork to drizzle the pastries with the glaze. Let the glaze set for at least 15 minutes before serving. Bear claws are best eaten the day they are made.

Store in an airtight container at room temperature for up to 2 days. Do not freeze.

ALMOND PASTE

MAKES ABOUT 1 CUP [230 G]

Almond paste is a common filling for pastries, but I've found it difficult to find a commercial product that doesn't contain wheat starch. This gluten-free version is easy to make.

1 cup [145 g] blanched almonds (see page 43)
½ cup [60 g] confectioners' sugar
1 egg white
⅛ tsp almond extract

In the bowl of a food processor or a blender, pulse the almonds into a fine meal. Add the confectioners' sugar and pulse until combined. Add the egg white and pulse until the mixture starts to come together. Add the almond extract and pulse until it comes together into a thick paste.

Store in an airtight container in the refrigerator for up to 1 month, or in the freezer for up to 3 months. Before using, remove the paste from the refrigerator and bring it to room temperature.

SIMPLE GLAZE FOR PASTRIES

MAKES 1 CUP [240 ML]

This glaze is used for all of the Danish pastries.

1 cup [120 g] confectioners' sugar, sifted
3 Tbsp water or freshly squeezed lemon juice

In a small bowl, whisk together the confectioners' sugar and water until smooth and uniform.

Store, covered, at room temperature for up to 48 hours. Do not freeze.

PASTRY SNAILS

So named because their shape looks like a whorled snail shell, these are based on a favorite treat of mine from childhood. The bakery in my hometown made Danish pastries of all types, and their version of pastry snails contained a cinnamon-pecan mixture, which I've replicated here.

½ cup [60 g] pecans, toasted (see page 42) and chopped

½ cup [100 g] lightly packed dark brown sugar

½ tsp ground cinnamon

Tapioca flour for dusting

1 recipe Master Danish Pastry Dough (page 154)

4 Tbsp [55 g] unsalted butter, softened

1 egg beaten with 1 Tbsp water, for egg wash

1 recipe Simple Glaze for Pastries (page 127)

1. In a small bowl, mix together the pecans, brown sugar, and cinnamon.

2. Line a large baking sheet with parchment paper. Dust a rolling board lightly but thoroughly with tapioca flour.

3. Place the dough, with the folded edges at the top and bottom (with a long side facing you), on the rolling board. Using a sharp knife, cut the dough down the middle. Rewrap half the dough in plastic wrap and return it to the refrigerator while you're rolling and shaping the other half.

4. Turn the dough so that the cut edge is facing you. Carefully roll out the dough until it is about 13 in [33 cm] long by about 9 in [23 cm] wide and ¼ in [6 mm] thick. Tidy the edges by cutting off about ½ in [12 mm] on all sides. You should now have a rectangle that is approximately 12 in [30 cm] long and 8 in [20 cm] wide.

5. Turn the dough so that a long side is facing you. Spread 2 Tbsp of the butter on the dough, leaving a ½-in [12-mm] border all around. Scatter half of the nut mixture over the butter, again leaving a ½-in [12-mm] border all around. Use a finger dipped in water to moisten the top border of the dough. Starting from the bottom edge, carefully roll the dough toward the top to make a log.

6. Lightly press the open ends of the log toward the middle to tidy them. Make 1½-in [4-cm] notches along the top of the log and use a sharp knife to slice the log into eight equal disks.

7. Place each piece, cut-side up, on the prepared baking sheet, at least 1 in [2.5 cm] apart.

8. Cover with plastic wrap and let sit at room temperature for 30 minutes to proof. If the temperature in your kitchen is above 70°F [21°C], monitor the pastries. If they become sweaty or look like they are coming apart, place the baking sheet in the refrigerator for the remaining proofing time.

9. While the rolls are proofing, preheat the oven to 450°F [230°C].

10. Remove the plastic wrap. Brush the pastries with the egg wash.

11. Place the baking sheet in the oven and lower the oven temperature to 425°F [220°C]. Bake until the pastries are golden brown, 20 to 25 minutes.

12. Transfer the pastries to a wire rack to cool completely. Repeat the process with the remaining Danish dough.

13. Once the pastries have cooled, place a large baking sheet under the wire rack and use a fork to drizzle the pastries with the glaze. Pastry snails are best eaten the day they are made.

Store in an airtight container at room temperature for up to 2 days. Do not freeze.

CREAM CHEESE PASTRY POCKETS

MAKES 12 PASTRIES

Pastry pockets are like edible breakfast presents. They look so cute on the plate and are, of course, scrumptious. My favorite filling for them is the sweetened cream cheese that is often used in sweet rolls.

Tapioca flour for dusting

1 recipe Master Danish Pastry Dough (page 154)

1 recipe Sweetened Cream Cheese Filling for Pastries (page 133)

1 egg beaten with 1 Tbsp water, for egg wash (optional)

1 recipe Simple Glaze for Pastries (page 127)

1. Line a large baking sheet with parchment paper. Dust a work surface lightly but thoroughly with tapioca flour.

2. Place the dough, with the folded edges at the top and bottom (with a long side facing you), on the work surface. Using a sharp knife, cut the dough down the middle. Rewrap half the dough in plastic wrap and return it to the refrigerator while you're rolling and shaping the other half.

3. Turn the dough so that the cut edge is facing you. Carefully roll out the dough until it is about 13 in [33 cm] long by about 9 in [23 cm] wide and ¼ in [6 mm] thick. Tidy the edges by cutting off about ½ in [12 mm] on all sides. You will now have a rectangle that is roughly 12 in [30 cm] long and 8 in [20 cm] wide.

4. Cut the dough into six squares, each about 4 in [10 cm] square, by measuring 4 in [10 cm] across the width of the dough and cutting the dough in half from top to bottom. Then measure 4-in [10-cm] increments down the vertical side of the dough, making two cuts horizontally from side to side in the dough. Stack the squares on top of one another so they retain their coolness.

5. Lightly dust the work surface with tapioca flour again. Roll out a square of dough once, flattening it a bit. Place 1 Tbsp of filling in the middle of the square. Fold one corner up so that the tip of the corner is on top of the filling. Use a finger dipped in water to moisten the tip and then fold the opposite corner up so that its tip lays on top of the first tip. Press lightly to seal the two tips together. Repeat the process with the other two corners, moistening the tops of the corner that came before. When all four corners have been folded up, use your index finger to press down on the final corner to make sure it is sealed to the one underneath it. Next, squeeze together each of the four newly created corners to make sure the filling doesn't leak out while baking. Place the finished pocket on the prepared baking sheet.

6. Repeat the process with the remaining squares of dough and place on the prepared baking sheet at least 1 in [2.5 cm] apart.

7. Cover with plastic wrap and let sit at room temperature for 30 minutes to proof. If the temperature in your kitchen is above 70°F [21°C], monitor the pastries. If they become sweaty or look like they are coming apart, place the baking sheet in the refrigerator for the remaining proofing time.

8. While the pastry pockets are proofing, preheat the oven to 450°F [230°C].

9. After 30 minutes, remove the plastic wrap. Lightly brush each pocket with the egg wash (if using).

10. Place the baking sheet in the oven and lower the oven temperature to 425°F [220°C]. Bake until the pockets are golden brown, 20 to 25 minutes.

11. Transfer the pastry pockets to a wire rack to cool completely. Repeat the process with the remaining half of the dough.

12. Once the pockets have cooled, place a large baking sheet under the wire rack and use a fork to drizzle the pastries with the glaze. Let the glaze set for at least 15 minutes before serving. Pastry pockets are best eaten the day they are made.

Store in an airtight container at room temperature for up to 2 days. Do not freeze.

SWEET ROLLS (A.K.A. THE CLASSIC DANISH)

MAKES 8 PASTRIES

As I researched Danish pastries, I realized that sweet rolls are the pastry that is most often called a Danish. Growing up, they were ubiquitous in our house. We called them "sweet rolls." I'm not sure if it was because my mom loved them or because they were just popular in our town, but it seemed like we often had them for breakfast. And I remember that when my mom ordered them at our local coffee shop, they seemed to be as big as my head (when I was really young, they probably were). She always shared them with me until I was big enough to order my own. This version is as buttery, flaky, and decadent as the ones I remember from childhood.

Tapioca flour for dusting

1 recipe Master Danish Pastry Dough (page 154)

1 recipe Sweetened Cream Cheese Filling for Pastries (recipe follows) or 3 Tbsp jam of your choice

1 egg beaten with 1 Tbsp water, for egg wash

1 recipe Simple Glaze for Pastries (page 127)

1. Line a large baking sheet with parchment paper. Dust a work surface lightly but thoroughly with tapioca flour.

2. Place the dough, with the folded edges at the top and bottom (with a long side facing you), on the work surface. Using a sharp knife, cut the dough down the middle. Rewrap half the dough in plastic wrap and return it to the refrigerator while you're rolling and shaping the other half.

3. Turn the dough so that the cut edge is facing you. Carefully roll out the dough until it is about 13 in [33 cm] long by about 9 in [23 cm] wide and ¼ in [6 mm] thick. Tidy the edges by cutting off about ½ in [12 mm] on all sides. You will now have a rectangle that is roughly 12 in [30 cm] long and 8 in [20 cm] wide.

4. Measure and mark 2-in [5-cm] increments along the top of the dough. Using the marks as a guide, use a sharp knife to cut the dough at each mark. You will now have four strips of dough that are 2 in [5 cm] wide by 12 in [30 cm] long. Stack the strips on top of one another so that they retain their coolness.

5. Lightly dust the work surface with tapioca flour again. Place a strip of dough on the surface. Spread 2 tsp of filling on the strip, leaving a small (about ¼ in [6 mm]) border all around. You might need to use a finger to hold down the dough while you spread the filling. Carefully roll the dough into a log along the long edge. Use a pastry brush to brush off any excess tapioca flour.

6. Make a spiral by curling one end of the log tightly toward the other end of the log. The pastry may break—repair the breaks and keep going. Use a finger dipped in water to moisten the end of the log to the side of the spiral. Carefully place the sweet roll on the prepared baking sheet.

7. Repeat the process with the remaining strips of dough. You will now have four pastries.

8. Cover with plastic wrap and let sit at room temperature for 30 minutes to proof. If the temperature in your kitchen is above 70°F [21°C], monitor the pastries. If they become sweaty or look like they are coming apart, place the baking sheet in the refrigerator for the remaining proofing time.

9. While the rolls are proofing, preheat the oven to 450°F [230°C].

10. Remove the plastic wrap. Gently make an indentation in the middle of the rolls and spoon either 1 tsp filling or 1 tsp jam into each. Brush each pastry with the egg wash.

11. Place the baking sheet in the oven and lower the oven temperature to 425°F [220°C]. Bake until the rolls are golden brown, 20 to 25 minutes.

12. Transfer the pastries to a wire rack to cool completely. Repeat the process with the remaining dough.

13. Once the pastries have cooled, place a large baking sheet under the wire rack and use a fork to drizzle the pastries with the glaze. Sweet rolls are best eaten the day they are made.

Store in an airtight container at room temperature for up to 2 days. Do not freeze.

SWEETENED CREAM CHEESE FILLING FOR PASTRIES

MAKES 1¼ CUPS [290 G]

This is a simple yet delicious pastry filling. You can also use it for Cream Cheese Pastry Pockets (page 130) and Crêpes (page 110).

8 oz [230 g] cream cheese
¼ cup [50 g] granulated sugar
1 egg yolk
1 tsp freshly squeezed lemon juice
½ tsp pure vanilla extract

In the bowl of a stand mixer fitted with the whisk attachment, combine the cream cheese, sugar, egg yolk, lemon juice, and vanilla and beat on medium speed until smooth.

Store in an airtight container in the refrigerator for up to 3 days. Do not freeze.

ENGLISH MUFFINS

MAKES 8 MUFFINS

Brimming with nooks and crannies and pleasantly crunchy yet chewy when toasted, these are everything you want from an English muffin. I slather them in butter and top them with some of my homemade jam.

3 cups [435 g] Jeanne's Gluten-Free All-Purpose Flour (page 39)

½ tsp xanthan gum

1 tsp salt

2 Tbsp granulated sugar

1 Tbsp aluminum-free double-acting baking powder

1 tsp baking soda

1 Tbsp plus 1 tsp instant yeast

2 Tbsp unsalted butter, melted and cooled slightly

1¾ cups [420 ml] warm buttermilk (about 95°F [35°C])

Tapioca flour for dusting

Vegetable oil for brushing

1. In the bowl of a stand mixer fitted with the dough hook, combine the all-purpose flour, xanthan gum, salt, sugar, baking powder, baking soda, yeast, and butter. Add the buttermilk, mix on low speed for a few seconds to combine, then increase the speed to medium-high and mix for 4 minutes. The dough should be moderately stiff but fluffy.

2. Using an oiled rubber spatula, scrape the dough into a large oiled bowl. Cover the bowl lightly with plastic wrap and let the dough rise in a warm, draft-free place for 1 hour. The dough should be puffy.

3. While the dough is rising, line two large baking sheets with parchment paper. Dust each with a thin layer of tapioca flour. Dust a work surface with tapioca flour.

4. Scoop a heaping ¼-cup [90-g] ball of dough onto the work surface. Dust your hands with tapioca flour and gently pat and shape the dough into a disk that is about 3 in [8 cm] wide by ¾ in [2 cm] thick. Transfer the disk to a prepared baking sheet. Repeat the process with the remainder of the dough and place the disks on the baking sheet at least 1 in [2.5 cm] apart. Lightly cover the disks with plastic wrap and place in a warm, draft-free place to rest for 30 minutes..

5. Preheat the oven to 400°F [200°C].

6. Heat a 12-in [30-cm] cast-iron skillet over medium-high heat. Brush the skillet lightly with vegetable oil. Carefully peel four disks of dough from a baking sheet (you may need to push on the underside of the parchment paper to release them) and gently (they are delicate— you want to preserve the rising they have done) place them in the skillet, leaving space in between each—they shouldn't touch. If you're using a smaller pan, adjust the number of disks accordingly. Cook until the bottoms are brown but not burned, about 3 minutes. Use a metal spatula to carefully flip each muffin and cook on the other side for another 3 minutes, or until the bottoms are brown but not burned.

CONTINUED >>

7. Once both sides are cooked, use a metal spatula to gently transfer the muffins to the other prepared baking sheet, leaving 1 in [2.5 cm] between each muffin. Bake until they are puffy in the middle, golden brown on top, and an instant-read thermometer inserted into the side of a muffin registers at least 205°F [95°C], about 12 minutes.

8. Carefully transfer the muffins to a wire rack and let cool for at least 30 minutes. Be patient— the muffins are still baking during this time. If you open them too early, they will be gummy inside.

9. To cut, pierce the perimeter of a muffin with the tines of a fork. This method will give you the nooks and crannies that are expected of English muffins. Toast and enjoy.

Store in a paper bag at room temperature for up to 24 hours, or tightly wrapped in plastic wrap in the freezer for up to 3 months. Defrost for 24 hours in the refrigerator before serving.

ENGLISH MUFFIN BREAD

MAKES 1 LOAF

Sometimes you want the taste of an English muffin without the fuss of making individual muffins. This recipe will satisfy your craving for an English muffin, but in loaf form. One of the many advantages of this bread is that like English Muffins (page 134), it contains no eggs—so egg-free folks can indulge along with everyone else!

Butter for greasing, plus 2 Tbsp melted and cooled slightly

Tapioca flour for dusting

3 cups [435 g] Jeanne's Gluten-Free All-Purpose Flour (page 39)

½ tsp xanthan gum

1 tsp salt

2 Tbsp granulated sugar

1 Tbsp aluminum-free double-acting baking powder

1 tsp baking soda

1 Tbsp plus 1 tsp instant yeast

1¾ cups [420 ml] warm buttermilk (about 95°F [35°C])

Vegetable oil for brushing

1. Grease an 8½-by-4½-in [22-by-11-cm] pan with butter and dust with tapioca flour.

2. In the bowl of a stand mixer fitted with the dough hook, combine the all-purpose flour, xanthan gum, salt, sugar, baking powder, baking soda, yeast, and melted butter. Add the buttermilk and mix on low speed for a few seconds to combine, then increase the speed to medium-high and mix for 2 minutes.

3. Scrape the dough into the prepared pan. Smooth the top with an oiled spatula and lightly brush the top with vegetable oil. Cover the pan with plastic wrap and let the dough rise in a warm, draft-free place for 30 minutes. The dough should be puffed and reach to just about the top of the rim of the pan.

4. While the dough is rising, preheat the oven to 400°F [200°C].

5. Remove the plastic wrap. Bake until the top of the bread is golden brown, about 45 minutes, or until an instant-read thermometer inserted into the center of the bread registers at least 205°F [96°C].

6. Let the bread cool in the pan. After 10 minutes, turn it out onto a wire rack and let cool for at least 1 hour. Be patient—the bread is still baking during this time. If you cut it while it's warm, it will be gummy inside.

Store cut-side down on a cutting board for up to 2 days, or tightly wrapped in plastic wrap in the freezer for up to 3 months. To defrost, place the bread in the refrigerator for 24 hours before serving.

BAGELS

When I attended graduate school in New York City, I came to love the dense, chewy, flavorful bagels found at the bagel shops that seemed to be located every few blocks. Of course, I had a favorite shop near my apartment where I stocked up each week. When I first moved to Seattle, I often bought a few bagels from this shop to bring home every time I visited New York. Of course, I can't do that now, so I've developed the following recipe. These bagels are like the traditional-style bagels I remember from New York. Variations for Cinnamon Raisin Bagels as well as Bagel Chips are also given.

5 cups [725 g] Jeanne's Gluten-Free All-Purpose Flour (page 39)

1 tsp xanthan gum

4 tsp aluminum-free double-acting baking powder

2 tsp salt

2 Tbsp dark brown sugar

1 Tbsp instant yeast

3 tsp apple cider vinegar

2 Tbsp unsalted butter or vegetable shortening, melted

2 cups plus 3 Tbsp [525 ml] warm water (about 95°F [35°C])

Tapioca flour for shaping

¼ cup [50 g] granulated sugar

1 tsp baking soda

1 egg beaten with 1 tbsp water, for egg wash

Assorted toppings such as poppy seeds, sesame seeds, kosher salt, rehydrated minced garlic, or onions (optional)

1. In the bowl of a stand mixer fitted with the dough hook, mix together the all-purpose flour, xanthan gum, baking powder, salt, brown sugar, and yeast. Add the vinegar, butter, and water and beat on medium-high speed for 4 minutes. Stop the mixer once or twice and use an oiled rubber spatula to scrape down the sides of the bowl. The dough will be dense and sticky.

2. Use an oiled rubber spatula to scrape the dough into a large oiled bowl. Cover with plastic wrap and let the dough rise in a warm, draft-free place for 1½ hours.

3. Bring a heavy-bottomed pot of water to a boil, covered with a lid. (I use a saucepan that is 9 in [23 cm] wide by 5 in [10 cm] high.)

4. Place a baking stone or cast-iron skillet on the center rack and an 8-in- [20-cm-] square metal baking pan on the bottom rack of the oven and preheat to 500°F [260°C]. Line a large baking sheet with parchment paper. Place a wire rack over a second large baking sheet.

5. Divide the dough into ten baseball-size balls and place them on a corner of the work surface. Cover the balls of dough with plastic wrap.

6. Using your palm, roll a ball of dough on a rolling surface (don't flour the rolling surface) to smooth out any folds and bumps in the dough. The bagels won't smooth out much while they're baking, so the time you take to roll the dough now will pay off in smooth, good-looking bagels. When the dough looks smooth, the ball will probably be a bit pointed at the top and bottom. Press it into a round ball and press it down lightly into a fat disk that is about 3¼ in [8 cm] in diameter. Dip your index finger into tapioca

CONTINUED >>

flour and plunge your finger into the middle of the disk, poking through to the other side. Slowly rotate your finger against the sides of the hole, increasing it to about 1 in [2.5 cm] in diameter. Turn the bagel over and use your fingers to smooth out the hole on that side. Turn the bagel over a couple of times, each time letting it rest on the rolling surface—this smooths the outside of the bagels a bit more. Use your fingers to lightly press any parts that look misshapen. Carefully place the bagel on the prepared baking sheet. Repeat the rolling and shaping process until you have ten bagels.

7. Check the water in the pot—it should be boiling. Pour the granulated sugar in the water. It will briefly foam and then subside. Stir a few times with a spoon to dissolve the sugar. Add the baking soda. Again, the water will foam up and then subside. Stir again to dissolve the baking soda. (If the water is no longer boiling, cover and bring it back to a boil.) Carefully slide as many bagels into the water as the pot can handle with room between each bagel. (My pot holds three bagels at a time.) Cover and boil for 1 minute. Remove the lid and gently flip the bagels with a slotted spoon. Re-cover and boil for 1 minute more. Use the slotted spoon to transfer the bagels to the prepared wire rack. If the water is no longer boiling, cover and bring it back to a boil before cooking the next batch. Repeat the boiling and turning process.

8. Fill a 2-cup [480-ml] glass measuring cup with ice cubes and pour in enough water to reach the 1-cup [240-ml] mark. Open the preheated oven and carefully pour the ice water into the hot baking pan. The water will create the steam that helps make a nice crust on the bagels. Quickly close the door.

9. Using a pastry brush, lightly brush the egg wash on the bagels. If desired, lightly sprinkle any toppings on the bagels now. Use less than you think you need—a little goes a long way.

10. Using a metal spatula, transfer the bagels to the baking stone (my stone is 14½ in [37 cm] in diameter and comfortably fits five bagels with 1 in [2.5 cm] between each) or cast-iron skillet.

11. Lower the oven temperature to 450°F [230°C]. Bake the bagels for 25 minutes, then turn off the oven and let the bagels rest in the oven for another 5 minutes. An instant-read thermometer inserted into the side of a bagel should read at least 205°F [95°C]. Transfer the bagels to a wire rack to cool.

12. Repeat the process with the remaining bagels.

Store in a paper bag at room temperature for 24 hours, or in an airtight container in the freezer for up to 3 months.

VARIATIONS

CINNAMON RAISIN BAGELS: Add 1½ cups [180 g] raisins and 1 tsp ground cinnamon to the dough and proceed as directed. Brush with the egg wash, if desired, but do not add any other toppings.

BAGEL CHIPS: Preheat the oven to 375°F [190°C]. Place a large wire rack over a large baking sheet. Slice as many bagels as you want into ¼-in [6-mm] slices through the middle. Brush one side of the slices with melted butter or vegetable oil and sprinkle lightly with coarse salt (use less salt than you think you need—a little goes a long way). Set the bagels on the wire rack. Put the baking sheet and rack in the oven and bake the chips until they are uniformly crisp and golden brown. Start checking after 10 minutes—some bagel slices can take up to 20 minutes. Remove from the oven and let cool on the wire rack.

Store in an airtight container at room temperature for up to 3 days. Do not freeze.

POPOVERS

Popovers are a light and airy egg bread with an almost hollow interior. They can be eaten in a variety of ways, sweet or savory—with whipped cream and jam for a decadent breakfast or an afternoon tea treat, or with butter (and/or meat drippings) for dinner. They get their name from the fact that the batter pops over the pan while they're baking. The ingredients for popovers, more than any other recipe, must be at the temperatures indicated. Cold ingredients will negatively affect the rise of the popovers.

1 cup [145 g] Jeanne's Gluten-Free All-Purpose Flour (page 39)

½ tsp salt

4 extra-large eggs, at room temperature

1 cup [240 ml] milk, at room temperature

1½ Tbsp unsalted butter, melted

1. Place a 6-cup popover pan in the oven and preheat to 425°F [220°C] for 30 minutes.

2. In a small bowl, mix together the flour and salt.

3. In a large bowl, whisk the eggs until just barely bubbly—do not overwhisk. Add the milk and whisk to combine. Add 1 Tbsp of the butter and whisk to combine. Add the flour mixture and whisk for 100 strokes (no more). The mixture should be fairly smooth, but might still have some tiny lumps in it—that's okay.

4. Remove the heated popover pan from the oven (use a potholder; the pan will be very hot). Brush the inside of the popover cups with the remaining butter. (You might not need all of the remaining butter.)

5. Divide the batter evenly between the cups. Each cup will be a little more than half full.

6. Immediately place the pan in the oven and bake for 25 minutes. After 25 minutes, lower the oven temperature to 400°F [200°C] and bake for another 15 minutes. Do not open the oven door to check the popovers—this will release heat and cause problems with the popovers' rise.

7. When the popovers are done, they should be golden brown and puffed up above the rims of the cups. Turn out the popovers onto a wire rack to cool. They will be lying on their sides on the rack. Insert a sharp knife into the side of each popover to release steam while they cool (the slit should be facing up while they are cooling). Popovers are best eaten the day they are baked.

Store in a paper bag at room temperature for up to 2 days, or in an airtight container in the freezer for up to 3 months.

TOASTER TARTS

MAKES 12 **OR** 13 **TARTS**

I grew up eating Pop Tarts for breakfast. With their sweet filling and thick sugar glaze, they were irresistible. I can picture boxes of them in my childhood kitchen, lining the shelves. Foreshadowing the baker I was to become, I spent more time than my siblings fussing with the toaster settings, insisting that my tarts have the perfect filling temperature and crust—warm but not too hot, crunchy without being burned. At some point as an adult, I realized that Pop Tarts are basically just small, portable versions of pie and that they can be made at home. What's more, they can be eaten as a breakfast treat, snack, or dessert. And the fillings are virtually limitless. I've given you a few suggestions, but feel free to experiment with your own ideas. A cool kitchen (one that is 60° to 67°F [15° to 19°C]) is helpful for the success of this recipe.

Tapioca flour for dusting
1 recipe Pie Crust (page 246)
1 cup [240 ml] jam, preserves, or fruit butter of your choice or 1 cup [170 g] semisweet chocolate chips
Simple Glaze for Pastries (page 127)

1. Dust two large baking sheets with tapioca flour.

2. Keep one disk of dough in the refrigerator and unwrap the other disk and place it on a rolling surface. Sprinkle the dough with tapioca flour and roll it out into a rough rectangle about ⅛ in [4 mm] thick. (You can also place the dough between two large pieces of plastic wrap and roll the dough.)

3. Measure and cut as many 4-by-3-in [10-by-8-cm] rectangles as you can. To do this, cut off the irregular edges and set those scraps aside to be re-rolled. Using a ruler, measure across the dough in 3-in [8-cm] increments and make notch at each with a sharp knife. Then use the ruler to measure 4-in [10-cm] increments along one of the vertical edges. With the knife, cut off any extra dough in either direction and place that dough in a pile to be re-rolled.

4. Next, use the knife to make vertical cuts in the dough at each notch in the top edge of the dough. Then make horizontal cuts at each notch along the side edge of the dough. You will now have several rectangles. Use a metal spatula to move the rectangle to one of the prepared baking sheets.

5. Gather the dough scraps, dust the rolling surface with more tapioca flour (or place the dough between two pieces of plastic wrap), and re-roll and cut more dough rectangles. Transfer to a baking sheet. Cover with plastic wrap and place the first sheet in the refrigerator while you roll and cut the second disk of dough. You should now have 24 to 26 rectangles (you need an even number of rectangles to pair together for the tarts). Cover the second sheet of rectangles with plastic wrap and place in the refrigerator.

6. Remove the first sheet of rectangles. Place as many pairs of rectangles on the work surface as will comfortably fit. Put 1 Tbsp jam in the middle of one rectangle of each pair. Dip your index finger in water and moisten the edge of each filled rectangle. Carefully place the companion rectangle on top of its mate.

CONTINUED >>

7. Gently but firmly press down along the perimeter of each tart with your fingers to make sure the pairs are aligned and fit together, then use the tines of a fork to press along the edges of each tart. This will complete the seal and create a decorative edge. Be sure you've sealed them well so that they don't leak while they're baking.

8. Make four small slashes on the top of each tart with a sharp knife to allow steam to escape during baking. (I like to make a cross or star pattern.) Return the rectangles to the baking sheet. When all of the tarts have been made, cover them with plastic wrap and place in the refrigerator. Remove the second tray of unfilled tart rectangles and repeat the filling, sealing, and slashing process. (At this point you can carefully stack the tarts in a freezable container with pieces of wax paper layered between each and freeze for up to 3 months. No need to defrost before baking.)

9. Preheat the oven to 450°F [230°C]. Line a large baking sheet with parchment paper.

10. With a pastry brush, lightly brush the top of each tart with the glaze (no need to be perfect about it—it will melt and be almost invisible after baking). Place the tarts on an ungreased baking sheet with about 1 in [2.5 cm] between each. Bake for 10 minutes, lower the oven temperature to 350°F [180°C], and bake until the tarts look light brown in the middle and slightly darker brown around the edges, about 10 minutes longer. Remove from the oven and place the tarts on a wire rack to cool completely.

Store in a stiff-sided freezable container, with a piece of wax paper layered between each, in the freezer for up to 3 months. When you're ready to serve, take out as many as are needed from the freezer (no need to defrost them) and toast on the "toast" function in a toaster oven for about 5 minutes.

CROISSANTS

MAKES 8 MEDIUM CROISSANTS OR 12 SMALL CROISSANTS

Buttery and delectable, croissants are probably the fussiest type of pastry to make. You are creating the layers of pastry by hand, so precision and patience are called for. But I've found that if you follow the directions, pay attention to the temperature requirements (an instant-read thermometer will come in handy here), and are careful with your technique, croissants come together beautifully. And although the croissant is fussy, it takes pity on the dedicated baker—regardless of experience—and most of the time, it rises to the challenge and comes out flaky on the outside and doughy on the inside. Persevere, dear reader. Your first batches of croissants may not be perfect and may look funny, but they will be delicious and well worth the effort. And once you have the techniques under your belt? Your results will be spectacular.

Some people have different or faster or easier ways of making croissants, but those methods may not work with gluten-free croissant dough, which is quite tricky to get right, so I've given you detailed instructions to give you the best chance of success. Before making this recipe, read the Laminated Dough Primer (page 94). You'll see three French terms in this recipe: *détrempe*, which refers to the water-flour dough; *beurrage*, which is the package of butter that you'll create; and *pâton*, the dough that is a laminated combination of the *détrempe* and *beurrage*.

It is important to prepare the croissants in a cool environment. A kitchen that is 60° to 67°F [15° to 19°C] is ideal. A kitchen that is too warm will make preparing the croissants more difficult, because the butter in the dough will melt. If you are making the croissants on a day that is supposed to be very warm, start early in the morning and cool the dough in the refrigerator as often as needed.

DÉTREMPE

2¼ cups [325 g] Jeanne's Gluten-Free All-Purpose Flour (page 39)

1½ tsp xanthan gum

2 Tbsp granulated sugar

1½ tsp salt

2¼ tsp instant yeast

1 cup [240 ml] warm water (about 95°F [35°C])

Tapioca flour for dusting

BEURRAGE

¾ cup [170 g] cold unsalted European-style butter (with at least 82% milk fat)

Tapioca flour for dusting

1 egg beaten with 1 Tbsp water, for egg wash

1. **TO MAKE THE *DÉTREMPE*:** Mix together the all-purpose flour, xanthan gum, sugar, salt, and yeast in the bowl of a stand mixer using a spoon. Place the bowl into the mixer fitted with the dough hook. Add the water and mix on low speed to combine. Increase the speed to medium and beat for 4 minutes. You may need to stop the mixer once or twice to push

CONTINUED >>

the dough back into the bowl. The dough will be stiff.

2. Remove the bowl from the mixer and, with hands lightly dusted with tapioca flour, pick up and shape the dough into a fairly smooth ball. Place the dough back into the mixing bowl (or into a dough rising container), cover with plastic wrap (or with a lid) and let rest and rise for 1 hour at room temperature. After 1 hour, place the bowl in the refrigerator for 1 hour to cool the dough and to let it rest and rise.

3. TO MAKE THE *BEURRAGE*: Cut two pieces of parchment paper to about 12 in [30 cm] long by 13 in [33 cm] wide. Measure and draw a 7-in [18-cm] square on one side of one of the pieces of parchment paper.

4. Place the unmarked piece of parchment paper on a work surface. From here, you should work as quickly as possible so that the butter doesn't become too warm. Remove the butter from the refrigerator and place it in the middle of the piece of parchment paper. Cover the butter with the parchment paper with the square drawn on it, penciled-side up (not touching the butter), centering the middle of the square over the butter. You are now going to plasticize the butter, pounding on it until it develops a consistency that bends rather than breaks when it is cold.

5. Using a heavy rolling pin, pound the butter until it spreads to about 1 in [2.5 cm] outside the lines of the square. Lift up the parchment paper and, using a bench scraper, cut off a bit of each side of the mound to straighten the sides and ensure that the butter block is still smaller than the drawn square. Use a knife to scrape the trimmed pieces of butter off the bench scraper onto the top of the butter block (never touch the butter with your fingers because your body heat will warm it up). Replace the parchment paper and pound the butter some more until it spreads to about 1 in [2.5 cm] outside the lines of the square. Trim the sides again with the bench scraper and scrape the trimmed pieces onto the

top of the block of butter with the knife. Repeat this process a few times to make sure the butter is properly plasticized.

6. To test for plasticity, move the parchment paper with the butter block to the edge of the counter so that half the block is hanging over the edge. Use your hand to gently press the butter down a bit over the edge. The butter should bend rather than break.

7. Make sure the block of butter is at least 1 in [2.5 cm] inside the square on all sides before you proceed to the next step.

8. Fold both pieces of parchment paper down along the lines of the penciled square (do your best with the bottom piece of parchment paper), tucking the paper under the block of butter. Place the parchment packet on the work surface, still with the square on top. Using a rolling pin, carefully roll out the butter so that it fills the entire square (be sure to fill out the corners). Try to make the butter as even as you can inside the packet. Place the packet on a flat surface in the refrigerator to cool.

9. Lightly sprinkle the work surface with tapioca flour.

10. To prepare a *pâton*, remove the *détrempe* from the refrigerator and unwrap it. Place the dough on the work surface and sprinkle the top lightly with tapioca flour. With lightly dusted hands, press down on the dough and then shape it into a roughly 6-in [15-cm] square. Dust the top of the dough with tapioca flour. Roll the dough into a 12.5-in [32-cm] square. Lift up and check underneath the *détrempe* often during the rolling process to make sure that it is not sticking to the rolling surface and that there is tapioca flour under it. Every time you lift up the *détrempe,* it will shrink a bit in size—this is normal.

11. Remove the *beurrage* from the refrigerator, unwrap the top piece of parchment paper, and place the *beurrage* butter-side down on top of the *détrempe* so that the corners of the *beurrage* are pointing toward the sides of the *détrempe*, and remove the second piece of parchment. The temperature of the *beurrage* should be 60° to 64°F [16° to 18°C]. If the parchment paper sticks to the butter and can't be easily pried off, then the butter is too warm to roll and it needs to be refrigerated to cool down.

12. You are now going to fold over the corners of the *détrempe* on top of the *beurrage* so that the top looks like one end of a gift-wrapped package. Carefully lift the sides of the *détrempe*, one at a time, over the top of the *beurrage*. They will meet in the middle. Gently squeeze together any gaps at the corners and gently press the dough over any uncovered spot in the middle. This is called the French lock-in method—you are "locking in" the butter in the dough. From now on, you want to make sure that the butter is always firmly and completely encased in dough—the success of your croissants will depend on it.

13. Using the rolling pin, press down gently but firmly on the *pâton*, diagonally from corner to corner, and at the middle from side to side to stabilize the dough. Lightly pound the rolling pin across the surface of the *pâton* from top to bottom. Repeat the diagonal and side-to-side pressing procedure. Gently but firmly roll the pin across the *pâton*, first from top to bottom and then from side to side. Repeat this process until you have a firm package of dough in which the butter is not sliding around. The *pâton* will be roughly 9 in [23 cm] square.

14. If your kitchen is not too warm and the dough and butter are still cold, do your first single fold and turn. The key to the folds and turns is that the dough and the butter stay cool so that the butter does not melt into the dough. If the kitchen is warm and the dough has warmed up, wrap the *pâton* well in plastic wrap and place in the refrigerator to cool for 30 minutes before the first roll and turn. Generally, croissant dough

doesn't need as many folds as puff pastry dough because of the presence of the yeast. For this croissant recipe, I do three single folds and one double fold. This gives me the equivalent of four and a half folds (the double fold actually gives you the equivalent to one and a half folds—not two folds). With croissants, you want to make enough folds to create layers but not so many that you lose the layering altogether.

15. Dust the rolling surface and the top of the dough with more tapioca flour. Firmly and quickly roll the *pâton* into a rectangle that is roughly 18 in [45.5 cm] long by 9 in [23 cm] wide. It's best to use a top-to-bottom and bottom-to-top rolling method with the dough. If you start the rolling in the middle, you risk rolling the dough unevenly. The important thing here is to roll out the dough into as even a rectangle as possible. This means that you need to work with as much precision as you can. Also, you don't want to roll the rectangle too thin. Make sure that it is at least ¼ in [6 mm] thick at all times. Check often to ensure that the *pâton* is not sticking to the rolling surface and that the bottom and top of the *pâton* are adequately (but lightly) floured.

16. When the rectangle is about 18 in [45.5 cm] in length, use a dry pastry brush to brush off the extra flour from the surface (you don't want to fold in any more flour than you have to). Now you will make the first single fold. To make a single fold, fold the *pâton* in thirds, the same way you'd fold a letter. Fold one end one-third of the length of the dough, brush off any extra flour, and then fold the opposite end over the top of the first fold.

17. You should now have a *pâton* that is about 12 in [30 cm] by 9 in [23 cm]. Tidy the *pâton* by brushing off as much of the tapioca flour as possible. If the folded edges have cracked, carefully smooth them with your hands, and tidy the sides by pressing them with your hands and with your rolling pin. I usually hit the long side of

MUFFINS, PANCAKES, DANISH, AND OTHER BREAKFAST TREATS

CONTINUED >>

my rolling pin against the sides of the *paton* to even them out and to seal them. Use the pad of your finger (and not your fingernail) to make an indentation in one of the corners of the *paton*. This indicates that you have done one fold and turn. It's a good system to follow—especially if you need to put the dough into the fridge to cool down—you will be able to see how many folds you've made by looking at the number of indentations.

18. Wrap the *paton* in plastic wrap so that it is airtight. (I wrap the *paton* twice in plastic wrap and then place it in a cleaned plastic sack that I put my vegetables in at the grocery store.) Place in the refrigerator for 30 minutes to cool and rest. The dough temperature should be no higher than 64°F [18°C] and no lower than 55°F [13°C] for rolling.

19. After 30 minutes, remove the *paton* from the refrigerator, unwrap, and place on the rolling surface so that the dough is 90 degrees from the way it was facing during the previous fold. The folded edges should be at left and right.

20. Repeat the rolling and folding process two more times so you have a total of three single folds. Be sure to flour the rolling surface before each turn and to make the appropriate number of indentations with your finger to indicate the number of turns, and to rest the *paton* for 30 minutes between each fold and turn. Before you start each turn, position the dough 90 degrees from the way it was facing during the previous fold. The folded edges should be at left and right. Place the dough in refrigerator for 30 minutes.

21. For your final turn (this should be the fourth turn), make a double, or book, fold instead of a single fold (double folds are the equivalent of one and a half folds). To make a double fold, fold one end of the dough so that the edge reaches the middle of the *paton*. Then fold the other end so that its edge meets the other edge in the middle of the *paton*. Brush off any excess flour, tidy the edges, and fix any tears in the

folded sides. Now fold the *paton* in half by folding it where the two edges meet. The *paton* will measure approximately 10 in [25 cm] by 7 in [18 cm].

22. Brush off any extra flour and make four indentations with your fingertip in the corner of the *paton*—this indicates that you have made four folds. Carefully wrap the *paton* in plastic wrap and place it in the refrigerator for at least 30 minutes, or up to 12 hours.

23. Once the *paton* has been in the refrigerator for 30 minutes, line a large baking sheet with parchment paper and lightly flour the rolling surface.

24. Remove the *paton* from the fridge and unwrap. Work quickly—you don't want the *paton* to get too warm. Gently but firmly use the side of the rolling pin to tap the *paton* up and down the length of the dough to stabilize it so the layers don't move against each other. Firmly but gently roll the dough into a rectangle that is roughly 20 in [51 cm] long and 9 in [23 cm] wide and no thinner than ¼ in [6 mm]. Take care here—the thickness of the dough should be even throughout the rectangle. Also, the dough should be cold and firm enough that the rolling pin is not breaking through the dough into soft butter. If the dough seems too warm and sticky, rewrap it and place it in the refrigerator to firm up. At the other extreme, if the dough and the butter are too cold, the butter will break through because it's slicing the dough. If this happens, stop and let the dough warm up a bit before proceeding.

25. Tidy up the edges of the dough. Using a straight edge as a guide, carefully cut off the ragged edges with a sharp knife or a pastry wheel. You should have a fairly tidy rectangle that is roughly 18 in [46 cm] long by 8 in [20 cm] wide. Discard the scraps. The short side of the dough should be facing you.

26. **To make 3-in [8-cm] croissants:** With the short end of the rectangle facing you, measure and make small notches with a sharp knife at 3-in [7.5-cm] intervals along each long edge of the *pâton*. You should have five notches along each side. Using the straight edge as a guide, cut from the bottom left corner to the first notch on the right side. Place the triangle on an unused part of your cutting surface (or on a plate). Starting at the notch you just cut to, cut across the *pâton* to the first notch on the left side of the *pâton*. Place this triangle on top of the first cut triangle (stacking the triangles helps to maintain their cool temperature). Repeat cutting and stacking until you have twelve triangles.

To make 4½-in [11-cm] croissants: With the short end of the rectangle facing you, measure and make small notches with a sharp knife at 4½-in [11-cm] intervals along the long edge of the side of the *pâton* that's at your right. On the opposite (left) edge, measure and make a notch at 2¼-in [5.5-cm]. Thereafter, measure and mark in 4½-in [11-cm] increments. You will have a 2¼-in [5.5-cm] length at the end. Using the straight edge as a guide, cut from the bottom right corner to the 2¼-in [5.5-cm] notch on the left side. This will be one of two small triangles that will be made from this *pâton*. Place the triangle on an unused part of your cutting surface (or on a plate). Starting at the notch you just cut to, cut across the *pâton* to the first notch on the right side of the *pâton*. Place this triangle on top of the first cut triangle (stacking the triangles helps to maintain their cool temperature). Repeat cutting and stacking until you have seven large triangles and two small triangles. (You will eventually place the smaller triangles together and roll them as one croissant.)

27. Lightly dust the rolling surface with tapioca flour. Place a triangle on the rolling surface. Sprinkle tapioca flour on top. In the center of the base (not the tip) of the triangle, make a 1-in- [2.5-cm-] long cut. Using a small rolling pin (if you have one), gently but firmly roll across the triangle from the base to about 1 in [2.5 cm] from the tip (the tip stays unrolled). Roll the pieces on both sides of the notch away from the center toward the side, flattening them out a bit more. The triangle should now look a bit like the Eiffel Tower (or a skinny rocket ship). The thickness of the dough should be somewhere between ¼ in [6 mm] and ⅛ in [4 mm] (but no thinner). The top point of the triangle will be thicker than the rest of the triangle.

28. Slowly and carefully use your fingers to roll the dough on either side of the base toward the notch in the center and then roll the entire base straight up to the tip. Most croissant recipes instruct you to tuck the tip under the croissant to secure it. Don't do this here—gluten-free croissant dough is delicate and needs to be able to rise unimpeded. The pointed end of the croissant should be on top of the croissant and should not stick to the layer underneath.

29. Place the shaped croissants on the prepared baking sheet at least 1 in [2.5 cm] apart.

30. Repeat the rolling and shaping process with the remainder of the triangles. Place the two smaller triangles close together so that they are touching in the middle along the non-slanted long edge and roll and shape them together to make one triangle. (In France, a croissant with the two end points curved into the middle indicates the presence of shortening in the dough, while a croissant with straight sides indicates butter in the dough. I find that no matter what kind of fat is used in the croissants, curving the ends into the middle tends to break the dough, so I just leave them straight.)

CONTINUED >>

31. Lightly cover the shaped croissants with plastic wrap (use more than one piece if necessary to make sure all of the croissants are covered), and let proof at room temperature for 1 hour. If the temperature in your kitchen is above 70°F [21°C], monitor the croissants. If they become sweaty or look like they are coming apart, place the baking sheet in the refrigerator for the remaining proofing time.

32. After the croissants have been rising for 30 minutes, preheat the oven to 400°F [200°C].

33. After the croissants have risen for 1 hour, lightly brush the egg wash on the top of each croissant. Bake for 10 minutes, then lower the oven temperature to 350°F [180°F] and bake until the croissants are golden brown, 20 to 25 minutes. One or two of the croissants might split in the center at the top—that's fine. The structure of the dough for gluten-free croissants is more delicate than for wheat croissants.

34. Remove the croissants from the oven and transfer to a wire rack to cool for at least 15 minutes before eating (they will do some final cooking while they're cooling). Croissants are best the day they are baked.

Store in a paper bag at room temperature for up to 1 day. Do not freeze.

VARIATION

CHOCOLATE CROISSANTS: Sprinkle a line of semisweet chocolate chips across the base of each croissant, above the notch, before you roll it up.

OAT-FREE GRANOLA

MAKES ABOUT 2½ CUPS [330 G]

Granola is so handy to have around—I eat it for breakfast with milk or yogurt, and I eat it as a snack. I often carry a bag of it with me in case I get peckish as I do my errands throughout the day. Unfortunately, I react to oats—as do many gluten-intolerant people. Rather than give up granola, I developed this recipe using raw quinoa flakes instead of oat flakes. The quinoa flakes are smaller than oat flakes, but they have a wonderful whole-grain taste that matches nicely with the other elements of the granola. If you can't find quinoa flakes in your area, you can find them online (see Sources for Ingredients and Equipment, page 250).

¼ cup [60 ml] olive oil

¼ cup [60 ml] maple syrup

1½ cups [140 g] raw quinoa flakes

½ cup [60 g] nuts or seeds (any kind)

1 tsp whole flax or chia seeds

¼ tsp salt

¼ tsp ground cinnamon

1 cup [120 g] chopped dried fruit (any kind)

1. Preheat the oven to 325°F [170°C].

2. In a small bowl, whisk together the olive oil and maple syrup.

3. In a large bowl, mix together the quinoa flakes, nuts, flax seeds, salt, and cinnamon. Drizzle the oil mixture over the quinoa-flake mixture and mix until the dry ingredients are well coated.

4. Spread the granola on a large ungreased rimmed baking sheet and bake until the quinoa flakes are golden brown, about 30 minutes. Stir the granola once or twice while it's baking.

5. Let the granola cool on the baking sheet on a wire rack for 15 minutes. Stir in the dried fruit and let cool completely.

Store in a tightly sealed jar at room temperature for up to 1 week.

MASTER DANISH PASTRY DOUGH

The dough for Danish pastries is the most forgiving of the laminated doughs, because it contains eggs in addition to yeast. And I have found that making a quick, or blitz, Danish dough creates results that are comparable to the more time-consuming traditionally laminated dough. This quick Danish dough is made more like a pie-crust dough, in that the butter is cut into the flour in chunks. You still need to do three rolls, folds, and turns, but they aren't nearly as finicky as croissant or puff pastry folds and turns. Before making this recipe, read the Laminated Dough Primer (page 94).

It is important to prepare the Danish pastry dough in a cool environment. A kitchen that is 60° to 67°F [15° to 19°C] is ideal. A kitchen that is too warm will make preparing the Danish pastry dough more difficult, because the butter will melt in the dough. If you are making the dough on a day that is supposed to be very warm, start early in the morning and cool the dough in the refrigerator as often as needed.

3 cups [435 g] Jeanne's Gluten-Free All-Purpose Flour (page 39)

1 tsp xanthan gum

2 Tbsp granulated sugar

1½ tsp salt

1 Tbsp instant yeast

1 cup [230 g] unsalted European-style butter (at least 82% milk fat), cold and cut into 16 pieces

2 extra-large eggs, slightly beaten

½ cup [120 ml] ice-cold water

Tapioca flour for dusting

1. In the bowl of a food processor, combine the all-purpose flour, xanthan gum, sugar, salt, and yeast. Pulse several times to combine. Add the butter and pulse several times until the dough looks like sand mixed with pebbles of varying sizes. (Or place the dry ingredients in a large bowl and use a pastry cutter or your fingers to work in the butter.)

2. Turn out the dough into a large bowl and add the eggs. Mix with a fork until combined. Add the water and mix with the fork until the dough just barely comes together. The dough will be shaggy and you will need to use your hands to get everything to stick together.

3. Using your hands, shape the dough into a rough 8-in [20-cm] square. Wrap the dough well in a few layers of plastic wrap—make sure it is airtight—and let sit at room temperature for 30 minutes to rest and hydrate.

4. After 30 minutes, refrigerate the dough for at least 4 hours, or up to 2 days.

5. When you are ready to use the dough, it will be cold and somewhat hard to roll. That's okay—this is a quick-laminated dough and it isn't as fussy as other laminated doughs.

6. Dust a work surface lightly but thoroughly with tapioca flour. Turn the dough out onto the work surface and dust the dough with tapioca flour. Work quickly from here on so that the dough doesn't warm up too much during the rolling, folding, and turning process. If the dough becomes floppy and sticks to the rolling surface, it's too warm—rewrap it with plastic wrap and return it to the refrigerator for about 15 minutes to cool down before you proceed.

7. Pound the dough with a rolling pin to flatten it a bit. Roll it out to an 18-by-8-in [45-by-20-cm] rectangle. Fold the dough into thirds, as you would a letter. If the dough breaks at the folded edges, just smooth the breaks with your fingers. Pound the dough with your rolling pin a few times along the top to help stabilize the layers. Using the rolling pin, press diagonally across the dough, from corner to corner, and repeat from the other corner to corner. Use the pad of your finger (and not your fingernail) to make an indentation in one of the corners of the dough. This indicates that you have done one fold and turn. (This will help you keep track of how many turns you've completed. It's a good system to follow—especially if you need to put the dough into the fridge to cool down—you will be able to see how many folds you've made by looking at the number of indentations.)

8. Turn the dough 90 degrees so that what were the sides are now the top and bottom and carefully roll out the dough again to about 18 by 8 in [45 by 20 cm]. Fold into thirds again. Pound and roll the dough again. Use your fingertip to make two indentations in a corner of the dough to indicate that you've made two folds.

9. Repeat turning, rolling, and folding one last time. Smooth the folded edges, stabilize the dough, and tidy the outer edges by pressing on the sides with your hands and the rolling pin. You should now have a rectangle that is roughly 7 by 9 in [18 by 23 cm]. Use your fingertip to make three indentations in a corner of the dough to indicate that you've made three folds. Wrap well with plastic wrap and place in the refrigerator for at least 1 hour, or up to 24 hours, before using.

CHAPTER 4

DINNER

No matter how busy our days, my husband, daughter, and I sit down to dinner together every evening. It's our time to relax and catch up with each other. On the days that we don't have dinner together, I feel out of sorts and dissatisfied. It's important to me as an individual, as well as to us as a family, to share this meal at the end of the day.

I confess, as the primary dinner-maker, I sometimes find it hard to get the meal on the table during the week. We are all active people (a bit too active at times), and we tend to have more going on than we should during any one day. And with the added challenge of making a gluten-free meal, I've had to come up with some go-to recipes that I can rely on and know that my family will love.

For busy days, I tend to make soups and stews that can be made in a slow cooker, or simple meat/bean/veggie/rice dishes that require relatively little effort and thought on my part.

On slower days, I like to spend more time on dinner and prepare the recipes you'll find in this chapter. These are the dishes that take a bit more time and care to cook or bake homemade, but that are so satisfying to make and to eat. I love having the luxury of being able to putter in the kitchen on weekend evenings and seeing my husband and daughter fully enjoying the results.

VEGETABLE TEMPURA

MAKES 5 CUPS [1.2 L] BATTER

When we first moved to our current neighborhood, I frequently ordered noodle soup with tempura-fried vegetables from a nearby Japanese noodle shop. I love the simple crunchy coating on the lightly cooked vegetables. This meal became one of my go-to comfort and sick-day foods. Making gluten-free vegetable tempura at home is quite easy. It is also an excellent way to use leftover vegetables. I adapted this recipe from one by Tadashi Ono, Japanese chef and cookbook author. Before making the recipe, read the Deep-Frying Primer (page 20).

Vegetable oil for frying
2½ cups [360 g] Jeanne's Gluten-Free All-Purpose Flour (page 39)
2 egg yolks
2 cups [480 ml] ice-cold water
2 ice cubes
An assortment of vegetables, such as bell pepper, broccoli, cauliflower, mushrooms, asparagus, and carrots, cut or sliced into bite-size pieces, as well as large-leafed fresh herbs like sage and parsley (see Note)

1. Pour 3 in [7.5 cm] of vegetable oil into a heavy-bottomed saucepan fitted with a candy thermometer and heat the oil to 350°F [180°C]. Line a large baking sheet with paper towels and place a wire rack over it.

2. When the oil has reached temperature, in a large bowl, mix together 2 cups [290 g] of the flour, the egg yolks, water, and ice cubes until they are barely combined and have the consistency of heavy cream. The batter will be lumpy due to pockets of flour—this is okay. (The ice cubes will slowly melt as you use the batter, accomplishing two things: keeping the batter cold, which is important to crispy tempura, and keeping the batter appropriately thin. After the ice cubes have melted, the batter will become thicker as the flour absorbs the liquid. Watch the batter and add additional water 1 Tbsp at a time as needed to keep the batter thin.)

3. Place the remaining ½ cup [70 g] flour in a wide bowl. Dredge each vegetable in the flour, then pull it through the batter. Coat the vegetables and herbs very lightly with the batter—you don't want to coat them as thickly as you would onion rings or fish fillets. Use a finger to wipe off a bit of batter from any vegetable that seems too thickly coated. You should be able to see the vegetable or herb through the batter. Place the batter-dipped vegetables in the oil. They will probably sink to the bottom for a few seconds and then rise to the surface. (Mushrooms and herbs usually don't sink.) If the vegetables haven't risen to the surface after a few seconds, use a pair of metal tongs to nudge and unstick them. If any vegetables stick together, nudge them apart.

4. Fry the herbs for about 1 minute. Fry softer vegetables like bell peppers, asparagus, and mushrooms for about 2 minutes. Fry root vegetables and cauliflower for about 2½ minutes. Turn the items a few times in the oil to make sure they are evenly cooked. Watch them carefully—the vegetables and herbs will brown and burn if they're fried too long. (The batter itself will not brown.) Monitor the oil to make sure that it stays at temperature.

5. Use a slotted spoon to scoop out the vegetables when they've finished frying, allowing any excess oil to drip back into the pan. Transfer the vegetables to the wire rack to cool. Taste the first few vegetables to see if they are done to your liking. After frying each batch of vegetables, use the slotted spoon to remove any leftover fried batter or vegetable pieces that are floating in the oil. If you don't do this, these pieces will eventually burn in the oil and the succeeding vegetables will pick them up as they fry. Fried vegetables and herbs are best eaten within an hour (or less) of being fried.

···

NOTE: *All of the vegetables should be cut into thin slices, except for vegetables like broccoli and cauliflower, which should be cut into small florets (although you can slice the cauliflower if the head contains tightly packed florets). The asparagus should be cut into lengths short enough to fit into your frying pan. Slice the vegetables ½ in [12 mm] thick and as long as you want. If you are so inclined, cut the vegetables in attractive ways; e.g., cutting carrots on the diagonal. I cut vegetables that are already thin enough to fry (like bell peppers) into 1-in [2.5-cm] strips. If you are frying herbs, they should be separated into single large leaves.*

FRIED ONION RINGS

MAKES 6 SIDE SERVINGS

There are a few restaurants in town that have dedicated gluten-free fryers, so I'm able to indulge in french fries without worrying about cross-contamination with gluten. But fried onion rings are harder to find because they require more work on the part of restaurants. These can be made with regular yellow onions or with sweet onions like Vidalias. As for the beer, there are more gluten-free options than ever. Before making this recipe, read the Deep-Frying Primer (page 20).

1½ cups [215 g] Jeanne's Gluten-Free All-Purpose Flour (page 39)

1 Tbsp aluminum-free double-acting baking powder

1 tsp salt

⅛ to ¼ tsp cayenne pepper (optional)

One 12-oz [355-ml] bottle gluten-free beer

Vegetable oil for frying

2 large yellow onions (regular or sweet)

½ cup [60 g] tapioca flour

1. In a large bowl, mix together the all-purpose flour, baking powder, salt, and cayenne (if using). Add the beer and whisk until the batter is smooth. Let sit for at least 15 minutes, or up to 1 hour, to allow the batter to thicken.

2. Pour 3 in [7.5 cm] of vegetable oil into a heavy-bottomed saucepan fitted with a candy thermometer and heat the oil to 375°F [190°C]. Line two large baking sheets with a double layer of paper towels and place a wire rack over each.

3. Cut off the blossom and root ends of the onions. Remove the skin and the first tough layer or two. Slice the onions horizontally into rings ½ in [12 mm] thick. Push out the layers of rings from each other so you have single rings of varying sizes.

4. Place the tapioca flour in a large bowl. Place the bowl with the batter next to it and set a plate next to the bowl of batter.

5. Place the separated onion rings in the tapioca flour and toss to coat. (There will probably be some flour left in the bowl.) Battering the onions is a bit challenging—the batter is thick and it's difficult to coat the onion rings with just the right amount without battering them too much. The best strategy is to drag the onion rings through the batter and then brush off the excess with a finger. Coat the number of rings that will fit into your pan without crowding and place them on the plate.

6. When the oil has reached temperature, carefully place the battered onion rings in the oil. The oil will bubble dramatically. Fry for 30 seconds to let the batter set and then fry for 3 minutes more. The rings should rise to the surface fairly quickly. If they haven't risen to the surface after a few seconds, use a pair of metal tongs to nudge and unstick them. Once they've risen, turn them every 30 seconds until they're golden brown, 2½ to 3 minutes. Monitor the oil so that it stays at temperature. Raise or lower the burner temperature to keep the temperature steady.

CONTINUED >>

7. Use metal tongs to remove the rings when they're finished frying, allowing any excess oil to drip back into the pan. Transfer the onion rings to the wire rack to cool.

8. Repeat the battering, frying, and draining process until all the onion rings are fried. After frying each batch, use a slotted spoon to remove any leftover fried pieces of batter in the oil. If you don't do this, these pieces will eventually burn in the oil and the succeeding rings will pick them up as they fry.

9. Turn the fried onion rings on the wire racks to allow both sides to dry. Onion rings are best eaten within an hour or two of being fried.

FRIED CHICKEN

Making good fried chicken is something of an art. Over the years I've experimented with different flour and seasoning mixtures as well as battering techniques, but I was never really satisfied with the results. Then I came across a recipe in Thomas Keller's excellent cookbook *Ad Hoc at Home: Family-Style Recipes*. Finally, here was the combination I had been looking for. As Keller says, "If there's a better fried chicken, I haven't tasted it." I agree. I've been using an adapted version of his recipe ever since. This fried chicken is flawlessly seasoned on the outside and juicy and perfectly cooked on the inside. It's one of my family's favorite dinner meals. Be sure to cut the chicken breasts in half horizontally—otherwise, it will be very difficult to fry them all the way through. Before making this recipe, read the Deep-Frying Primer (page 20).

3 cups [435 g] Jeanne's Gluten-Free All-Purpose Flour (page 39)

2 Tbsp garlic powder

2 Tbsp onion powder

2 tsp salt

2 tsp paprika

½ tsp freshly ground black pepper

¼ tsp cayenne pepper, plus more to taste

2 cups [480 ml] buttermilk

Vegetable oil for frying

One 4- to 5-lb [1.8- to 2.25-kg] chicken cut into 10 pieces (fryer parts)

1. In a medium bowl, mix together the flour, garlic powder, onion powder, salt, paprika, black pepper, and cayenne. Pour half the flour mixture into another medium bowl.

2. Pour the buttermilk into a third medium bowl. (Each bowl should be large enough to accommodate a piece of chicken.) Line up the bowls as follows: flour mix, buttermilk, flour mix. Set a large plate next to the second bowl of flour for the floured pieces of chicken to rest before being fried.

3. Line a large baking sheet with two layers of paper towels and place a large wire rack on top.

4. Pour 3 in [7.5 cm] of vegetable oil into a heavy-bottomed saucepan fitted with a candy thermometer and heat the oil to 320°F [160°C].

5. Dredge each piece of chicken in the first flour mix, shake off the excess flour, dip in the buttermilk, let the excess drip back into the bowl, dredge in the second bowl of flour mix, shake off the excess, and place on the plate.

6. Fry the thighs and legs first. Carefully place the chicken pieces in the oil, which will bubble dramatically. Fry for 2 minutes to set the coating, then turn the pieces and fry, turning every 1 to 2 minutes, for another 12 minutes, or until the coating is golden brown. Monitor the oil so that the temperature stays constant. Raise or lower the burner temperature to keep the heat steady. Transfer the pieces to the wire rack to cool.

7. For the breast halves and wings, increase the oil temperature to 340°F [170°C].

CONTINUED >>

8. Once the oil reaches temperature, fry the breast halves and wings for 1 minute to set the coating, then turn the pieces and fry, turning every 1 to 2 minutes, for an additional 6 minutes, or until the coating is golden brown. Monitor the oil so that the temperature stays constant. Raise or lower the burner temperature to keep the heat steady. Transfer the pieces to the wire rack to cool.

9. Turn the fried chicken pieces on the wire rack to make sure each piece dries. Eat the fried chicken while it's hot.

Store in an airtight container in the refrigerator for up to 2 days; the coating will get soggy but it will still be tasty.

BATTERED AND FRIED FISH

I have been lucky in life—all the places I've lived have been near an ocean so I've enjoyed a ready supply of fresh fish. I love a good plate of beer-battered fish and chips every so often, but now that restaurant versions are off-limits, I created this recipe. Firm-fleshed fish such as cod or halibut are the traditional choices for this recipe. Luckily, gluten-free beer is easily available nowadays—I can find it at my neighborhood grocery store. Before making this recipe, read the Deep-Frying Primer (page 20).

1½ cups [215 g] Jeanne's Gluten-Free All-Purpose Flour (page 39)

1 Tbsp aluminum-free double-acting baking powder

1 tsp salt

⅛ to ¼ tsp cayenne pepper (optional)

One 12-oz [355-ml] bottle gluten-free beer

Vegetable oil for frying

1 to 1½ lb [455 to 680 g] firm white-fleshed fish

½ cup [60 g] tapioca flour

1. In a large bowl, mix together the all-purpose flour, baking powder, salt, and cayenne (if using). Slowly add the beer and whisk until the batter is smooth. Let sit for at least 15 minutes, or up to 1 hour, to allow the batter to thicken.

2. Pour 3 in [7.5 cm] of vegetable oil into a heavy-bottomed saucepan fitted with a candy thermometer and heat the oil to 350°F [180°C]. Line a large baking sheet with a double layer of paper towels and place a wire rack on top.

3. With a sharp knife, cut the fish into pieces that are about 1 by 3½ in [2.5 by 9 cm].

4. Place the tapioca flour in a medium bowl. Place the bowl of batter next to it and set a plate next to the bowl of batter.

5. When the oil has reached temperature, prepare the first batch of fish to be fried. Dredge a piece of fish in tapioca flour, shake off the excess flour, then dip it in the batter. The batter is thick—use your finger to brush off a bit of batter from the sides of the fish if it seems too heavily battered. Place the battered fish on the plate and repeat the process until you have battered the number of pieces that will fit into your pot without crowding.

6. Carefully place the fish pieces in the oil, which will bubble dramatically. Fry for 30 seconds to set the batter. The fish pieces will sink to the bottom as you add them to the oil. If they haven't risen to the surface after 30 seconds, use a pair of metal tongs to unstick them from the bottom. Fry for 2 minutes longer, turning them every 30 seconds until they are golden brown. Monitor the oil so that it stays at temperature. Raise or lower the burner temperature to keep the heat steady.

7. Use metal tongs to remove each piece, allowing any excess oil to drip back into the pan. Transfer the fish to the wire rack to cool.

8. Repeat the flouring, dredging, frying, and draining process until all the pieces of fish are fried. After frying each batch, use a slotted spoon to remove any leftover pieces of batter in the oil. If you don't do this, these pieces will eventually burn in the oil and the succeeding fish pieces will pick up them up as they fry.

9. Turn each piece on the wire rack once or twice to allow all the sides of the fish to dry. Serve hot—battered and fried fish doesn't store well.

CALZONES

MAKES 6 MEDIUM CALZONES

Calzones are basically pizza dough wrapped around a filling. The word *calzone* means "trouser leg," which I'm assuming refers to the fact that the half-moon shape of a calzone looks like the billowing pantaloon of an Italian commedia dell'arte character. Traditionally, calzones are filled with meat, vegetables, and cheese and then baked and sometimes served with a marinara sauce. I often make calzones to use up leftover spaghetti sauce, along with some grated cheese and maybe some cooked ground meat as well (don't tell the traditionalists, who usually serve them with the marinara sauce poured on the outside rather than stuffed on the inside). Stuff and top your calzones with your favorite fillings and sauce.

Tapioca flour for dusting

1 recipe Master Bread Dough (page 92), prepared through the first rise

2 cups [210 g] filling of any combination of cooked meat, cooked vegetables, spaghetti sauce, and grated cheese, at room temperature

Olive oil for brushing

1. Position a rack near the bottom of the oven and preheat to 450°F [230°C]. Line a large baking sheet with parchment paper.

2. Dust a rolling surface thoroughly with tapioca flour. Turn out the dough onto the rolling surface. Sprinkle tapioca flour on top of the dough and use your hands to shape it into a dome. Use a floured bench scraper or a large sharp knife to cut the dough into three approximately equal wedges. Cut each wedge in half, for a total of six wedges.

3. Flour your hands with tapioca flour and shape each wedge into a ball. Place the balls on a corner of the work surface.

4. Sprinkle the work surface well with more tapioca flour. Place a ball of dough on the surface and use a floured palm to press it down into a fat disk. Flour the top well and roll the dough out into a circle that is about 7 in [18 cm] in diameter. The dough will be very, very soft—it will seem almost too soft—but don't worry, it will work. The dough will also be quite sticky, so make sure that it and the rolling pin are well floured as you roll it out. Place ⅓ cup [35 g] of the filling in the center of the dough. Fold the dough over the filling to form a half-moon shape. Press the edges of the dough together to seal them. Next, fold the sealed edges back onto themselves. This will ensure that the filling is well sealed. The edges will look a bit messy—this is normal. They will smooth out during the baking process.

5. The completed uncooked calzone will be very soft and floppy. Carefully slide a floured metal spatula under the calzone and transfer it to the prepared baking sheet.

6. Repeat the rolling, folding, and sealing process with the remaining dough and filling and place the calzones on the baking sheet at least 1 in [2.5 cm] apart. With a *lame* or a sharp knife, make a small slit in the middle of each calzone near the folded edge. This will allow the steam from the filling to escape while the calzones are baking. Lightly brush the calzones with olive oil.

7. Bake until the calzones are golden brown, about 15 minutes. Remove from the oven and use a metal spatula to transfer the calzones to a wire rack to cool for about 15 minutes. Calzones are best eaten the day they are made.

Store in an airtight container in the refrigerator for up to 2 days, or in the freezer for up to 2 months. Defrost in refrigerator for 24 hours. Calzones may be reheated in the microwave on high in 1-minute increments until the filling has reached the temperature you'd like.

DEEP-DISH PIZZA

MAKES **1** DEEP DISH PIZZA

When I attended college in Los Angeles, there was a local pizza chain that had the best deep-dish pizza crust. It was slightly sweet and satisfyingly doughy, and my roommates and I loved it. Over the years, I've often thought of that pizza crust and have finally replicated it with this recipe.

Olive oil for brushing and drizzling

1 recipe Master Bread Dough (page 92), prepared through the first rise

Tapioca flour for dusting

About ⅔ cup [160 ml] Simple Tomato Sauce (page 180)

Vegetables (any kind; optional)

Meat (any kind; optional)

Grated or sliced cheese (any kind; optional)

1. Preheat the oven to 425°F [220°C] for 30 minutes.

2. While the oven is preheating, brush a deep-dish pizza pan or cast-iron skillet, with sides at least 2 in [5 cm] high, thoroughly with olive oil.

3. Turn out the dough into the middle of the pizza pan. Dust some tapioca flour on the dough and use your fingers to push it into the sides of the pan. Sprinkle more tapioca flour on the dough whenever your hands start to stick to the dough. Push the dough up the sides of the pan until it's just shy of the rim. Press down on the dough in the bottom of the pan and use your fingers to fix any tears. Pay particular attention to pressing the dough into the crease around the perimeter of the pan. I also use the tip of my index finger to press the top edge of the dough down a little bit to tidy it.

4. Cover the pan with plastic wrap and let the dough rise for the remainder of the oven preheating time.

5. Unwrap the dough and place it in the oven. Bake for 15 minutes. The crust should be brown.

6. Remove the pan from the oven. If the dough has billowed up at the bottom, use a fork to prick the dough to release the bubbles of gas.

7. Top the crust with the tomato sauce and your choice of vegetables, meat, and cheese. Drizzle a little olive oil over the top. Lightly brush the edges of the crust with olive oil so they will become a deeper brown during the second bake.

8. Return the pan to the oven. Bake for about 10 minutes—watch carefully so that the cheese and toppings don't burn. (I find that fresh mozzarella has a tendency to burn very quickly.)

9. Remove from the oven and let sit for 10 minutes to cool. Cut the pizza into wedges and serve from the pan. The pizza is best eaten the day it is baked.

Store in an airtight container in the refrigerator for up to 2 days. Do not freeze.

NYC-STYLE PIZZA

This dough creates a thin crust that is crunchy on the bottom and chewy in the middle. The key to this crust is to bake it twice—once by itself and then again with toppings.

1⅓ cups [195 g] Jeanne's Gluten-Free All-Purpose Flour (page 39)

½ tsp xanthan gum

½ tsp salt

1½ tsp aluminum-free double-acting baking powder

1 Tbsp granulated sugar

2 Tbsp instant yeast

¾ cup [180 ml] warm water (about 95°F [35°C])

1 tsp olive oil, plus more for brushing

1 tsp cider vinegar

Tapioca flour for dusting

About ⅔ cup [160 ml] Simple Tomato Sauce (page 180)

Vegetables (any kind; optional)

Meat (any kind; optional)

Grated or sliced cheese (any kind; optional)

1. Place the all-purpose flour, xanthan gum, salt, baking powder, sugar, and yeast in the bowl of a stand mixer fitted with the paddle attachment and beat on low speed for a few seconds to mix. Add the water, olive oil, and vinegar and beat on low speed for a few seconds more to combine, then increase the speed to medium-high and mix for 3 minutes. After 3 minutes, the dough should be fairly loose and resemble a smooth batter.

2. Tear off a large piece of parchment paper that is 12½ in [32 cm] wide by about 16 in [41 cm] long. Turn out the dough onto the parchment paper. You can now either shape the dough or let it rise for up to 1 hour. If you let it rise, the baked crust will be a bit lighter.

3. When you are ready to shape the dough, dust it with tapioca flour to prevent sticking. Using your fingers, carefully push the dough into a circle that is about 12 in [30 cm] in diameter, keeping the thickness even throughout. It will feel soft and pillowy. Use more tapioca flour if necessary to prevent sticking. Mound the edges a bit to create a wall to prevent the toppings from oozing off during baking.

4. Let the dough rise in a warm, draft-free place for at least 20 minutes, or up to 2 hours. The crust will become fuller and more puffy.

5. As the dough is rising, position a rack in the middle of the oven and preheat to 475°F [240°C]. If you're using a baking stone, place it in the oven to preheat.

6. Once the dough has risen, pierce the middle a few times with a fork to prevent bubbles from forming in the crust. If you're using a baking stone, transfer the dough to the stone by lifting the parchment paper on both sides and carefully and slowly placing the dough (still on the parchment paper) in the oven. If you're not using a baking stone, place the dough and parchment paper onto a pizza pan or baking sheet.

7. Bake for 15 minutes, then remove from the oven and set it on a heatproof surface. Remove the parchment paper from the bottom of the crust.

8. Top the crust with the tomato sauce and your choice of vegetables, meat, and cheese. Lightly brush the edges of the crust with olive oil so they will become brown and crispy during the second baking.

9. If you're using a baking stone, use a pizza peel (or two large metal spatulas) to transfer the crust back to the stone in the oven. If you're not using a baking stone, place the pizza pan back in the oven. Bake for 6 to 10 minutes—watch carefully so that the cheese and the toppings don't burn. (I find that fresh mozzarella has a tendency to burn very quickly.)

10. Use the pizza peel to remove the crust from the baking stone, or remove the pizza pan from the oven. Cut into wedges and serve. The pizza is best eaten the day it is baked.

Store in a zip-top bag in the refrigerator for up to 2 days (it will become somewhat soggy, but will still be tasty).

POTATO GNOCCHI WITH TOMATO-PORCINI MUSHROOM SAUCE

MAKES 250 GNOCCHI

When I was in high school, I had a friend of Italian descent who would often invite me over for a dinner of gnocchi with her family. After a while, I asked if she would teach me to make the little pillowy potato dumplings. She did, and I began making gnocchi for my family. These gnocchi are cooked by steaming rather than boiling—because they disintegrate in the boiling water. I've designed this recipe to make a lot, so you can either make them for a crowd or make them for family dinner and then freeze the remainder for future dinners.

This recipe uses russet potatoes, which are starchy baking potatoes. In the United Kingdom, King Edwards, Rooster, and Maris Piper would be good choices. Waxy potatoes, such as Yukon gold, will not work for this recipe. Also, the potatoes are baked rather than boiled. This cooks the potatoes without adding extra water—too much water makes the gnocchi dough too loose and difficult to form.

4 lb [1.8 kg] russet potatoes

2 extra-large eggs, lightly beaten

3½ cups [505 g] Jeanne's Gluten-Free All-Purpose Flour (page 39)

1 tsp salt

Tomato-Porcini Mushroom Sauce (page 176)

1. Preheat the oven to 400°F [200°C].

2. Wash and dry the potatoes thoroughly and place them on a large baking sheet. Bake for 30 minutes, prick them all over with a fork, return them to the oven, and bake for another 45 minutes.

3. Remove the potatoes from the oven. You want to work as quickly as possible, but be aware that the potatoes are very hot. Cut each potato in half and use a spoon to scrape out the insides into a bowl. Force the potatoes through a ricer into a large bowl. (I don't recommend using a potato masher if you have a ricer, because the masher tends to leave hard lumps that make forming the gnocchi difficult.) Let the potatoes cool until just warm.

4. Add the eggs and stir to combine. Add 1½ cups [215 g] of the flour and the salt and mix together with a fork until smooth. Add another 1 cup [145 g] flour and, using your hands, knead the flour into the dough until it is completely absorbed. Add the remaining flour, ¼ cup [35 g] at a time, using your hands to knead it into the dough. At this point you should have a stiff dough that is somewhat tacky—it shouldn't be wet or overly sticky.

5. Roll ¼ cup [35 g] of the dough into a ball with your hands. Place the dough on a clean rolling surface. The dough should not be so sticky that it sticks to the surface in a problematic way. (You can use a tiny amount of all-purpose flour to dust the rolling surface and the surface of your dough, but if it really sticks to the surface, return the dough to the larger lump of dough and add another ¼ cup [35 g] flour, knead until the flour is absorbed, and try again.)

6. Carefully roll the ball into a uniform log that is 12 in [30 cm] long and ½ in [12 mm] in diameter. (I put a clean 12-in [30-cm] ruler on the rolling surface and roll the log to match the length of it.)

7. Cut the log into 1-in [2.5-cm] segments. Roll each segment into a ball. Using a fork, gently mash down each ball so that it forms a fat disk with a tine pattern on top. The bumps created by the tines of the fork will serve to catch and hold more sauce on the gnocchi.

8. Repeat until all of the gnocchi are cut and rolled. (I know this seems like a lot of dough to work with, but the process goes quickly once you get started. At this point, you can place the gnocchi in a single layer on baking sheets lined with wax paper and freeze for 1 hour, then transfer to zip-top bags and freeze for up to 3 months.)

9. Place a steamer (I use a folding metal steamer) in a large pot. Pour in enough water to reach the underside of the steamer (don't cover the steamer with water). Bring the water to a boil over high heat. Place a single layer of gnocchi in the steamer. Cover the pot, turn the heat to medium-high, and steam for 9 minutes. Use a slotted spoon to transfer the gnocchi to a plate. Repeat until you have as much gnocchi as you need.

10. Top with the sauce and serve.

TOMATO-PORCINI MUSHROOM SAUCE

MAKES 5 CUPS [1.2 L]

Dried mushrooms provide the perfect umami complement to the tomatoes' tang.

One 1-oz [28-g] package dried porcini mushrooms

¼ cup [60 ml] extra-virgin olive oil

1 medium yellow onion, diced

4 medium garlic cloves, minced

One 26- to 28-oz [737-g to 794-g] box or can strained tomatoes or plain tomato sauce

1 Tbsp dried parsley

1 Tbsp dried basil

1 tsp freshly ground black pepper

Salt

1. Place the mushrooms in a medium bowl and cover with boiling water. Let the mushrooms soak for at least 30 minutes.

2. Heat the olive oil in a heavy-bottomed saucepan over medium heat. Add the onion and garlic and sauté until the onion is translucent, about 8 minutes.

3. Once the mushrooms are hydrated, strain the liquid into another bowl and reserve. Chop the mushrooms and add them to the saucepan. Sauté for 5 minutes. Add the tomatoes, parsley, basil, pepper, and a pinch of salt and stir to combine. Add ¼ cup [60 ml] of the reserved porcini soaking liquid and stir to combine.

4. Let the sauce simmer, stirring occasionally, over low heat for at least 1 hour, or up to 3 hours. Season with salt.

Store in an airtight container in the refrigerator for up to 3 days, or in the freezer for up to 3 months.

PASTA WITH SIMPLE TOMATO SAUCE

MAKES 4 SERVINGS

It may sound odd, but I associate fresh pasta with my maternal grandmother who lived not in Italy, but in Des Moines, Iowa. When I was young, I went to Iowa for several weeks each summer to visit my grandparents. I loved those Midwest summers. They seemed to be an endless stream of fun. There were a slew of kids my age whom I could hang out with and a grandmother who did all sorts of things that storybook grandmothers did—hosting taffy pulls and keeping the freezer full of Popsicles. In addition to both of these things, she made homemade pasta. Of course, she called them *noodles* and didn't fuss over them too much. She just mixed, rolled, and cut the dough into thick, "rustic" noodles, boiled them, and served them with melted butter and salt—and maybe some Parmesan cheese from the ubiquitous green can. Every time I make my own noodles, I am transported back to those childhood Iowa summers. This recipe is equally nonfussy, and the resulting dough is malleable enough to be cut by machine or by hand. It stands up to a moderate amount of shaping, allowing it to be made into ravioli (see page 181).

PASTA

2 cups [290 g] Jeanne's Gluten-Free All-Purpose Flour (page 39), plus more for dusting

Large pinch of salt

4 extra-large eggs, at room temperature

Tapioca flour for dusting

Simple Tomato Sauce (page 180)

1. **TO MAKE THE PASTA:** Place the all-purpose flour in a medium bowl. Make a large well in the center of the flour. Add the salt and eggs to the well. Using a fork, pierce the yolk of each egg and then beat the flour into the well by slowly stirring around the well and gradually pulling more and more flour from the sides into the eggs in the middle. When the dough becomes too stiff to work with the fork, use your hands to mix the remaining flour into the dough.

2. Dust a work surface with additional all-purpose flour and turn out the dough onto the work surface.

3. Dust the lump of dough with all-purpose flour. Pull a corner of the dough from the back to the front of the lump and press it into the opposite corner of the lump just as if you were kneading wheat bread. Give the dough a quarter turn, dust with more all-purpose flour, and repeat pulling a corner from the back to the front and pressing it into the opposite corner of the lump. Make sure the work surface is adequately floured with all-purpose flour the entire time.

CONTINUED >>

4. The dough will be stiff during this process, so it will take some effort to knead it. After a few minutes of kneading and dusting the dough with flour, the dough will become smooth and will no longer feel sticky. Press your finger into the center of the ball to see if the inside is tacky. If it is, continue the turning and kneading process for a few more turns. Check the inside again. It might feel the slightest bit tacky—that's okay, but it shouldn't be overly tacky inside.

5. Form the dough into a disk, wrap it tightly in plastic wrap so that it's airtight, and let it rest on the counter at room temperature for at least 1 hour, or up to 24 hours. (If you let it rest for longer than about 4 hours, place the dough in the refrigerator.) This resting period will give the dough time to relax and hydrate. When you unwrap the dough, you will be surprised at how much more supple it is than it was before its rest.

6. When you're ready to roll out and cut the dough, unwrap it, place it on a work surface (no need for flouring), and cut it into four equal wedges. Wrap three wedges in plastic wrap so that they don't dry out while you work on the fourth wedge.

7. **Rolling and cutting the pasta by hand:** Dust a work surface with all-purpose flour. Use your hands to shape the wedge into a small rectangular block. It's best to do this with your hands in order to avoid adding any more flour than necessary to the dough. Place the block on the work surface, sprinkle it with all-purpose flour, and roll it into a long rectangle. The dough will be elastic and will bounce back a bit as you roll it. Keep rolling, making sure you roll it out to the sides as well. Sprinkle the dough with all-purpose flour as needed so the dough doesn't stick to the rolling pin. Roll the dough out to a rectangle that is about ⅛ in [4 mm] thick, then fold the dough in thirds from the long side. Turn the dough so that an open edge is facing you, roll it out some more, and fold it into thirds

again. Repeat this process a few more times to build the strength and structure of the dough and create a smooth and fairly even rectangle of dough. After folding and rolling the dough at least four times, and until it looks very smooth, roll the dough into a rectangle about ⅛ in [4 mm] thick.

Now, cut the pasta into any (flat) shape you want. I usually cut it with a sharp knife into noodles ¼ to ½ in [6 to 12 mm] wide. If you want the pasta to look uniform, use a ruler to measure the width you want and use a straight edge to guide the knife.

Pile the cut noodles into a medium bowl and toss with some tapioca flour. Cover the bowl with a damp dish towel while you are rolling and cutting the other noodles so that they don't dry out. Repeat the rolling and cutting process until you have used all four wedges. (If you need less pasta, you can also use just the number of wedges you need and store the rest, tightly wrapped, in the fridge for up to 2 days.)

Rolling and cutting the pasta with a manually operated pasta machine: Use your hands to form a wedge of dough into a ball. Lightly dust a work surface with all-purpose flour. Roll the ball into a fairly even oblong shape that is about ⅛ in [4 mm] thick.

Set the pasta rollers to the largest size. (On my Atlas machine this is setting 1.) Carefully and slowly roll the pasta through the rollers, catching it as it comes out. It shouldn't stick—but if it does, it needs to be dusted with more all-purpose flour. Take the rolled dough, fold it into thirds, and run it through the machine again leading with an open edge of the folded dough. Repeat the rolling and folding process at least four times to build the strength and structure of the dough and to form it into a rectangle that is smooth and fairly even on all sides. As you run it through the machine, the dough may become too long to fold into thirds—this is okay. Make as many folds as is necessary to create a rectangle that is a width that will fit easily through the machine.

After repeating this initial rolling, folding, and shaping process with the machine set at the largest size, set the rollers to one size smaller. (On my machine this is setting 2.) Carefully and slowly roll the pasta through the rollers once, catching it on the other side. Set the machine to one size smaller again and repeat the process until you have rolled the pasta through the fifth smallest setting (or the smallest setting the dough will roll well through on your machine; on my machine this is setting 5). On my machine, the sheet of pasta usually breaks somewhere around the third or fourth setting because it has become too long. This is okay. Just roll each of the broken pieces individually, keeping track of what setting each piece is on.

After rolling the dough through the fifth setting, run the sheets of pasta through the cutters, set at the noodle size and type you want. I have a flat noodle cutter, a smaller flat spaghetti cutter, and a round spaghetti cutter, and each works fine with this dough. Place each batch of cut pasta in a bowl. I usually make the whole recipe for one meal, so it all goes into the same bowl. (At this point, you can place the noodles in small serving-size piles on a baking sheet lined with parchment paper, cover with plastic wrap, and freeze for 2 hours, then transfer to zip-top bags and freeze for up to 3 months.)

8. Bring a large pot of well-salted water to a rolling boil over high heat. Add as much pasta as will fit without crowding, and stir gently to distribute the noodles in the water. Cook the pasta for 3 to 4 minutes, or until it has a bit of resistance in the middle when you bite into a test noodle. Drain and rinse lightly with hot water (to remove any leftover starch).

9. Top with the sauce and serve.

SIMPLE TOMATO SAUCE

This is one of my family's favorite pasta and pizza sauces. The honey gives it a subtly sweet taste that serves as a perfect foil for the tang of the tomatoes. It's mellow enough to pair well with meatballs yet flavorful enough to be delightful on its own. We usually like the sauce with chopped tomatoes, but it's equally as delicious with puréed tomatoes. Use this sauce to top Calzones (page 168), too.

¼ cup [60 ml] extra-virgin olive oil

1 medium yellow onion, diced

2 large garlic cloves, minced

One 26- to 28-oz [737- to 794-g] box or can chopped tomatoes

1 Tbsp neutral-tasting honey

1 tsp salt

¼ tsp freshly ground black pepper

⅛ tsp fennel seeds

1 tsp dried oregano

1 tsp dried marjoram

½ tsp dried thyme

1 bay leaf

Heat the olive oil in a medium heavy-bottomed saucepan over medium heat. Add the onion and sauté until the onion is transparent, about 8 minutes. Add the garlic and sauté for 1 minute. Add the tomatoes, honey, salt, pepper, fennel seeds, oregano, marjoram, thyme, and bay leaf and stir to combine. Lower the heat and bring to a simmer. Cover and cook for 1 hour to meld the flavors, stirring occasionally. Remove the bay leaf before serving.

Store in an airtight container in the refrigerator for up to 3 days, or in the freezer for up to 3 months.

RAVIOLI

MAKES ABOUT 30 RAVIOLI

When my daughter was little, she called ravioli "pillows of pasta"—which is a perfect (and charming) description. The shapes can differ—this recipe calls for rectangles—but the shape matters less than the filling and the sauce. I've included two easy and flavorful fillings in this book: Ricotta-Spinach Filling and Simple Meat Filling, along with Simple Tomato Sauce. Gluten-free pasta dough is a little less elastic than wheat dough, so it's important to add less filling than you think you need for each raviolo.

1 recipe pasta dough (see page 177), prepared through the rolling of the dough

Ricotta-Spinach Filling (page 183) or Simple Meat Filling (page 183), at room temperature

Simple Tomato Sauce (facing page) or sauce of your choice

Parmesan cheese for garnish

1. Line a large baking sheet with parchment paper.

2. Tidy the edges of one rolled sheet of dough and use a sharp knife and a straight edge to square off the sides and ends.

3. Cut the rectangle of dough in half lengthwise, creating two roughly 3-in [7-cm] wide lengths. Using a ruler, make a notch every 2 in [5 cm] along the long side of one of the pieces of dough. Cut the dough at each notch, creating small rectangles of dough. Repeat the measuring, notching, and cutting process with the second length of dough. You should now have two equal amounts of pasta rectangles.

4. Place 1 tsp of filling in the middle of half of the pasta rectangles. Use a finger dipped in water to moisten the edges of the dough. Place an unfilled rectangle on top of each filled square. Gently but firmly press down around the perimeter of the rectangles to seal the two pieces together. If the dough tears at any point, use a finger to smooth out the tear. Use the tines of a fork to complete the seal and make a decorative edge. Make sure the ravioli are well sealed. Any unsealed edge will open up in the cooking water and release the filling into the water.

5. Place the ravioli on the prepared baking sheet and cover with plastic wrap so they don't dry out while you repeat the process with the remainder of the dough and filling. (At this point, you can freeze them for 2 hours, then transfer to a zip-top bag and freeze for up to 3 months. Cook as directed, adding a minute or two to the cooking time.)

6. Bring a large pot of well-salted water to a rolling boil over high heat. Add as many ravioli as will fit without crowding, and nudge them gently with a spoon to make sure they don't stick to each other. Cook the ravioli for 4 to 6 minutes, or until they are just barely cooked through when you test one. The pasta should be slightly firm and the filling should be hot.

7. Top with the sauce, garnish with Parmesan, and serve.

RICOTTA-SPINACH FILLING

MAKES 2¼ CUPS [605 G]

This is a classic filling for ravioli. It is light and ethereal and pairs nicely with Simple Tomato Sauce (page 180). Some brands of ricotta cheese that come packaged in tubs are a bit watery, which can make the filling runny. Before using it, place the ricotta in a fine-mesh strainer set over a large bowl. Cover with plastic wrap and let drain in the refrigerator for about 8 hours, or overnight. Discard the liquid. After cooking the spinach, be sure to squeeze out any liquid the leaves retain. Otherwise, the filling will be runny.

2 cups [455 g] ricotta cheese, well drained

8 Tbsp [80 g] grated Parmesan cheese

2 cups [85 g] fresh spinach leaves, lightly steamed, drained, and finely chopped

In a large bowl, mix together the drained ricotta cheese, Parmesan cheese, and spinach until well blended.

Store in an airtight container in the refrigerator for up to 3 days. Do not freeze.

SIMPLE MEAT FILLING

MAKES 2 CUPS [430 G]

This is a simple ground meat filling that can be used in ravioli or in wontons (see page 190). It is mildly seasoned so that it won't fight with the flavors of the sauce used with the pasta. It goes especially well with the Simple Tomato Sauce (page 180). If you're using ground chicken or ground turkey, use a combination of white meat and dark meat so that the filling isn't dry.

¼ cup [60 ml] olive oil

12 oz [340 g] ground meat of your choice

1 small yellow onion, diced

2 garlic cloves, minced

1 tsp dried basil

Salt and freshly ground black pepper

¼ cup [40 g] grated Parmesan cheese (optional)

1. Heat the olive oil in a medium heavy-bottomed saucepan over medium heat. Add the meat and sauté until the meat is almost, but not quite, fully cooked, about 7 minutes. Add the onion and cook for 2 minutes. Add the garlic and cook until the onion is transparent and the meat is fully cooked, 7 to 10 minutes. Add the basil and mix to combine. Remove from the heat. Season with salt and pepper.

2. Transfer the mixture to a large, heatproof bowl. Add the cheese (if using) and mix with a large spoon to combine thoroughly. Let cool to room temperature.

Store in an airtight container in the refrigerator for up to 3 days. Do not freeze.

CHICKEN AND DUMPLING SOUP

My family is a soup family. We are so busy during most of the year with work, school, and activities that I turn to hearty soups and stews for satisfying one-dish meals on our busiest nights. This is one of our favorites. The beauty of this soup is that it is delicious on its own, or you can customize it by adding seasonal vegetables (add them when you add the seasonings to the broth). You can also replace the dumplings with cooked pasta (see page 177) or rice.

½ cup [120 ml] extra-virgin olive oil

2 boneless chicken breasts and 2 boneless chicken thighs

Salt and freshly ground black pepper

1 medium yellow onion, chopped

2 large carrots, chopped

2 large celery stalks, chopped

2 large garlic cloves, minced

2 qt [2 L] gluten-free chicken or vegetable broth

1 Tbsp dried dill

2 tsp dried thyme

2 tsp dried basil

1 bay leaf

¼ cup [65 g] tomato paste

Soup Dumplings (facing page)

1. Heat ¼ cup [60 ml] of the olive oil in a large stockpot over medium heat. Add the chicken, season with salt and pepper, and sauté until just cooked through, about 15 minutes. Transfer the chicken to a plate, cover with aluminum foil, and refrigerate until ready to use.

2. Heat the remaining olive oil in the stockpot and use a spoon to dislodge any browned chicken bits that are left in the pot. Add the onion, carrots, and celery and sauté until the onion is translucent, about 8 minutes. Add the garlic and sauté for 1 minute more.

3. Add the broth, dill, thyme, basil, bay leaf, 2 tsp salt, and 1 tsp pepper and stir to combine. Simmer for at least 1 hour for the flavors to meld.

4. Remove the chicken pieces from the refrigerator, cut them into bite-size pieces, and add them to the broth. Stir the tomato paste into the broth and let simmer for another 15 minutes to heat the chicken and meld the flavors. Test one piece of chicken to make sure it's heated through, and adjust the seasonings.

5. Add the dumplings to the individual serving bowls, ladle in the soup, and serve.

Store in an airtight container in the refrigerator for up to 3 days, or in the freezer for up to 2 months.

SOUP DUMPLINGS

Soup dumplings seem to be a popular comfort food for my readers. There are few things more soothing than a steaming bowl of soup and dumplings. I didn't grow up eating dumplings, but many of my friends and readers did. I came to dumplings as an adult, and once I experienced them I couldn't believe what a treat I'd been missing. These fluffy dumplings are delicate and need to be steamed on their own to cook thoroughly before they're added to a soup. I like to pair them with a traditional chicken vegetable soup, but you can add them to any kind of soup that suits your fancy.

1¼ cups [180 g] Jeanne's Gluten-Free All-Purpose Flour (page 39)

½ tsp salt

1 Tbsp aluminum-free double-acting baking powder

1 Tbsp chopped fresh parsley or 1 tsp dried parsley

1 Tbsp plus 1½ tsp unsalted butter, melted

⅓ cup [80 ml] milk

1 extra-large egg, beaten

1. In a medium bowl, mix together the flour, salt, baking powder, and parsley. Add the butter, milk, and egg and mix. The dough will be stiff but moist.

2. Place a steamer (I use a folding metal steamer) in a large pot. Pour in enough water to reach the underside of the steamer (don't cover the steamer with water). Bring the water to a boil over high heat.

3. While the water is coming to a boil, shape the dumplings. Scoop out a scant 1 Tbsp of dough, shape it into a ball with your hands, and place it on a plate. Repeat with the remainder of the dough; you should get about 20 dumplings. Place a piece of plastic wrap over the plate of dumplings so they don't dry out.

4. Once the water is boiling, place a single layer of dumplings in the steamer. Cover the pot and steam for 19 minutes. Use a slotted spoon to transfer the dumplings to a large plate. Repeat until all of the dumplings are cooked.

Store in an airtight container in the refrigerator for up to 2 days. Do not freeze.

RAMEN SOUP

....

MAKES 2 QT [2 L]

....

Nearly every region of Japan has its own version of ramen soup, which is an umami-rich broth with meat and vegetables that serves as a vehicle for the slurpable ramen noodles. This is a very flavorful yet basic and easy-to-make version of chicken ramen soup.

1 bunch scallions, cleaned

2 qt [2 L] gluten-free chicken broth

1-in [2.5-cm] knob ginger root, peeled and minced

3 garlic cloves, minced

¼ cup [60 ml] gluten-free tamari or soy sauce

1 tsp salt

1 cooked boneless chicken breast, shredded

1 recipe Ramen Noodles (page 188)

2 hard-boiled eggs, halved

1 cup [60 g] mung bean sprouts

Sesame oil for drizzling

Chili oil for drizzling

1. With a sharp knife, cut off and discard the roots and ½ in [12 mm] of the green stalks from the scallions. Cut off the white bulbs and finely chop them. Reserve the green stalks.

2. Put the broth, ginger root, garlic, and chopped scallion bulbs in a large pot set over medium-high heat and bring to a boil. Cover, turn the heat to low, and simmer for 30 minutes to let the flavors meld.

3. After 30 minutes, add the tamari, salt, and chicken and simmer for 30 minutes to heat the chicken and meld the flavors.

4. While the soup is simmering, finely slice the reserved scallion stalks into thin rings.

5. Ladle the soup into four large soup bowls. Add one portion of ramen noodles to each bowl and top each bowl with half a hard-boiled egg, some mung bean sprouts, and some sliced scallions. Drizzle a small amount of sesame oil and chili oil into each bowl and serve hot.

Store, without noodles or toppings, in an airtight container in the refrigerator for up to 3 days, or in the freezer for up to 2 months.

RAMEN NOODLES

MAKES ABOUT 4 SERVINGS

Ramen noodles are one of the elusive holy grails of the gluten-free world. Up until now, gluten-free folks had to settle for regular rice noodles in their ramen instead of genuine ramen noodles. Ramen noodles are typically made with a preparation of lye water called *kansui*, which strengthens the protein in the wheat and gives the noodles their flavor and sturdy texture. Nowadays, home cooks often use baked baking soda to make ramen noodles instead of *kansui*, which can be difficult to find and use. This recipe uses a combination of baked baking soda and egg whites (note the precise measure) to give the noodles their flavor and chewy texture. Gluten-free ramen lovers can slurp away—ramen noodles are back on the menu!

2 cups [290 g] Jeanne's Gluten-Free All-Purpose Flour (page 39)
½ tsp xanthan gum
½ tsp salt
½ cup [120 ml] cool water
1 tsp Baked Baking Soda (page 43)
¼ cup [60 ml] egg whites
Tapioca flour for dusting

1. In a medium bowl, mix together the all-purpose flour, xanthan gum, and salt.

2. In a small bowl, whisk together the water and baking soda. Some of the baking soda may not dissolve—that's fine.

3. In the bowl of a stand mixer, whisk together the egg whites and water mixture. Add the flour mixture and place the bowl into the mixer fitted with the dough hook. Beat on low speed to combine the ingredients. Use a spatula to scrape down the sides of the bowl if necessary. Increase the speed to medium-high and beat

for 5 minutes. Watch the mixer carefully—the dough is very stiff and my mixer usually starts to travel across the counter due to the dough bumping against the sides of the bowl.

4. After 5 minutes, the dough should be smooth and very stiff. Use your hands to form the dough into a ball and wrap it well in plastic wrap. Let the dough rest at room temperature for at least 1 hour. (If you plan to store for longer than 4 hours, place it in the refrigerator for up to 24 hours. Bring the dough to room temperature before using.)

5. After 1 hour, unwrap the dough (reserve the plastic wrap) and cut the ball into four equal wedges. Rewrap three pieces in plastic wrap and set them aside.

6. Dust the work surface with tapioca flour. Use your hands to shape a wedge of dough into a small rectangular block. Place the block on the work surface, sprinkle it with tapioca flour, and start to roll it into a long rectangle. The dough will be elastic and will bounce back a bit as you roll it. Keep rolling, making sure you roll it out to the sides as well, until it is about ¼ in [6 mm] thick. Sprinkle the dough with tapioca flour as needed so the dough doesn't stick to the rolling pin.

7. Rolling and cutting the noodles by hand: Fold the rectangle in thirds the same way you would fold a letter. Turn the dough so that an open edge faces you, roll out to ¼ in [6 mm] thick, and again fold into thirds. Repeat this process a few more times—this folding process will strengthen the structure of the noodles and create a smooth and relatively even rectangle of dough. After folding and rolling the dough at least four times (and when the dough looks fairly smooth), roll the dough into a rectangle that is about ¼ in [6 mm] thick.

Now cut the dough. I usually cut it, using a sharp knife, into noodles ¼ in [6 mm] wide. If you want your noodles to look uniform, measure the dough with a ruler and then cut the noodles using a straight edge to guide the knife. Or, you can create rustic-looking noodles by cutting them freehand to roughly the same width. It doesn't really matter—they will taste delicious either way.

Rolling and cutting the dough in a manually operated pasta machine: Set the pasta rollers to the largest size. (On my Atlas machine, this is setting 1.) Carefully and slowly roll the dough through the rollers, catching it as it comes out. It shouldn't stick—but if it does, it needs to be dusted with more tapioca flour. Take the rolled dough, fold it into thirds, turn it, and run it through the machine again, leading with the open edge of the folded dough. Repeat the rolling and folding process at least six times to build the strength and structure of the dough and to form it into an even rectangle. As you run it through the machine, the dough may become too long to fold it into thirds—this is okay. Use as many folds as is necessary to create a rectangle that is a width that will easily fit through the machine.

Set the machine rollers to 2 and run the dough through. Cut the dough by running it through the desired cutter on the pasta machine.

8. Once the dough has been cut into noodles, toss in a bowl with some tapioca flour and set aside. This is enough noodles for one batch of soup.

9. Repeat the rolling, cutting, and tossing process with the remaining three portions of dough.

10. Cook the noodles one batch at a time. Bring a medium saucepan of water to a rolling boil over high heat. Carefully place the first batch of noodles in the water, stir a bit to separate, cover, and let boil for 1½ minutes (no longer). After 1½ minutes, use a slotted spoon to quickly transfer the noodles to a bowl.

11. Bring the water back to a rolling boil and repeat the process with the remaining batches of noodles. The water will become cloudy due to the starch coming off the noodles—this is okay.

Store in separate batches in zip-top bags in the refrigerator for up to 24 hours. Do not freeze.

WONTONS

Traditional wonton wrappers are versatile wheat-based Asian dumpling wrappers. They are sturdy and hold up to heavy fillings. Currently, there are no commercial gluten-free options available. Which is just fine because I enjoy making this gluten-free version by hand. They are easy to prepare, I can control the size and shape of my homemade wrappers, and they can be frozen for long-term storage. I adapted this recipe from one in Andrea Nguyen's excellent book *Asian Dumplings: Mastering Gyoza, Spring Rolls, Samosas, and More.* Use these wrappers with your choice of fillings. They can be boiled in a soup or fried and served with the Garlic-Ginger Dipping Sauce.

1⅓ cups [195 g] Jeanne's Gluten-Free All-Purpose Flour (page 39)

¾ tsp salt

¼ cup [60 ml] water

1 extra-large egg

Tapioca flour for dusting

Simple Meat Filling (page 183) or filling of your choice

1. In the bowl of a food processor, combine the all-purpose flour and salt and pulse a few times to mix. In a small bowl, whisk together the water and egg until foamy. Add the egg mixture to the flour mixture in a slow stream through the feed tube with the processor running. Run the machine until the dough comes together. If you don't have a food processor, mix the flour and salt in a medium bowl with a fork. In a small

bowl, whisk together the water and egg until foamy. Add the egg mixture to the flour mixture and mix thoroughly with a fork.

2. Turn out the dough into a medium bowl (or keep the dough in the bowl you've mixed it in) and use your hands to do the final mixing. Squeeze the dough together into a ball. The dough should be stiff and just the slightest bit tacky.

3. Wrap the dough well in plastic wrap and let rest at room temperature for at least 1 hour, or up to 24 hours. (If you plan to let it rest for more than 3 hours, place it in the refrigerator, but bring it back to room temperature before shaping.)

4. When you're ready to shape the dough, place it on a work surface and use your hands to shape it into a fairly even dome. Cut the dough into four wedges. Cut each wedge into eight equal wedges (they will be thin). You should now have 32 wedges. Using your hands, roll each wedge into a ball and place the balls into a zip-top bag and seal so they don't dry out. Have ready a second, large zip-top bag for the shaped wontons.

5. Lightly dust a rolling surface with tapioca flour. Remove a ball of dough from the bag and place it on the rolling surface. With the palm of your hand, press down on the ball to flatten it into a fat disk. Sprinkle a little bit of tapioca flour on top of the dough. Use a small Asian rolling pin to roll the dough into a 3- to 3¼-in [8- to 9-cm] circle by rolling over the disk once. Pick up the dough and turn it slightly. Roll the dough again and pick it up and turn it slightly. This will create an evenly rolled round of dough. If the dough starts to stick, use a little bit of tapioca flour to dust the rolling surface and the top of the dough. (At this point, you can place the wrappers in a zip-top bag and refrigerate for up to 3 days, or freeze for up to 2 months. Defrost in the refrigerator for 24 hours before using.)

6. Place 1 tsp of filling in the middle of the wrapper. Use a finger dipped in water to moisten the edges of the wrapper. Fold the wrapper over the filling to form a half-moon shape. Gently but firmly press the edges together. Use the tines of a fork to complete the seal and make a decorative edge. Place the wonton in the large zip-top bag.

7. Repeat the rolling, filling, and storing process with the remaining wrappers.

8. Bring a large pot of water to a rolling boil over high heat. Gently slip in as many wontons as will fit without crowding, and nudge them with a wooden spoon to make sure they don't stick to each other. If the water is no longer boiling, increase the heat so that it comes to a gentle boil. The wontons will probably sink to the bottom of the pot when you first add them, but they should rise to the surface after a few seconds. If they don't, use a wooden spoon to nudge them to the surface. Cook the wontons for about 2 minutes, or until they are slightly translucent. Use a slotted spoon to remove the cooked wontons from the water, allowing any excess water to drip into the pot, and transfer the wontons to a bowl. Repeat the process until all of the wontons are cooked.

Store in an airtight container in the refrigerator for up to 2 days, or in the freezer for up to 2 months. Defrost in the refrigerator for 12 hours before serving.

GARLIC-GINGER DIPPING SAUCE

MAKES ½ CUP [120 ML]

A piquant sauce that pairs beautifully with wontons.

- **2 Tbsp granulated sugar**
- **2 Tbsp gluten-free tamari or soy sauce**
- **2 Tbsp rice vinegar**
- **2 Tbsp water**
- **½ tsp sesame oil**
- **1 large garlic clove, minced**
- **1 tsp minced fresh ginger**
- **⅛ to ¼ tsp crushed red pepper flakes**

In a small bowl, whisk together the sugar, tamari, vinegar, water, and sesame oil until the sugar is dissolved. Add the garlic, ginger, and red pepper flakes and whisk to combine.

Store in an airtight container in the refrigerator for up to 5 days. Do not freeze.

CHAPTER 5

COOKIES, BARS, CREAM PUFFS, PIES, AND OTHER DESSERTS

Dessert is probably what drew me to baking as a kid. I had a strong sweet tooth and, when I was quite young, I would often use a chair to climb up on the counters in our big yellow kitchen and look through the cupboards for the ingredients to bake something for dessert that night.

Dessert falls into a special category of food. Dessert is something that you don't eat for any purpose other than pleasure. Allowing yourself a bit of sweetness at the end of a meal gives you a moment of bliss in the midst of a day that is probably filled with "have-tos" and "shoulds."

Of course, for me, part of the enjoyment is the process of making the dessert. The fact that I get to eat it afterward is, as they say, icing on the cake.

CHOCOLATE CHIP COOKIES

MAKES ABOUT 50 COOKIES

It can be argued that chocolate chip cookies are the quintessential American cookie. They were invented in the 1930s at the Toll House Inn in Massachusetts. There are conflicting stories of how the chocolate chips came to be included in what were originally butter-scotch cookies. One is that chocolate was added to liven up a cookie that was to be served with ice cream, while another claims that bars of semisweet chocolate fell off an overhead shelf while a batch of cookies was being mixed in a large mixer. Regardless, they are my favorite cookie. Sometimes I add chopped and toasted nuts. Feel free to do whatever tickles your fancy!

2 cups [290 g] Jeanne's Gluten-Free All-Purpose Flour (page 39)

1 tsp baking soda

1 tsp salt

¾ cup [170 g] unsalted butter, at room temperature

½ cup [100 g] lightly packed dark brown sugar

½ cup [100 g] granulated sugar

1 tsp pure vanilla extract

¼ cup [60 ml] milk, at room temperature

1 extra-large egg, at room temperature

2 cups [340 g] semisweet chocolate chips or chocolate chunks

½ cup [60 g] pecans or walnuts, toasted (see page 42) and chopped (optional)

1. Preheat the oven to 350°F [180°C]. Line two large baking sheets with parchment paper.

2. In a small bowl, mix together the flour, baking soda, and salt.

3. In a large bowl, beat together the butter, brown sugar, and granulated sugar with a wooden spoon until well combined. Add the vanilla and milk and beat until combined. Add the egg and beat until well combined. Add the flour mixture and beat until well combined and smooth. Add the chocolate chips and nuts (if using) and mix until combined.

4. Drop the dough by tablespoons onto the prepared sheets, spacing them about 1 in [2.5 cm] apart (I do 12 cookies per sheet).

5. Bake until the cookies are a bit puffed up and light brown, 15 minutes. Let the cookies cool slightly on the baking sheets, then transfer to wire racks to cool. Let the baking sheets cool completely and repeat with the remaining dough.

Store in an airtight container at room temperature for up to 5 days, or in the freezer for up to 3 months.

CHOCOLATE WAFER COOKIES

These cookies are the little black dress of the baking world. They are perfect on their own (and addictive, I might add), but they can be gussied up and turned into Jeanneos (page 205) or Chocolate Chocolate Mint Cookies (page 203).

1½ cups [215 g] Jeanne's Gluten-Free All-Purpose Flour (page 39)

¾ cup [75 g] unsweetened cocoa powder (not Dutch process cocoa powder), sifted

1 cup [200 g] granulated sugar

¼ tsp baking soda

½ tsp salt

¾ cup [165 g] unsalted butter, slightly softened and cut into 14 pieces

3 Tbsp milk

½ tsp pure vanilla extract

1. In the bowl of a food processor, combine the flour, cocoa powder, sugar, baking soda, and salt. Pulse a few times to mix. Add the butter and pulse until the mixture looks like sand mixed with pebbles. Add the milk and vanilla and run the food processor until everything is combined and the mixture looks like clumpy, wet sand (it should just take a few seconds). If you're not using a food processor, place the dry ingredients in a bowl and mix with a spoon until combined. Add the butter and rub into the dry mixture with your fingers or a pastry cutter until the mixture looks like sand mixed with pebbles. Add the milk and vanilla and mix with a spoon until everything is combined and the mixture looks like clumpy wet sand.

2. Gather the dough in your hands and knead it until it holds together. Don't knead the dough so long that the butter in the dough begins to melt and becomes too soft—you want the dough to stay cool. Divide the dough into two roughly equal pieces. Shape one piece into a round ball and place it between two large pieces of wax paper. Roll out the dough until it is about ¼ in [6 mm] thick. Place the rolled dough, still between the pieces of wax paper, in the refrigerator to chill. Repeat the process with the other piece of dough.

3. Chill the dough for at least 1 hour, or up to 3 days. (If you're chilling the dough for more than 1 hour, wrap the dough, still between the sheets of wax paper, in plastic wrap so it doesn't dry out.)

4. Position racks in the middle and bottom of the oven and preheat to 350°F [180°C]. Line two large baking sheets with parchment paper. Remove one piece of dough from the refrigerator and place on a work surface. With a 2-in- [5-cm-] round cookie cutter, cut out as many rounds as you can and place them on the prepared baking sheets 1 in [2.5 cm] apart. Place a baking sheet on each oven rack.

5. Bake for 7 minutes, then switch the position of the baking sheets and bake an additional 6 to 8 minutes, depending on how crisp you would like the cookies to be. Remove from the oven and let cool on the baking sheets for a few minutes before transferring the cookies to a wire rack to cool completely.

6. Let the baking sheets cool completely and then repeat the rolling, cutting, and baking process with the remaining dough.

Store in an airtight container at room temperature for up to 5 days, or in the freezer for up to 6 months.

QUINOA FLAKE COOKIES

MAKES 36 COOKIES

These are a deliciously different take on traditional oatmeal cookies. When I was in Girl Scouts as a kid, our scout leader often had us make homemade cookies as our activity (she was my kind of scout leader). My favorite cookies to make with her turned out to be oatmeal cookies. This was a revelation because I was a die-hard chocolate fan and even though I baked a lot at home, I had never made oatmeal cookies. When we made oatmeal cookies at scouts, it was as if the world became a bit brighter. The cookies were an unexpected treat for me—the only way I had eaten oats before this was in oatmeal. When I found out that I was sensitive to oats, I turned to raw quinoa flakes to satisfy my oatmeal cookie cravings. Quinoa flakes are smaller and a bit nuttier in flavor than oatmeal, but they create cookies with a texture similar to and every bit as delectable as oatmeal cookies. If you can't find quinoa flakes in your area, you can find them online (see Sources for Ingredients and Equipment, page 250).

1 cup [145 g] Jeanne's Gluten-Free All-Purpose Flour (page 39)

½ tsp baking soda

½ tsp aluminum-free double-acting baking powder

½ tsp salt

¾ tsp ground cinnamon

¼ tsp ground nutmeg

½ cup [110 g] unsalted butter, at room temperature

½ cup [100 g] lightly packed dark brown sugar

½ cup [100 g] granulated sugar

1 tsp pure vanilla extract

1 extra-large egg

1 cup [85 g] raw quinoa flakes

½ cup [70 g] raisins (optional)

1. Place racks in the middle and bottom of the oven and preheat to 350°F [180°C]. Line two large baking sheets with parchment paper.

2. In a medium bowl, mix together the flour, baking soda, baking powder, salt, cinnamon, and nutmeg.

3. In the bowl of a stand mixer fitted with the paddle attachment, beat the butter, brown sugar, and granulated sugar until creamy. Add the vanilla and beat to combine. Add the egg and beat to combine. Add the flour mixture and beat to combine. Add the quinoa flakes and beat to combine. Remove the bowl from the mixer, add the raisins (if using), and mix with a spoon to combine.

4. Drop the dough by tablespoons on the prepared baking sheets, spacing them about 1in [2.5 cm] apart. Place a baking sheet on each oven rack.

5. Bake for 12 minutes for a chewy cookie or 15 minutes for a crisp cookie. Switch the positions of the sheets halfway through the baking time so the cookies are evenly baked. Transfer the cookies to a wire rack to cool.

Store in an airtight container at room temperature for up to 5 days, or in the freezer for up to 6 months.

FIG-FILLED COOKIES

MAKES 12 COOKIES

Fig cookies are another flavor of childhood that I've missed. I don't think figs would have ever been on my radar if it weren't for these cookies. They are cakey and sweet with a dried-fruit filling, so they have the illusion of being healthier than other cookies. These are terrific travel or lunch box cookies. This recipe uses figs, but you can use any dried fruit in the filling.

DOUGH

1½ cups [215 g] Jeanne's Gluten-Free All-Purpose Flour (page 39)

1 tsp salt

½ tsp aluminum-free double-acting baking powder

⅛ tsp ground cinnamon

6 Tbsp [85 g] unsalted butter, at room temperature

½ cup [100 g] granulated sugar

1 extra-large egg

1 tsp pure vanilla extract

FILLING

1 cup [140 g] roughly chopped dried figs

1 tsp mild honey

¼ tsp orange extract

⅛ tsp ground cinnamon

1. **TO MAKE THE DOUGH:** In a small bowl, mix together the flour, salt, baking powder, and cinnamon.

2. In the bowl of a stand mixer fitted with the paddle attachment, beat the butter and sugar on medium-high speed for 1 minute. Add the egg and beat for 1 minute. Add the vanilla and beat until combined.

3. Add the flour mixture and beat on medium speed until combined. Turn out the dough onto a piece of plastic wrap, wrap tightly, and place in the refrigerator for 1 hour to firm.

4. **TO MAKE THE FILLING:** Place the figs in a small bowl and add hot water to cover. Let sit for 15 minutes to soften. After 15 minutes, pour 1 Tbsp of the soaking liquid into the bowl of a food processor or blender. Drain the remaining soaking liquid from the figs and place the figs in the food processor. Add the honey, orange extract, and cinnamon. Purée the mixture for about 1 minute. Scrape the mixture into a small bowl and cover with plastic wrap. Let sit at room temperature.

5. Place a rack in the middle of the oven and preheat to 350°F [180°C]. Line two large baking sheets with parchment paper. Place two pieces of wax paper, each about 15 in [38 cm] long, on the rolling surface.

6. Remove the dough from the refrigerator. Unwrap (but keep the plastic wrap) and cut the dough in half. Rewrap one piece of dough in the plastic wrap and return it to the refrigerator.

CONTINUED >>

7. With your hands, quickly shape the dough into a rough rectangle. This will help you roll it into the proper shape. Place the dough between the two sheets of wax paper. You are going to roll the dough into a 12-by-5-in [30-by-13-cm] rectangle. This may take a bit of fussing. First, tap a rolling pin all over the top of the dough. Then slowly and carefully roll out the dough until it reaches 12 in [30 cm] long. If the dough is drastically out of rectangle shape, cut the wonky pieces off the sides, place them on top of the dough, and roll again. When the dough has reached 12 in [30 cm] long, roll side to side until the dough is about 5 in [13 cm] wide.

8. Measure 2.5 in [6 cm] in from a short side of the dough (halfway to the middle) and use a ruler and a knife to lightly mark a line down the middle of the dough. Do not cut.

9. Place 6 Tbsp of filling down the middle of one side of the dough. Use a butter knife or a small spatula to carefully spread the filling in an even layer along the length of the dough, leaving a ¼-in [6-mm] border around the outer edges.

10. Using the wax paper to help you, lift up and fold the unfilled half of dough over the filled half. Use your fingers to press the dough down along the edge of the long side (but not the short sides—leave those open). Cut a narrow strip of dough off the outer long edge to tidy it a bit. Using the ruler and sharp knife, make 1-in [2.5-cm] marks along the length of the dough. Then use the knife to cut the dough into bars at each mark. Transfer the bars to one of the prepared baking sheets, placing them at least 1 in [2.5 cm] apart.

11. Bake until the cookies are lightly browned, about 25 minutes.

12. Place a 12-in [30-cm] piece of parchment paper on the counter. Remove the cookies from the oven. Using a spatula, transfer the hot cookies to the parchment paper, placing them close together. Wrap the cookies with the parchment paper and then place the packet in a large zip-top bag. This helps to steam the cookies a bit while they cool, giving them the cakey texture found in commercial versions. If you want a more crunchy texture, transfer the hot cookies to a wire rack to cool.

13. Repeat with the remaining dough and filling.

Store in an airtight container at room temperature for up to 5 days. Do not freeze.

CHOCOLATE CHOCOLATE MINT COOKIES

MAKES ABOUT 50 **COOKIES**

These are a version of my preferred Girl Scout cookie, Thin Mints. The combination of mint and chocolate is one of my favorites. When my daughter was in Girl Scouts, it was so ironic that she had to sell cookies that neither she nor I could eat—she because of her peanut allergy and me because of my gluten intolerance. During cookie season, our living room was filled with cases of Girl Scout cookies. After that first season, I couldn't stand it anymore so I developed a gluten-free version of Thin Mints. These cookies are addictive. Also, they are spectacular frozen. Make sure to use peppermint oil, not extract—the latter may cause the chocolate to "seize up," or become grainy.

3 cups [510 g] semisweet chocolate chips or chopped semisweet chocolate

1 to 1½ tsp peppermint oil, or more to taste

1 recipe Chocolate Wafer Cookies (page 196)

1. In a heavy saucepan over very low heat, melt the chocolate chips. Watch them carefully so that the chocolate doesn't burn. Just before all of the chocolate is melted, remove the pan from the heat and add the peppermint oil. Whisk until the peppermint oil is combined and the chocolate is smooth.

2. Line two large baking sheets with wax paper.

3. Place a cookie in the melted chocolate and use a fork to turn it over to coat completely. Use the fork to remove the cookie from the chocolate, tapping the fork once or twice on the side of the pan to allow any excess coating to drip back into the pan. Don't tap too hard—the cookies are delicate and might break. Carefully place the coated cookie on a prepared baking sheet to set.

4. Repeat the dunking process with the remaining cookies. You may place the baking sheets in the refrigerator or freezer to speed up the hardening process.

Store in an airtight container at room temperature, or in the refrigerator for up to 5 days, or in the freezer for up to 6 months.

COOKIES, BARS, CREAM PUFFS, PIES, AND OTHER DESSERTS

JEANNEOS

I used to call these cookies something boring like Chocolate Sandwich Cookies. Then one day I was on Facebook and saw that my editor had baked a batch and called them Jeanneos—and thus these cookies were christened. These are a more sophisticated version of Oreos. I took my cue from the brilliant Thomas Keller and made the filling out of cream and white chocolate, which bumps up the deliciousness factor.

⅓ cup [80 ml] heavy cream

8 oz [230 g] gluten-free white chocolate chips or chunks

1 recipe Chocolate Wafer Cookies (page 196)

1. In a small, heavy-bottomed saucepan over medium heat, bring the cream to just boiling (this will not take long—watch it carefully so it doesn't burn). Turn off the heat and pour in the chocolate. Use a spoon to push the chocolate around so it is evenly distributed in the cream. Let sit for 1 minute, then whisk the melting chocolate into the cream until it is smooth. Let the mixture sit on a counter for about 30 minutes, until it firms up a bit and is no longer runny. (You may also place it in the refrigerator to accelerate this process, but monitor it closely; the filling will become solid if left too long in the refrigerator. If this happens, heat the filling a bit over low heat and whisk it again until smooth.)

2. Have ready a large baking sheet to hold the assembled cookies. With small spatula or a butter knife, spread 1 tsp of the filling onto a cookie and place another cookie on top of the filling to make a sandwich. Place the cookie on the baking sheet.

3. Repeat the process until all the cookies are used.

Store in an airtight container at room temperature for up to 3 days, or in the freezer for up to 3 months.

STROOPWAFELS

MAKES ABOUT 22 FILLED COOKIES

Literally, "syrup-waffles," these are a delightful Dutch treat that consists of a caramel filling sandwiched by light and crispy waffle cookies. Often, you see them served as edible lids for coffee here in the United States. The heat of the coffee warms up the caramel inside the cookie, making it gooey and irresistible when you bite into it. You can also eat the cookies unfilled. This recipe uses a specialty waffle-cone iron (see Sources for Ingredients and Equipment, page 250).

COOKIES

1¾ cups [250 g] Jeanne's Gluten-Free All-Purpose Flour (page 39)

2 tsp aluminum-free double-acting baking powder

½ tsp ground cinnamon

¼ tsp salt

3 extra-large eggs

¾ cup [150 g] lightly packed dark brown sugar

½ cup [110 g] unsalted butter, melted

2 tsp pure vanilla extract

FILLING

2 Tbsp water

1 cup [200 g] lightly packed dark brown sugar

¼ cup [60 ml] maple syrup

1 tsp ground cinnamon

6 Tbsp unsalted butter, at room temperature and cut into 12 pieces

1. **TO MAKE THE COOKIES:** In a small bowl, mix together the flour, baking powder, cinnamon, and salt.

2. In a large bowl, whisk together the eggs and brown sugar until combined. Add the melted butter and whisk to combine, about 1 minute. Add the vanilla and whisk to combine.

3. Add the flour mixture to the egg mixture and whisk to combine. Cover with plastic wrap and let sit for 15 minutes at room temperature to allow the flavors to meld and the batter to thicken.

4. Preheat a waffle-cone iron according to the manufacturer's instructions. (I heat mine to setting 4.) Oil the waffle-cone iron, if needed.

5. Place 1 Tbsp of batter in the upper middle of the waffle maker (a portion scoop is very handy here) and then slowly close and lock the lid. Cook for 2 to 2½ minutes, or until the cookie is brown. Open the lid and use metal tongs to transfer the cookie to a wire rack to cool completely.

6. Repeat with the remaining batter. The cookies will crisp as they cool. Once the cookies have cooled a bit, you can stack them on top of one another to make room on the rack for more cookies. It may take a few batches to get the hang of centering the cookies on the waffle-cone iron. You will probably need to cook a few cookies before you find the optimal cooking time for your iron. (At this point, you can transfer the cookies to an airtight container at room temperature for up to 5 days, or freeze for up to 3 months.)

CONTINUED >>

7. **TO MAKE THE FILLING:** In a small heavy-bottomed pot fitted with a candy thermometer, combine the water, brown sugar, maple syrup, and cinnamon and gently stir over medium heat for about 5 minutes to dissolve the sugar. Once the sugar is dissolved, raise the heat to medium-high and boil until the syrup reaches 225°F [110°C] (no higher). Once the mixture has reached temperature, remove the pan from the heat, add the butter, and whisk gently until combined. Allow the mixture to cool and firm a bit to spreading consistency. In my kitchen, it takes at least 30 minutes.

8. Place 1 tsp of the filling on a cookie. Top with a second cookie, gently pressing together to spread the filling. Stroopwafels are best eaten the day they are made—they start to get soggy after a few hours.

ANIMAL CRACKERS

MAKES ABOUT 40 SMALL (1-IN [2.5-CM]) COOKIES,

20 MEDIUM (2-IN [5-CM]) COOKIES, OR 15 LARGE (3-IN [8-CM]) COOKIES

There is something so charming about animal crackers. When I was a kid, they came in a box shaped and decorated like a circus train car filled with animals. The box had a handle and I remember carrying it around long after the cookies were gone. I learned later that the handle was designed to hang the box on a Christmas tree. When my daughter was younger, animal crackers were still available in the same kind of box, although the handle was no longer part of the packaging. As I developed this recipe, I couldn't put my finger on the elusive yet signature flavor of the animal crackers from my childhood. Finally, a friend suggested I try orange extract. She was right! Orange is the undertone flavor. You can find orange extract in the grocery store next to the vanilla and almond extracts. I give options for making small, medium, or large cookies due to the variety of animal cookie cutters that are available.

1 cup [145 g] Jeanne's Gluten-Free All-Purpose Flour (page 39)

¼ cup [35 g] sorghum flour (also known as sweet sorghum flour)

½ tsp aluminum-free double-acting baking powder

¼ tsp baking soda

¼ tsp salt

¼ cup [55 g] unsalted butter, cut into pieces

¼ cup [85 g] mild honey

¼ cup [60 ml] milk

½ tsp pure vanilla extract

⅛ tsp orange extract

1. In a large bowl, mix together the all-purpose flour, sorghum flour, baking powder, baking soda, and salt. Add the butter and use your fingers or a pastry cutter to rub it into the dry ingredients until the mixture looks like a coarse meal. Add the honey and mix quickly with a fork. (I find that mixing quickly helps to overcome the stickiness of the honey and mixes it well.) Add the milk and mix well with the fork. Add the vanilla and orange extract and mix to combine. Use your hands to do the final mixing to bring the dough together.

2. Shape the dough into a disk and place it between two pieces of wax paper. Roll out the dough to ⅛ in [4 mm] thick. Place in the refrigerator for 15 minutes to firm up.

3. Place racks in the middle and bottom of the oven and preheat to 400°F [200°C]. Line two large baking sheets with parchment paper.

4. Remove the top sheet of wax paper (reserve for future rollings). Cut the dough into shapes using cookie cutters. Transfer to a prepared baking sheet, placing them 1 in [2.5 cm] apart. Repeat with the remaining dough until both baking sheets are filled. Place the dough in the refrigerator as needed to firm.

5. Bake until the cookies are a bit brown, about 5 minutes for small cookies; 5 to 7 minutes for medium cookies; and 7 to 10 minutes for large cookies. Carefully transfer the cookies to a wire rack to cool completely. They will crisp as they cool.

Store in an airtight container at room temperature for up to 5 days, or in the freezer for up to 3 months.

GRAHAM CRACKERS

Originally, graham crackers were made from graham flour, which is a combination of finely ground white flour and coarsely ground wheat bran and germ. They have an interesting history. Apparently, the Reverend Sylvester Graham, who lived in Connecticut during the late eighteenth century through the mid-nineteenth century, was an early advocate for dietary reform. He promoted vegetarianism and temperance, and he eschewed additives in food all in order to curb lust (instead of simply for good health). Graham crackers were part of the diet he developed. Originally they were not nearly as sweet as modern graham crackers and were considered bland. They were kind of a mix between a savory cracker and a sweet cookie. Today's graham cracker is a sweet-but-not-too-sweet cookie that is a staple in the diets of children in the United States. Of course, graham flour has gluten, so I've substituted sorghum flour for part of the flour in this recipe.

1¼ cups [180 g] Jeanne's Gluten-Free All-Purpose Flour (page 39)

1 cup [140 g] sorghum flour (also known as sweet sorghum flour)

½ tsp baking soda

½ tsp aluminum-free double-acting baking powder

½ tsp salt

¼ tsp ground cinnamon

½ cup [100 g] packed dark brown sugar

½ cup [110 g] unsalted butter, cold and cut into 8 pieces

1 Tbsp mild honey

1 tsp pure vanilla extract

3 to 6 Tbsp ice water

¼ tsp ground cinnamon mixed with ¼ cup [50 g] granulated sugar (optional)

1. In the bowl of a food processor, combine the all-purpose flour, sorghum flour, baking soda, baking powder, salt, and cinnamon and pulse a few times to mix. Sprinkle the brown sugar over the flour mixture and pulse a few more times to mix. Make sure the brown sugar is evenly distributed. If you don't have a food processor, mix the ingredients in a large bowl with a spoon.

2. Add the butter and pulse until the mixture looks like coarse sand. Add the honey and pulse a few more times to combine. Add the vanilla and pulse to combine. If you're mixing by hand, use your fingers or a pastry cutter to rub the butter into the flour mixture and use a fork to mix in the honey and vanilla.

3. Add the water 1 Tbsp at a time and pulse after each addition to combine—add more as needed until you have a stiff dough that is starting to hold together fairly well. Be sure not to add too much water—you do not want a dough that is sloppy and dripping wet. If you're mixing by hand, add the water in the same way and use a spoon to mix.

4. Dump the dough into a large bowl (keep the dough in the bowl if you're mixing by hand) and use your hands to do the final mixing, squeezing the dough to bring it together.

5. Divide the dough into two disks. Wrap each disk in plastic wrap and place in the refrigerator to chill for 15 minutes to firm up for rolling.

6. Place racks at the middle and bottom of the oven and preheat to 350°F [180°C]. Line two large baking sheets with parchment paper.

7. Unwrap a disk of dough and place it between two large sheets of wax paper. Roll out the dough to ⅛ in [4 mm] thick. With a 2-in [5-cm] straight or scalloped square cookie cutter, cut out as many crackers as you can. Gently prick each cracker three times down the center with a fork to give them the appearance of a commercial graham cracker (do not prick all the way through the dough). Lightly sprinkle each with the cinnamon-sugar mixture (if using). Use a metal spatula to carefully transfer the cut crackers to a lined baking sheet, leaving 1 in [2.5 cm] between each.

8. Gather the leftover scraps of dough, form them into a ball, and reroll the dough between the sheets of wax paper. Repeat the cutting and pricking process until both baking sheets are filled. Monitor the temperature of the dough. If it starts to become too sticky and floppy and is becoming difficult to roll and cut, it is too warm—return it to the refrigerator to firm up a bit.

9. Bake for 8 minutes, switch the positions of the baking sheets, and bake another 7 to 9 minutes, or until the crackers are a bit brown (it will be hard to tell because the dough is so dark, but you will be able to see a slight increase in the browning).

10. Let the graham crackers cool on the baking sheets for 5 minutes and then transfer them to a wire rack to cool completely. The crackers will crisp as they cool. Allow the baking sheets to cool and then repeat the rolling, cutting, pricking, and sprinkling process with the other disk of dough.

Store in an airtight container at room temperature for up to 3 days, or in the freezer for up to 3 months.

NANAIMO BARS

This no-bake treat hails from the Canadian city of Nanaimo, British Columbia (although there is some controversy about whether it was originally created there). I love layered treats—the many tastes and textures satisfy just about any sweet craving. These layers contain all things good: cookies, nuts, custard, and chocolate.

BOTTOM LAYER

½ cup [110 g] unsalted butter

¼ cup [50 g] granulated sugar

⅓ cup [25 g] unsweetened cocoa powder

1 extra-large egg, lightly beaten

1¼ cups [175 g] crushed Graham Crackers (page 210)

½ cup [60 g] almonds, toasted (see page 42) and finely chopped

1 cup [85 g] shredded coconut (sweetened or unsweetened)

MIDDLE LAYER

½ cup [110 g] unsalted butter, at room temperature

2 Tbsp heavy cream

2 Tbsp gluten-free vanilla instant pudding powder or custard powder (such as Bird's Custard Powder)

2 cups [240 g] confectioners' sugar, sifted

TOP LAYER

⅔ cup [115 g] semisweet chocolate chips or chopped semisweet chocolate

2 Tbsp unsalted butter

1. **TO MAKE THE BOTTOM LAYER:** In a heavy-bottomed saucepan over very low heat, melt the butter. Add the sugar and cocoa powder and whisk to combine. Add the egg and whisk continuously to cook the egg slightly and to thicken the mixture.

2. Once the mixture has thickened, remove from the heat and stir in the crushed graham crackers, almonds, and coconut. Turn out the dough into an ungreased 8-in [20-cm] square pan and press it firmly and evenly into the corners.

3. **TO MAKE THE MIDDLE LAYER:** In the bowl of a stand mixer fitted with the whisk attachment, beat the butter, cream, and pudding powder on medium speed until combined and fluffy. Gradually add the confectioners' sugar and beat until smooth and spreadable. Turn out the mixture over the first layer and use a rubber spatula to spread it evenly over the crust. Smooth the top.

4. **TO MAKE THE TOP LAYER:** In a heavy-bottomed saucepan over very low heat, melt the chocolate and butter. Watch them carefully so they don't burn. Just before the chocolate has completely melted, remove from the heat and whisk until the mixture is combined and smooth. Let cool to room temperature, then pour the mixture over the middle layer and use a rubber spatula to spread it evenly over the filling.

5. Place the pan in the refrigerator until the top has hardened and the filling is chilled, about 1 hour. Cut into 2-in [5-cm] squares.

Store in an airtight container in the refrigerator for up to 4 days. Do not freeze.

BROWNIES

MAKES 16 BROWNIES

For me, this recipe makes the perfect brownie: cakey and moist, verging on the edge of, though not quite entering, the realm of the fudgey. It is sublimely chocolaty with a crumb that melts in your mouth.

¾ cup [110 g] Jeanne's Gluten-Free All-Purpose Flour (page 39)

1 tsp aluminum-free double-acting baking powder

¼ tsp salt

⅔ cup [115 g] semisweet chocolate chips or chunks

½ cup [110 g] unsalted butter, at room temperature

1 cup [200 g] granulated sugar

2 extra-large eggs, at room temperature

1 tsp pure vanilla extract

1 cup [120 g] walnuts or pecans, toasted (see page 42) and chopped (optional)

1. Place a rack in the middle of the oven and preheat the oven to 350°F [180°C]. Butter an 8-in [20-cm] square baking pan.

2. In a small bowl, mix together the flour, baking powder, and salt.

3. In a small, heavy-bottomed saucepan over very low heat, melt the chocolate and butter. Watch them carefully so they don't burn. Just before the chocolate has completely melted, remove from the heat and whisk until the mixture is combined and smooth. Let cool to room temperature.

4. In a medium bowl, use a wooden spoon to beat together the sugar and eggs until smooth and well combined. Add the chocolate mixture and beat until smooth. Add the vanilla and beat until combined. Add the flour mixture and beat until combined and smooth. Add the nuts (if using) and stir until combined.

5. Using a rubber spatula, scrape the batter into the prepared pan, pushing the batter into the corners of the pan and making sure it is even and has a smooth top.

6. Bake until a tester inserted into the middle comes out clean, 30 to 35 minutes. Place the pan on a wire rack to cool. Cut into 2-in [5-cm] squares.

Store in the pan, covered with plastic wrap, for up to 3 days, or in an airtight container in the freezer for up to 3 months.

BLONDIES

The blondie, also known as a blond brownie, is a bar dessert much like brownies, but they are based on brown sugar rather than chocolate. Food history timelines claim that blondies came before brownies as a home-baked confection. At some point, brownies overtook them in popularity once chocolate became more accessible and affordable as an ingredient. Even though brownies are delicious, I've always had a special place in my heart for blondies—for some reason, I made them as a kid more often than I did brownies. My love for chocolate is matched only by my love for butterscotch—which is basically made with brown sugar and butter, the two main ingredients in blondies. The blondies I used to make as a kid included nuts but not chocolate. In this recipe, I've included chocolate chips as well as nuts.

Tapioca flour for dusting

1½ cups [215 g] Jeanne's Gluten-Free All-Purpose Flour (page 39)

1 tsp aluminum-free double-acting baking powder

¼ tsp salt

¾ cup [170 g] unsalted butter

1 cup [200 g] lightly packed dark brown sugar

2 tsp pure vanilla extract

2 extra-large eggs

1 cup [170 g] semisweet chocolate chips

½ cup [60 g] pecans or walnuts, toasted (see page 42) and chopped (optional)

1. Place a rack in the middle of the oven and preheat to 350°F [180°C]. Butter a 9-in [23-cm] square pan and dust it with tapioca flour.

2. In a small bowl, mix together the all-purpose flour, baking powder, and salt.

3. In the bowl of a stand mixer fitted with the paddle attachment, beat together the butter and brown sugar on medium-high speed until fluffy, about 2 minutes. Add the vanilla and beat until combined. Add the eggs and beat for 1 minute more. Add the flour mixture to the butter mixture and beat until well combined.

4. Remove the bowl from the stand mixer and add the chocolate chips, using a spoon to stir until combined. Add the nuts (if using) and stir until combined.

5. Using a rubber spatula, scrape the batter into the prepared pan, pushing the batter into the corners of the pan and making sure it is even and has a smooth top.

6. Bake until a tester inserted into the middle comes out clean, about 35 minutes. Remove from the oven and place the pan on a wire rack to cool. Cut into 1½-in [4-cm] squares.

Store in the pan, covered with plastic wrap, for up to 3 days, or in an airtight container in the freezer for up to 3 months.

ICE-CREAM SANDWICHES

MAKES 9 ICE-CREAM SANDWICHES

Chocolate cookies and ice cream are an enduringly popular combination. Once again, I went back to my childhood memories for inspiration for this recipe. This is a simple and adaptable recipe that allows you to choose a cookie shape and ice cream flavor. Vanilla ice cream is the conventional choice for ice-cream sandwiches, but one of the nifty things about making your own ice-cream sandwiches is that you can choose whatever flavor of ice cream you like!

2 cups [290 g] Jeanne's Gluten-Free All-Purpose Flour (page 39)

½ cup [50 g] unsweetened cocoa powder, sifted

1½ tsp aluminum-free double-acting baking powder

¾ tsp salt

¾ cup [170 g] unsalted butter, at room temperature

¾ cup [150 g] granulated sugar

1½ tsp pure vanilla extract

1 extra-large egg, plus 1 egg yolk, at room temperature

2 pt [1 L] ice cream, softened

1. Position racks in the middle and bottom of the oven and preheat to 350°F [180°C]. Line two large baking sheets with parchment paper.

2. In a medium bowl, mix together the flour, cocoa powder, baking powder, and salt.

3. In the bowl of a stand mixer fitted with the paddle attachment, beat together the butter and sugar on medium-high speed for 1 minute. Add the vanilla and beat until combined. Add the egg and egg yolk and beat for 1 minute. Add the flour mixture and beat on low speed to combine.

4. Remove the bowl from the mixer and use a rubber spatula to do a final mix to make sure all the ingredients are well combined.

5. Shape the dough into a disk and place it between two large pieces of wax paper. Roll out the dough to ¼ in [6 mm] thick (no thicker). Place in the refrigerator for 15 minutes to firm up.

6. Remove the top sheet of wax paper (reserve for future rollings). Using a 2¾- to 3-in [7- to 7.5-cm] square or round cookie cutter, cut out as many pieces as you can. The cookies retain their edge when baked, so feel free to use a cutter with a scalloped edge for a decorative look. Transfer to the prepared baking sheets, placing them 1 in [2.5 cm] apart. Prick the center of each cookie three times with the tines of a fork. Gather the dough scraps, form into a disk, place the disk back onto the bottom piece of wax paper, and replace the top piece of wax paper. Repeat the rolling, cutting, transferring, and pricking process until all the dough has been

CONTINUED >>

used. If the dough becomes too floppy to work with, place it in the refrigerator for 5 to 15 minutes to firm up. You should have 18 cookies (you want to end up with an even number of cookies to make the sandwiches), 9 per baking sheet. The ice cream will accommodate 9 sandwiches, so 18 is the ideal number of cookies. Place the baking sheets on each oven rack.

7. Bake for 15 minutes, switching the positions of the baking sheets halfway through. The cookies should be puffed up a bit. Remove from the oven and let the cookies cool on the baking sheets for 10 minutes to firm up, then transfer them to a wire rack to cool completely. Do not assemble the sandwiches until the cookies are completely cool.

8. While the cookies are baking, line a 9-in [23-cm] square pan with two large pieces of parchment paper, each folded to the width of the pan. Place the first piece up and over two sides opposite each other and then the second piece up and over the other two sides opposite each other (this will allow you to pick up the ice-cream block out of the pan later). I find that it's easiest to spread the softened ice cream on the parchment paper if the paper is clipped to the pan because the parchment paper tends to slide around. I use binder clips to clip the paper to all four sides of the pan.

9. Place the softened ice cream in a stand mixer fitted with the paddle attachment and beat until smooth. This should take less than 1 minute—you don't want the ice cream to melt too much. Turn out the whipped ice cream into the prepared pan and use a rubber spatula to spread it into an even layer. Any hills and bumps in the ice cream will result in uneven ice-cream sandwiches. Use a rubber spatula to smooth the top (remove the binder clips, if using), cover with plastic wrap, and freeze until firm (in my freezer it takes about 1 hour for the ice cream to become firm).

10. When the ice cream is firm and you are ready to assemble the sandwiches, use the parchment paper to lift the ice-cream block out of the pan and onto the work surface. Work quickly—you don't want the ice cream to melt very much.

11. Use the same cookie cutter you used for the cookies and cut out 9 ice-cream rounds or squares. It will be tight—make the cuts very close to each other—but you will be able to get 9 rounds or squares. Use a metal spatula to lift an ice-cream round and place it on the bottom (the unpricked side) of one of the cookies. Place the bottom of another cookie on top of the ice cream (pierced-side up), creating a sandwich. Wrap the sandwich in plastic wrap and place it in a large zip-top bag. Place the bag with the finished sandwich in the freezer while you're assembling the next sandwich.

12. Repeat the cutting, lifting, sandwiching, and wrapping process with the remainder of the ice-cream rounds and cookies. Place the bag of wrapped sandwiches in the freezer to firm. The sandwiches are quite hard once frozen. Test one and, if you like, let the ice cream in the middle soften a bit before eating.

Store, tightly wrapped, in the freezer for up to 3 months.

WAFFLE ICE-CREAM CONES

MAKES 4 LARGE WAFFLE CONES

Making waffle cones at home never fails to delight me. They seem like something you can buy only at a specialty ice-cream store, so making them myself feels a bit like magic. They are made by cooking a simple batter on a special waffle-cone iron (see Sources for Ingredients and Equipment, page 250) that imprints the iconic grid pattern. The iron comes with a plastic roller that is used to shape the hot waffle into a cone. The homemade cones are moderately sweet and satisfyingly crunchy. What I like about making my own cones is that not only can I have a gluten-free cone, but I can go wild and create a sundae in my cone—including a couple scoops of ice cream, hot fudge sauce, chopped nuts, whipped cream, and a cherry on top. Now that's how to do a waffle cone. This recipe can be easily doubled.

⅔ cup [95 g] Jeanne's Gluten-Free All-Purpose Flour (page 39)

¼ tsp salt

1 extra-large egg, plus 1 egg white

¼ cup [50 g] granulated sugar

2 Tbsp unsalted butter, melted and cooled slightly

Vegetable oil for brushing

1. Place a clean kitchen towel on a dinner plate.

2. In a small bowl, mix together the flour and salt.

3. In a medium bowl, whisk together the egg and egg white until foamy. Add the sugar and whisk until well combined.

4. Add the flour mixture to the egg mixture and whisk until well combined and there are no lumps. Add the butter and whisk until well combined.

5. Heat the waffle-cone iron according to the manufacturer's directions. (I heat mine to the 3.5 setting.) Lightly brush with oil, if necessary.

6. My waffle-cone iron makes large cones, so I use 3 Tbsp of batter for each cone. You may have to experiment with how much batter to use. Place the batter on the iron, close and lock, and let cook for 2 to 2½ minutes, or until the cone begins to brown.

7. Once the waffle has cooked, use metal tongs to transfer it to the towel-covered plate. Working quickly, place the pointed end of the roller in the middle of one edge of the waffle. Use the kitchen towel to help you wrap the waffle around the roller and then roll the waffle until the two sides overlap. Let sit, seam-side down, for 1 minute for the cone to cool a bit in its shape. After 1 minute, transfer the cone to a wire rack and let cool completely, seam-side down. The cones will crisp as they cool.

8. Wait until the waffle-cone iron comes back to temperature and then repeat the process with the remaining batter. Waffle cones are best eaten the day they are made.

Store in an airtight container at room temperature for up to 2 days. Do not freeze.

FUNNEL CAKES

MAKES 4 OR 5 FUNNEL CAKES

Funnel cakes are one of my favorite festival and fair foods. My siblings and I would get them on big paper plates, piled high with confectioners' sugar, and we'd wander around the county fair eating them, eventually becoming covered with confectioners' sugar and huge smiles. Before making this recipe, read the Deep-Frying Primer (page 20). Funnel cakes are different from other fried foods—they will expand to the diameter of your pan. So choose your pan wisely. I recommend one that is 7 in [18 cm] in diameter, which makes funnel cakes that are about 6.5 in [16.5 cm] in diameter.

1⅓ cups [190 g] Jeanne's Gluten-Free All-Purpose Flour (page 39)

2 Tbsp granulated sugar

½ tsp salt

1 tsp aluminum-free double-acting baking powder

1 extra-large egg, at room temperature

1½ cups [360 ml] milk

½ tsp pure vanilla extract

Vegetable oil for frying

1 cup [120 g] confectioners' sugar

1. In a small bowl, whisk together the flour, granulated sugar, salt, and baking powder.

2. In a large bowl, whisk together the egg, milk, and vanilla until combined and the mixture is foamy.

3. Whisk the flour mixture into the egg mixture until just combined. The batter may have some flour lumps in it—this is fine. The consistency of the batter should resemble thick pancake batter.

4. Cover with plastic wrap and let the batter rest and thicken at room temperature. (At this point, you can transfer the batter in an airtight container and refrigerate for up to 2 days. Bring to room temperature before frying. Do not freeze.)

5. Pour 3 in [7.5 cm] of vegetable oil into a heavy-bottomed pan fitted with a candy thermometer and heat the oil to 375°F [190°C]. Line two large baking sheets with paper towels and place a large wire rack over each.

6. When the oil has reached temperature, pour the batter into a pastry bag fitted with a medium-round tip. Carefully squeeze about ¼ cup [60 ml] of batter into the oil, moving the bag in a zigzag and circular motion. The dough will separate into pieces, which will sink to the bottom and then quickly rise to the surface. These pieces form the base layer of the cakes (trust me, it will work).

7. As soon as the first pieces rise to the surface, squeeze another ¼ cup [60 ml] of batter on top of them, again moving the bag in a zigzag and circular motion. This layer holds the bottom pieces together, so be sure to squeeze out the batter across the width of the pan to let the top layer of batter grab on to and hold together the bottom pieces of dough. The cake should now look like a crazy lattice of dough in the oil. Fry until the cake is golden brown on the bottom, 1 to 2 minutes. Use metal tongs to lift one side of the cake out of the oil to check the color. The cake will be fairly delicate. Using a slotted spoon or metal spatula, carefully and gently lift one side of the cake up and turn it over in the oil.

CONTINUED >>

(Imagine turning over a not-quite-fully-inflated inner tube in water—this is what turning over the fried batter will seem like.) Fry for another minute or so, until the second side of the cake is golden brown. The oil will probably drop in temperature to about 350°F [180°C]—this is fine; don't worry about bringing the temperature back up to 375°F [190°C]. The temperature drops because the dough covers the entire surface of the oil.

8. Using a large slotted spoon or spatula, carefully transfer the funnel cakes to a prepared rack to cool. The cakes are delicate and pieces may drop off—if they do, just place all of the pieces on the wire rack near the cake they came off of.

9. Bring the oil back to 375°F [190°C]. Repeat the piping, frying, turning, draining, and skimming process for the remainder of the dough. After frying each batch, use a slotted spoon to remove any leftover fried batter in the oil. If you don't do this, these pieces will eventually burn and adhere to subsequent cakes.

10. Place each cake (and its pieces) on its own plate and scatter about ¼ cup [30 g] of confectioners' sugar on each (this will basically be a pile of confectioners' sugar on top of each cake). The cakes don't need to be completely cool. You can use less confectioners' sugar, if you like. Funnel cakes are best eaten the day they are made.

CHURROS

Churros are known as Spanish doughnuts. They are traditionally made with a tool called a *churrera*, which is a syringe that pushes lengths of dough into hot oil for frying. Using a pastry bag fitted with a star tip also works well, but I find that piping the dough directly into the oil creates curled churros instead of the straight churros sold by street vendors. To make a straight churro, I pipe the dough onto parchment pieces that go into the oil with the dough. (The parchment paper helps the churros hold their straight shape.) Of course, you can experiment and pipe the dough directly into the oil and see what you think. Before making this recipe, read the Deep-Frying Primer (page 20).

1 recipe Pâte à Choux Dough (page 248)
Vegetable oil for frying
1 recipe Cinnamon-Sugar for Doughnuts and Pastries (page 117)

1. Line two large baking sheets with parchment paper. Fit a pastry bag with a small star tip (I use an Ateco #18). Churros expand to almost three times the size of the dough, so choose a tip that is much smaller than you want your churros to be.

2. Fill the prepared pastry bag with half of the dough. Pipe out twelve 5-in [13-cm] logs of dough onto a prepared baking sheet about 1 in [2.5 cm] apart. Repeat with the remaining dough. You should have about 12 logs per sheet. With a pair of scissors, cut the parchment paper around each churro.

3. Pour 3 in [7.5 cm] of vegetable oil into a heavy-bottomed saucepan fitted with a candy thermometer and heat the oil to 375°F [190°C]. Line a large baking sheet with a double layer of paper towels and place a large wire rack on it.

4. When the oil has reached temperature, place as many churros with their attached parchment as will fit into the pan without crowding. After about 30 seconds, the parchment paper should be easy to remove—peel it off with a pair of metal tongs. (I keep a plate next to the stove to hold the used parchment pieces as they come out of the oil.)

5. Fry the churros, turning every minute or so, until golden brown, 5 to 7 minutes. Transfer the churros to the wire rack to cool. Monitor the oil temperature while you're working and let the oil come back to temperature after frying each batch of churros.

6. When the churros are just cool enough to handle, roll them in the cinnamon-sugar mixture. Churros are best eaten the day they are fried.

Store in a paper bag for up to 3 days. Do not freeze.

YELLOW LAYER CAKE WITH CHOCOLATE FUDGE FROSTING

MAKES 1 (9-IN [23-CM]) LAYER CAKE

To my mind, this cake is *the* classic layer cake. It's a fluffy, light, yellow cake paired with dense, chocolaty frosting. Not only do the flavors work together in consummate harmony, but the cake slices look pretty on a plate due to the light cake and the dark frosting. This is wonderful for any occasion, but it is perfect as a birthday cake. A variation for cupcakes follows.

CAKE

2 cups [290 g] Jeanne's Gluten-Free All-Purpose Flour (page 39)

1 Tbsp aluminum-free double-acting baking powder

½ tsp salt

1 cup [220 g] unsalted butter, at room temperature

2 cups [400 g] granulated sugar

5 extra-large eggs, at room temperature

1 tsp pure vanilla extract

1 cup [240 ml] buttermilk

FROSTING

2 cups [480 ml] heavy cream

½ cup [100 g] lightly packed dark brown sugar

1 lb [455 g] semisweet chocolate chips or chopped semisweet chocolate

1. **TO MAKE THE CAKE:** Preheat the oven to 350°F [180°C]. Line the bottom of two 9-in [23-cm] round cake pans with parchment paper.

2. In a medium bowl, mix together the flour, baking powder, and salt.

3. In the bowl of a stand mixer fitted with the paddle attachment, beat the butter on medium-high speed until it is light and fluffy, about 2 minutes. Add the granulated sugar and beat until fluffy, about 2 minutes. Add the eggs, one at a time, and beat on low speed until combined. Add the vanilla and beat on medium-high speed until combined.

4. Turn the mixer speed to low and add the flour mixture alternately with the buttermilk in small batches, beginning and ending with the flour mixture, and beat to combine. Beat for a few seconds more to be sure the mixture is completely combined. Divide the batter evenly between the two prepared pans.

5. Bake for 40 minutes, or until a tester inserted into the centers of the cakes comes out clean. Transfer the pans to wire racks to cool for 10 minutes, then turn the cakes out onto the wire racks, carefully peel off the parchment paper, and let cool completely. (At this point, you can freeze the cake layers, tightly wrapped in plastic wrap, for up to 3 months.)

CONTINUED >>

6. TO MAKE THE FROSTING: In a medium heavy-bottomed saucepan over medium heat, bring the cream to a simmer. Watch it carefully so it doesn't burn. Once it begins to simmer, turn off the heat, add the brown sugar, and whisk briefly until just combined. Add the chocolate chips and let sit for about 4 minutes until the chocolate has melted. After 4 minutes, whisk until the mixture is smooth and shiny.

7. Depending on the temperature in your kitchen, you can leave the mixture on the counter and whisk every so often as it cools to a spreadable consistency. If it is hot in your kitchen or you want to speed up the process, place the saucepan in the refrigerator and whisk every so often until it reaches a spreadable consistency. With either method, watch the frosting closely—it can go from a bit too runny to too hard to spread quite quickly.

8. Once the frosting has reached a spreadable consistency, place one of the cake layers on a serving plate, bottom-side up (this is the flat side that the parchment paper was on). If you want to keep the plate clean, tuck some pieces of wax paper or parchment paper under the perimeter of the cake before frosting it. (Remove them once the cake is frosted.)

9. Use a pastry brush to brush off any crumbs that might be clinging to the cake. Spread the top of the cake with an even layer of frosting

that is about ¼ in [6 mm] thick. Place the next cake layer on top of the frosted layer, again bottom-side up. If you like, apply a crumb coat (see box below) before applying the final layer of frosting.

10. Frost the top of the cake first, and then the sides, with an even ¼-in- [6-mm-] thick layer of frosting (or a bit more, if you like). Once the cake is frosted, tidy it up and add swirls or swooshes to the frosting, if desired.

Store, lightly covered, at room temperature for up to 3 days. Do not freeze the frosted cake.

VARIATION

CUPCAKES: Line 24 standard-size muffin cups with paper liners or grease with butter. Divide the batter evenly among the cups. Bake at 350°F [180°C] for 25 to 30 minutes, or until a tester inserted into one of the cupcakes comes out clean. Remove from the oven and turn the cupcakes out onto wire racks to cool.

Once the cupcakes are completely cool, frost as desired.

Store as you would the cake. Makes 24 cupcakes.

CRUMB COATS

Professional cake makers like to frost cakes with a crumb coat, a very thin layer of frosting spread over the top and sides of the cake to seal any loose crumbs in place. There's no need to worry about how a crumb coat looks—its job is to make the final layer of frosting look smooth and free of crumbs (crumbs are often a different color from the frosting). Once the crumb coat is applied, the next layer of frosting goes on easily and looks beautiful.

SAVOIARDI

MAKES ABOUT 36 COOKIES

These are the delicate Italian version of ladyfingers, the crispy sponge cookies that are used for tiramisu. *Savoiardi* are also lovely cookies to eat on their own. Fragile and airy, savoiardi are perfect for an afternoon treat with tea, or after dinner as a light dessert. The entire recipe is needed for the tiramisu recipe on page 229. If you want extras for snacking, make two batches.

3 extra-large eggs, separated
6 Tbsp [75 g] granulated sugar
¾ cup [110 g] Jeanne's Gluten-Free All-Purpose Flour (page 39)
6 Tbsp [45 g] confectioners' sugar

1. Position racks in the middle and bottom of the oven and preheat to 350°F [180°C]. Line two large baking sheets with parchment paper. Fit a pastry bag with a medium-size round tip (I use an Ateco #804).

2. Place the egg whites in the clean and dry bowl of a stand mixer (any stray fat in the bowl will inhibit the whites from increasing in volume) fitted with the whisk attachment. Beat the whites on medium-high speed until stiff peaks form. Turn the speed to low and slowly add the granulated sugar and beat until combined, then increase the speed to medium-high and beat until the mixture is stiff and glossy.

3. In a small bowl, whisk the egg yolks until they are foamy. Remove the bowl with the egg white mixture from the mixer. Add the beaten yolks slowly at one side of the bowl and carefully fold the yolks into the egg whites. Be gentle, but do

this as quickly as possible so as not to deflate the egg whites any more than you have to.

4. Carefully sift the flour over the egg mixture and fold in gently, again doing so as quickly as possible so you don't deflate the mixture any more than you have to.

5. Place half the batter in the pastry bag and pipe out 3½-in- [9-cm-] long strips of dough onto a prepared baking sheet about 1 in [2.5 cm] apart. Hold the tip above the sheet as you pipe out the batter so that you don't squish the batter—you want each strip to be as fluffy as possible. Repeat with the remaining batter and baking sheet. Each baking sheet should have about 18 strips of dough on it.

6. Sift half the confectioners' sugar over the strips of dough. Wait for 5 minutes, then sift the remaining confectioners' sugar over the strips of dough. The coating of sifted confectioners' sugar gives the cookies their crispness. Place a baking sheet on each oven rack.

7. Bake for 10 minutes, then switch the positions of the baking sheets as well as their orientation (rotating the ends that were in the back to the front) and bake for another 10 minutes. The cookies should be light brown on the bottom.

8. Carefully transfer the savoiardi to wire racks to cool. If they stick to the parchment paper, use a metal spatula to gently lift them off the paper. Let the cookies cool completely.

Store in an airtight container, layered with wax paper, for up to 3 days. Do not freeze.

TIRAMISU

Tiramisu ("pick me up" in Italian) is a popular dessert that was developed in the Veneto region of Italy, probably in the late 1960s or early 1970s. It is a confection of ladyfinger cookies dipped in espresso layered with a *zabaione* (also called zabaglione, a Marsala-flavored custard) mixed with mascarpone cheese and whipped cream and topped with a dusting of unsweetened cocoa powder.

1 cup [240 ml] boiling water

2 Tbsp instant espresso or coffee powder (decaffeinated is fine)

1½ tsp granulated sugar, plus ½ cup [100 g]

1½ tsp rum (optional)

4 egg yolks

⅓ cup [80 ml] Marsala (or a good red table wine)

1 lb [455 g] mascarpone, cold

1 cup [240 ml] heavy cream, cold

1 recipe Savoiardi (page 227)

Unsweetened cocoa powder for dusting

1. In a medium bowl, stir together the water, instant espresso, 1½ tsp sugar, and rum (if using) until combined and the sugar has dissolved. Let cool.

2. In a metal bowl set over a saucepan of simmering (not boiling) water, use a hand mixer on medium speed or a whisk to beat together the egg yolks, Marsala, and remaining ½ cup [100 g] sugar until tripled in volume, about 5 minutes.

3. Remove the bowl from the heat and use a hand mixer on medium speed or a whisk to beat in the mascarpone until just combined. You may want to set the bowl on a clean kitchen towel to stop the bowl from moving around on the counter.

4. In the bowl of a stand mixer fitted with the whisk attachment, beat the cream until it forms stiff peaks. Remove the bowl from the mixer. Use a rubber spatula to gently fold the mascarpone mixture into the cream until thoroughly blended.

5. Submerge a savoiardo in the espresso mixture quickly. Don't let the savoiardo sit in the mixture too long—it will disintegrate. Place the savoiardo in an 8-in [20-cm] square pan. Dip another savoiardo in the espresso mixture and place it in the pan next to the first one. Repeat the process until the bottom of the pan is covered with savoiardo. I usually place the savoiardi side by side in two rows across the bottom of the pan and then fill in the middle space with a couple more savoiardi. I usually get about 16 savoiardi per layer.

6. Spread half the mascarpone mixture over the layer of savoiardi. Place another layer of dipped savoiardi over the mascarpone. Spread the remaining mascarpone mixture on top of the savoiardi and smooth the top. Dust with a layer of cocoa powder.

7. Cover the pan with plastic wrap and refrigerate for at least 6 hours to allow the flavors to meld.

8. Before serving, let the tiramisu sit at room temperature for about 30 minutes. Dust with more cocoa powder just before serving.

Store, lightly covered, in the refrigerator for up to 4 days. Do not freeze.

CREAM PUFFS

MAKES 36 CREAM PUFFS

Cream puffs are lighter-than-air pastry pillows made from pâte à choux dough. They are usually filled with whipped cream and topped with a chocolate glaze. There is nothing more cheerful than seeing a plate full of cream puffs. The fact that they are delicious just adds to their charm.

1 recipe Pâte à Choux Dough (page 248)
1 recipe Sweetened Whipped Cream (facing page)
1 recipe Chocolate Ganache Glaze (facing page)

1. Preheat the oven to 425°F [220°C]. Line two large baking sheets with parchment paper.

2. Drop the pâte à choux dough by the table-spoon onto the prepared baking sheets at least 1 in [2.5 cm] apart. I find that it's easiest to do this using a 1-Tbsp portion scoop or a pastry bag fitted with a ⅜-in [1-cm] tip (I use an Ateco #804). Tidy the mounds of dough by lightly pressing down on any points with a fingertip dipped in water.

3. Bake, one sheet at a time, for 10 minutes, or until the dough puffs up, and then lower the oven temperature to 350°F [180°C] and bake for another 20 to 25 minutes, or until the puffs are golden brown. Do not open the oven while the cream puffs are baking except to check their color after 20 minutes. Transfer to a wire rack to cool completely.

4. Bring the oven temperature back to 425°F [220°C] and bake the second sheet of puffs. (At this point, you can transfer the cream puffs to a paper bag at room temperature for up to 3 days, or to an airtight container in the freezer for up to 2 months. Recrisp in a 350°F [180°C] oven for about 10 minutes before filling.)

5. Once the cream puffs are completely cool, fill them with whipped cream. Do this one of two ways: Cut each puff in half horizontally and spoon about 2 tsp whipped cream onto the bottom half of the puff and cover with the top half of the puff. Or, fill them using a pastry bag fitted with a ¼-in [6-mm] tip (I use an Ateco #801). Insert the tip in the bottom center of the puffs and slowly pipe in the cream until it starts to come back out of the puff. Filled puffs quickly become soft and soggy, so repeat the process only with as many puffs as are to be eaten within an hour.

6. Dip the top of each cream puff in the ganache glaze and place on the wire rack for about 30 minutes for the ganache to set before serving.

SWEETENED WHIPPED CREAM

MAKES ABOUT 1½ CUPS [360 ML]

This filling is also a nice topping for Crêpes (page 110) and for fresh berries.

1 cup [240 ml] heavy cream

2 Tbsp confectioners' sugar, sifted

½ tsp pure vanilla extract

Pour the cream into a chilled bowl and add the confectioners' sugar and vanilla. Using a hand mixer, beat the cream to the desired consistency. For a cream puff filling, beat to stiff peaks. For a topping for crêpes or berries, beat to soft peaks.

Store tightly covered with plastic wrap in the refrigerator for up to 1 day. If liquid separates from the cream, whip it again to incorporate. Do not freeze.

CHOCOLATE GANACHE GLAZE

MAKES ⅔ CUP [160 ML]

This soft chocolate glaze can also be used for the tops of Éclairs (page 232).

½ cup [120 ml] heavy cream

⅔ cup [115 g] semisweet chocolate chips or chopped semisweet chocolate

Heat the cream in a small heavy-bottomed saucepan over low heat. Just as it begins to simmer, remove from the heat and add the chocolate chips. Let sit for 1 minute to allow the chocolate to melt and then whisk until the mixture is combined and smooth.

Store in an airtight container in the refrigerator for up to 3 days. Before using, bring back to room temperature. Do not freeze.

ÉCLAIRS

MAKES 24 ÉCLAIRS

When I was in high school, I was involved in community theater. One summer, I ran lighting for a play at an outdoor theater that was near an authentic French pastry shop. Whenever I had the time, I would stop by the shop and pick up an éclair to treat myself at the end of the night's performance. Those éclairs were amazing. They contained a delicate chocolate pastry cream and had a chocolate ganache glaze on top. I've often thought of those éclairs in the years since, and I've re-created them. These éclairs have the signature light and crispy pastry shell filled with a silky pastry cream and topped with a just-sweet-enough chocolate glaze. *Éclair* is French for "lightning," which is thought to refer to how quickly they tend to be eaten. Although I am partial to éclairs with a chocolate pastry cream, you may use the vanilla variation instead.

1 recipe Pâte à Choux Dough (page 248)
1 recipe Chocolate Pastry Cream (page 234)
1 recipe Chocolate Ganache Glaze (page 231)

1. Preheat the oven to 425°F [220°C]. Line two large baking sheets with parchment paper.

2. Fill a pastry bag fitted with a ½-in [12-mm] round pastry tip (I use an Ateco #807) with half of the dough. Pipe out 5-in [13-cm] logs of dough onto a prepared baking sheet, about 1 in [2.5 cm] apart. Repeat with the remaining dough. You should have about 12 logs per sheet.

3. Bake, one sheet at a time, for 10 minutes, until the dough puffs up, and then lower the oven temperature to 350°F [180°C] and bake for another 20 to 25 minutes, or until the puffs are golden brown. Do not open the oven while the éclairs are baking except to check their color after 20 minutes. Transfer to a wire rack to cool completely.

4. Bring the oven temperature back to 425°F [220°C] and bake the second sheet of éclairs. (At this point, you can transfer the éclairs to a paper bag at room temperature for up to 3 days, or to an airtight container in the freezer for up to 2 months. Recrisp in a 350°F [180°C] oven for about 10 minutes before filling.)

5. Once the éclairs are completely cool, use a sharp knife to cut along one long side of each. Leave the other long side intact—it will act as a hinge for opening and closing the éclair. Spoon 1 Tbsp pastry cream into the middle. Close the éclair and return it to the wire rack. Filled puffs quickly become soft and soggy, so repeat the process only with as many éclairs as are to be eaten within an hour.

6. Use a small spatula to smooth a bit of ganache glaze along the top of each éclair and place on the wire rack for about 30 minutes for the ganache to set before serving.

CHOCOLATE PASTRY CREAM

MAKES 3 CUPS [710 ML]

Pastry cream is a thick custard that is used in a variety of cakes, tarts, and pastries. In addition to éclairs, this cream can also be used instead of the Sweetened Whipped Cream in Cream Puffs (page 230).

½ cup [100 g] granulated sugar

6 egg yolks, at room temperature

½ cup [70 g] Jeanne's Gluten-Free All-Purpose Flour (page 39)

Pinch of salt

2½ cups [600 ml] milk

½ cup [85 g] semisweet chocolate chips, or chopped semisweet chocolate

1 Tbsp pure vanilla extract

1. In a large heatproof bowl, whisk the sugar and egg yolks. Sift in the flour and salt and whisk to combine. You will have a loose paste. Don't let the mixture sit too long or else the sugar will cook the egg by a chemical reaction. Place the bowl on a kitchen towel set on the counter—it will stop the bowl from moving around the counter during the next step.

2. In a heavy-bottomed saucepan, bring the milk to just simmering (do not boil). Remove from the heat and slowly add the milk to the egg mixture, whisking continuously in order not to cook the egg. Whisk until smooth.

3. Pour the mixture back into the saucepan and cook over medium heat until just boiling. Stir the mixture continuously with a whisk, but don't actually whisk it—the bubbles created will make it difficult to see when the mixture starts to simmer. Once it's simmering, continuously move the whisk through the mixture for 30 to 60 seconds, or until the mixture thickens. Add the chocolate chips and whisk until they melt. Remove from the heat and whisk in the vanilla until the mixture is smooth. If some of the egg did get cooked and chunks are appearing in the mixture, strain the cream into a bowl through a sieve to remove the chunks.

4. Pour the mixture into a bowl. Lay a circle of wax paper directly on the surface so that a film doesn't form on the cream. Let cool to room temperature.

Store in the refrigerator for up to 3 days. Whisk before using to get rid of any lumps that may have formed. Do not freeze.

VARIATION

VANILLA PASTRY CREAM: Simply omit the chocolate from the recipe.

BLUEBERRY GALETTE

MAKES 8 TO 10 SERVINGS

A galette is a free-form pie that looks a bit like a large cookie. It is made by wrapping a layer of pie crust around a fruit filling. Galettes are quick and easy to make and are the perfect answer to occasions when you want a pie but don't want to spend much time making one. Since a galette has only one layer of crust, it takes less time to make. Galettes are an ideal dessert to whip up at the last minute, and they look pretty on a plate. Just about any fruit can be used in a galette (my favorite choices are berries or peaches in summer and apples or pears in fall and winter). I've chosen blueberry here, but feel free to substitute your favorite berries or sliced fruit. This recipe doesn't include any spices—my goal is to let the flavor of the fruit shine, amplified by a bit of sugar and vanilla extract. Galettes are supposed to look rustic, so it doesn't matter if the crust is a bit ragged around the edges.

2 cups [285 g] fresh blueberries, rinsed

½ tsp pure vanilla extract

3 Tbsp granulated sugar, plus more for sprinkling

1 Tbsp Jeanne's Gluten-Free All-Purpose Flour (page 39)

½ recipe Pie Crust dough (see page 246)

Tapioca flour for dusting

1 egg beaten with 1 Tbsp water, for egg wash

1. Preheat the oven to 425°F [220°C]. Line a large baking sheet with parchment paper.

2. In a large bowl, mix together the blueberries and vanilla with a large spoon. Add the sugar and all-purpose flour and mix until combined.

3. Remove the disk of dough from the refrigerator and unwrap. Dust a work surface with tapioca flour and roll out the dough to about 12 in [30 cm] in diameter (or roll the dough out between two pieces of plastic wrap). Carefully transfer the crust to the prepared baking sheet (remove the plastic wrap if you used it for rolling).

4. Carefully spread the blueberry mixture on the dough, leaving a 2-in [5-cm] border around the perimeter. Gently fold the edges of the crust over the filling, pleating the dough as necessary. The outer crust will be folded over about 2 in [5 cm], leaving a portion of the fruit exposed in the middle. Gently brush the crust with the egg wash and sprinkle with additional sugar.

5. Bake until the crust is golden brown, about 25 minutes. Remove from the oven and place the baking sheet on a wire rack to cool.

6. The galette is fairly delicate, so if you want to transfer it to a plate for serving, use the parchment paper to help you move it. Grasp the edges of the parchment and gently lift up the galette and quickly place it on a serving plate. Then use scissors to cut the paper around the edges of the galette to tidy it up. Serve warm or at room temperature.

Store, lightly covered, at room temperature for up to 3 days. Do not freeze.

PEACH PIE

Peaches symbolize the height of summer and all of its pleasures. In Seattle, the weather can be dreary much of the year, but summers are spectacular. Seattleites look forward to the glory days of July and August when the weather is warm, dry, and sunny. So, when peaches come into season, it means summer is really here. I wanted to let the taste of the peaches shine through in this pie, so the spices are light and designed to showcase the fruits' sweet and slightly tart flavor notes. For a cold-weather pies, use apples instead of peaches. There's no need to peel the apples before slicing.

4 cups [800 g] peeled and sliced fresh peaches

¼ cup [35 g] Jeanne's Gluten-Free All-Purpose Flour (page 39)

¾ cup [150 g] granulated sugar, plus more for sprinkling

½ tsp ground cinnamon

¼ tsp ground nutmeg

⅛ tsp ground ginger

¼ tsp salt

1 recipe Pie Crust (page 246), lined into a pie pan for a double-crust pie and refrigerated

2 Tbsp unsalted butter, cold and cut into small pieces

1 egg beaten with 1 Tbsp water, for egg wash

1. Preheat the oven to 425°F [220°C].

2. Place the peaches in a large bowl. Add the flour, sugar, cinnamon, nutmeg, ginger, and salt and mix with a large spoon to combine—be sure that the peaches are well coated with the mixture.

3. Remove the lined pan from the refrigerator and pour in the filling. Dot the top of the filling with the butter. Place the dough for the top crust over the filling, seal the edges, and make small slits in the top of the dough in a few places to make vents for steam to escape. Brush the top of the dough with the egg wash and sprinkle with additional sugar.

4. Bake for 25 minutes. Lower the oven temperature to 350°F [180°C] and bake for another 35 minutes. The crust should be golden brown but not burned. Start watching it at around 25 minutes to make sure it doesn't burn. Transfer the pie to a wire rack to cool. Serve warm or at room temperature.

Store, lightly covered, at room temperature for up to 3 days. Do not freeze.

CHOCOLATE CREAM PIE

Chocolate cream pie is pure comfort. Crunchy bittersweet chocolate cookie crust, rich and creamy pudding in the middle, and lightly sweetened whipped cream on top. This is easy to put together the night before you present it since it needs to be chilled before serving. Also, the filling is basically chocolate pudding, which you can eat by itself for a creamy snack or dessert anytime you like.

CRUST
2½ cups [350 g] Chocolate Cookie Crumbs (recipe follows)
¼ cup [50 g] granulated sugar
¼ cup [55 g] unsalted butter, melted

FILLING
5 oz [140 g] semisweet chocolate chips or chopped semisweet chocolate
2 oz [55 g] chopped unsweetened chocolate
⅔ cup [130 g] granulated sugar
¼ cup [30 g] tapioca flour
¼ tsp salt
3 cups [720 ml] milk
2 tsp pure vanilla extract

TOPPING
1 cup [240 ml] heavy cream, cold
1 Tbsp granulated sugar

1. **TO MAKE THE CRUST:** Preheat the oven to 350°F [180°C].

2. In a medium bowl, mix together the cookie crumbs and sugar. Add the melted butter and stir until the crumb mixture is well coated.

3. Press the crumb mixture into a 9-in [23-in] pie pan so that it covers the bottom and goes partway up the sides.

4. Bake for 20 minutes. Transfer to a wire rack to cool completely.

5. **TO MAKE THE FILLING:** In a small heavy-bottomed saucepan, melt the semisweet chocolate and unsweetened chocolate over very low heat. Watch the chocolate closely so it doesn't burn. Just before both chocolates are completely melted, remove from the heat and whisk until smooth and free of lumps.

6. In a medium heavy-bottomed saucepan over medium heat, whisk the sugar, tapioca flour, and salt until combined. Add the milk in small amounts, whisking after each addition to make sure no lumps form—the mixture should be smooth. Add the vanilla and whisk to combine.

7. Increase the heat to medium-high and bring the mixture to a boil, whisking continuously. Once the mixture has reached the texture of heavy cream, remove from the heat. Add the melted chocolate to the milk mixture and whisk until the mixture is smooth and thick—the texture should be that of pudding.

8. Let the mixture cool to room temperature, whisking every so often. Once the mixture is at room temperature, lay a piece of a wax paper on the surface of the pudding so that a skin doesn't form and place in the refrigerator to chill completely, about 2 hours.

9. Once the filling has chilled, uncover and pour it over the crust. Use a rubber spatula to smooth it evenly. Cover lightly with plastic wrap and refrigerate for at least 2 hours, or up to 24 hours.

10. **TO MAKE THE TOPPING:** In the bowl of a stand mixer fitted with the whisk attachment, beat the cream on medium-high speed until thick. Sprinkle the sugar over the cream and beat just until the cream holds stiff peaks (do not beat any longer because you'll run the risk of beating it into butter).

11. Remove the pie from the refrigerator and unwrap. Use a large spoon to scrape the whipped cream onto the top of the filling. Use a rubber spatula to smooth the cream evenly over the top of the chocolate, leaving a 1-in [2.5-cm] border around the perimeter.

Store, covered, in the refrigerator for up to 3 days. Do not freeze.

CHOCOLATE COOKIE CRUMBS

MAKES ABOUT 3 CUPS [420 G]

(ENOUGH TO LINE A 9-IN [23-CM] SPRINGFORM PAN OR PIE PAN, WITH SOME LEFT OVER)

One thing that used to stop me from making a cheesecake or a cream pie was that I had to make a batch of cookies and then crush them in order to make the crust. Then I saw and adapted a recipe for making cookie crumbs in the excellent *Momofuku Milk Bar* cookbook by Christina Tosi. Making cookie crumbs themselves instead of making the cookies and then crushing them is a brilliant idea. Use these as you would any crushed cookies—for any type of tart, pie, or cheesecake that needs a chocolate cookie crust. This recipe makes a bit more than most recipes call for—which isn't a problem because my family likes them sprinkled over ice cream or even yogurt.

1 cup [145 g] Jeanne's Gluten-Free All-Purpose Flour (page 39)

¾ cup [150 g] granulated sugar

1 cup [100 g] unsweetened cocoa powder

1 tsp salt

1 tsp baking soda

6 Tbsp [85 g] unsalted butter, melted

1. Preheat the oven to 300°F [150°C]. Line a large rimmed baking sheet with parchment paper.

2. In the bowl of a stand mixer fitted with the paddle attachment, mix the flour, sugar, cocoa powder, salt, and baking soda on low speed until combined.

3. Add the butter and mix on low speed until the mixture starts to come together in lumps. Spread the lumps on the prepared baking sheet.

4. Bake for 30 minutes, using a metal spatula to break up the lumps every so often. The crumbs should be slightly moist to the touch, but they will dry and harden as they cool. Let the crumbs cool completely before using.

Store in an airtight container at room temperature for up to 5 days, or in the freezer for up to 4 months.

CHEESECAKE

Cheesecake is one of those recipes that has as many variations as there are cookbooks. But at the end the day, I like a basic cheesecake the best. Smooth and creamy, with the tang of the cream cheese playing off the sweetness of the sugar, and the crust providing a satisfying crunch, a cheesecake needs no embellishments to make it a perfect dessert.

CRUST

1 recipe Gingersnap Cookie Crumbs (facing page) or Chocolate Cookie Crumbs (page 239)

2 Tbsp granulated sugar

5 Tbsp [70 g] unsalted butter, melted

FILLING

2 lb [910 g] cream cheese, at room temperature

1 Tbsp Jeanne's Gluten-Free All-Purpose Flour (page 39)

¼ tsp salt

1¼ cups [250 g] granulated sugar

1 Tbsp pure vanilla extract

4 extra-large eggs

1. **TO MAKE THE CRUST:** Preheat the oven to 375°F [190°C].

2. In a medium bowl, mix together the cookie crumbs and sugar. Add the melted butter and mix until the crumb mixture is well coated. Turn the mixture out into a 9-in [23-cm] springform pan and use your fingers to press the mixture into an even layer on the bottom of the pan.

3. Bake for 12 minutes. Transfer the pan to a wire rack to cool.

4. **TO MAKE THE FILLING:** Lower the oven temperature to 300°F [150°C].

5. In the bowl of a stand mixer fitted with the paddle attachment, beat the cream cheese, flour, and salt on medium-high speed until smooth and fluffy, without any lumps, about 4 minutes. Add the sugar and beat until well combined and smooth, 1 minute more. Add the vanilla and beat until combined.

6. Add the eggs one at a time, beating after each addition until just combined and smooth. Be careful not to overbeat the eggs because it will cause the cake to rise too high and crack on top.

7. Scrape the filling over the crust. Bake for 60 to 65 minutes. When done, the edges should be puffed and the middle of the cheesecake should jiggle when the pan is shaken. Remove from the oven and place on a wire rack to cool completely. Once the cheesecake is completely cool, cover with plastic wrap and refrigerate for at least 5 hours, or up to 2 days.

8. When ready to serve, unclasp and remove the side of the pan. If you also want to remove the bottom of the pan before placing the cheesecake on a serving plate, run a long, thin metal spatula under the bottom of the cake to separate it from the bottom of the pan. Use a large metal spatula to slide the cake onto a serving plate (I usually just leave the cake on the bottom of the pan).

Store lightly wrapped in plastic wrap in the refrigerator for up to 3 days. Do not freeze.

GINGERSNAP COOKIE CRUMBS

MAKES ABOUT 3 CUPS [420 G]

**(ENOUGH TO LINE A 9-IN [23-CM] SPRINGFORM PAN OR PIE PAN,
WITH SOME COOKIE CRUMBS LEFT OVER)**

Okay, I admit it. After developing the recipe for Chocolate Cookie Crumbs (page 239), I couldn't stop making cookie crumbs. This is a recipe for gingersnap cookie crumbs that pairs excellently with cheesecake. Here, too, this recipe makes more than is usually needed for most recipes, so you'll have some leftover cookie crumbs for snacking or sprinkling over ice cream.

6 Tbsp [85 g] unsalted butter, melted

2 Tbsp unsulphured molasses

1 cup [145 g] Jeanne's Gluten-Free All-Purpose Flour (page 39)

1 tsp baking soda

¼ tsp salt

½ tsp ground cinnamon

1 tsp ground ginger

¼ tsp ground cloves

½ cup [100 g] granulated sugar

1. Preheat the oven to 300°F [150°C]. Line a large rimmed baking sheet with parchment paper.

2. In a small bowl, whisk together the butter and molasses.

3. In the bowl of a stand mixer fitted with the paddle attachment, mix the flour, baking soda, salt, cinnamon, ginger, cloves, and sugar on low speed until combined.

4. Add the butter mixture to the flour mixture and mix on low speed until the ingredients form small lumps. Spread the lumps on the prepared baking sheet.

5. Bake for 20 minutes, using a metal spatula to break up the lumps every so often. The crumbs should be slightly moist to the touch, but they will dry and harden as they cool. Let the crumbs cool completely before using.

Store in an airtight container at room temperature for up to 5 days, or in the freezer for up to 4 months.

Baklava is a delectable pastry of Turkish origin made from phyllo dough layered with a nut mixture that is then covered with a spiced sugar syrup. Originally only baked on holidays and special occasions, baklava has come to be a beloved dessert found at Mediterranean restaurants and delis. I am so proud of this recipe—it is impossible to find gluten-free commercial versions of baklava because no one makes gluten-free phyllo dough. But I do! My husband and daughter regularly order baklava from our neighborhood Afghani restaurant, and I am so happy to finally be able to make my own to enjoy with them. Feel free to mix two or more types of nuts—walnuts and/or pistachios are the most traditional, but I love to use pecans.

SYRUP

¼ cup [50 g] granulated sugar

¼ cup [85 g] honey

¾ cup [180 ml] water

1 lemon slice

½ cinnamon stick

1 Tbsp orange flower water, rose water, or vanilla extract

FILLING

1½ cups [185 g] nuts of your choice, toasted (see page 42) and coarsely chopped

2 Tbsp granulated sugar

1 tsp ground cinnamon

⅛ tsp ground cloves

1 recipe Phyllo Dough (page 245)

Tapioca flour for dusting

Unsalted butter for greasing, plus 1 cup [230 g], melted

1. **TO MAKE THE SYRUP:** In a heavy-bottomed saucepan over medium heat, combine the sugar, honey, water, lemon slice, cinnamon stick, and orange flower water. Simmer, stirring frequently, until the sugar and honey have dissolved and the mixture is somewhat thick. Do not boil. Once the syrup has simmered for about 30 minutes and is somewhat thick, turn off the heat, remove the lemon slice and the cinnamon stick, and let cool.

2. **TO MAKE THE FILLING:** In a medium bowl, mix together the nuts, sugar, ground cinnamon, and cloves and set aside.

3. Divide the phyllo dough into 11 Ping-Pong-ball-size balls. (You will be rolling out all 11 pieces of dough before you start to assemble the baklava. If possible, use a small Asian rolling pin to roll the dough.) Lightly dust a rolling surface and the top of the dough with tapioca flour. (The dough may stick to itself—if a piece of dough ends up on the rolling pin, it will also stick to the dough you're rolling and tear it. If this happens, I've found that it's best to scrape the dough off the rolling pin with a bench scraper after rolling each piece. Also, the rolling technique should be quick but careful. The more the rolling pin lingers on the dough, the more likely the dough is to stick to it.)

4. Roll out a ball of dough until it is thin enough to see through (it will be thinner than a piece of paper). I roll the dough until I can see the grain of my wooden rolling board under it. Then, using an 8-in [20-cm] square baking pan as a template, cut the dough into pan-size squares with a sharp knife. Remove the pan, pick up the

CONTINUED >>

cut piece of dough, and place it on a plate that is sprinkled lightly with tapioca flour.

5. Repeat the rolling and cutting process with the remaining ten pieces of dough, stacking them on top of each other on the plate. They shouldn't stick to each other. There's no need to cover them while you are rolling the other balls—it's good for them to dry out a little bit before assembling the baklava.

6. Preheat the oven to 375°F [190°C]. Grease an 8-in [20-cm] square baking pan with butter.

7. Place a piece of phyllo in the bottom of the prepared pan. Using a pastry brush, lightly brush the dough with some of the melted butter. Place another sheet of phyllo on top of the first sheet and lightly brush it with butter. Repeat the process until there are five sheets of phyllo in the pan.

8. Sprinkle half the filling over the stacked sheets of phyllo.

9. Place a sheet of phyllo on top of the filling and brush it lightly with melted butter. Sprinkle the remaining half of the filling on top of this piece.

10. Place another sheet of phyllo on top of the second layer of filling and brush lightly with melted butter. Continue layering the remaining four sheets of phyllo and brushing with melted butter. You should have the following layers: five sheets of phyllo on the bottom of the pan; a layer of filling; one sheet of phyllo; another layer of filling; and five sheets of phyllo on top. Carefully cut it into sixteen 2-in [5-cm] squares with a sharp knife.

11. Bake for 30 minutes, then increase the oven temperature to 475°F [240°C] and bake for 10 minutes longer, until the top is golden brown and the top layer of phyllo has shrunk a bit.

12. Remove the baklava from the oven. Carefully and slowly pour the syrup over the hot baklava and let sit until completely cool, at least 1 hour. Once the baklava is cool, cut the squares again.

Store covered with plastic wrap at room temperature for up to 3 days.

PHYLLO DOUGH

MAKES ABOUT 1 LB [455 G]

Phyllo comes from the Greek word for "leaf." Phyllo dough is considered to be almost impossible to make at home. Part of the reason for this is that traditional phyllo is rolled and then stretched and pulled into a gigantic sheet of transparent dough that is eventually draped over a large table or other huge surface. Then it's cut and layered in both sweet and savory dishes. Gluten-free dough isn't that elastic and it doesn't stretch like this. So I start with small portions of dough, which roll into small sizes. The dough is still rolled out very thinly—so thin that you can see through it—it's just not dining-table size. I've adapted the following recipe from the terrific cookbook *Kaffeehaus: Exquisite Desserts from the Classic Cafés of Vienna, Budapest, and Prague* by the inimitable Rick Rodgers.

This dough is best used by rolling out pieces to fit the recipe you're making. For example, when I make baklava, I roll out a Ping-Pong-ball–size ball of dough until it is very thin, then I place the pan in which the baklava will be assembled on the dough and cut around the perimeter of the pan with a sharp knife to create a piece that fits the pan exactly.

¾ cup plus 3 Tbsp [225 ml] water
¼ cup [60 ml] vegetable oil
1 tsp cider vinegar
2⅔ cups [385 g] Jeanne's Gluten-Free All-Purpose Flour (page 39)
¼ tsp salt

1. In glass measuring cup, whisk together the water, vegetable oil, and vinegar.

2. In the bowl of a stand mixer fitted with the dough hook, combine the flour and salt. Add the water mixture and beat on low speed to combine, then increase the speed to medium and beat for 5 minutes.

3. Remove the dough from the mixer. It should be smooth and very stiff. Using your hands, form it into a ball by holding it in one hand and hitting it with the heel of your other hand. Turn and hit it again with the heel of your hand. Repeat the process several times until the outside of the dough is smooth.

4. Wrap the dough tightly with plastic wrap and let sit for at least 1 hour, or up to 4 hours, to rest and hydrate before using. Phyllo does not freeze well.

PIE CRUST

A well-made pie crust is a joy to behold and a delight to eat. It is flaky and buttery and is the perfect partner for the filling inside, whether sweet or savory. That said, the amount of fear people seem to have of pie crust astounds me. Pie crusts are easy to make and yet people tell me all the time that they just "aren't a pie-crust person." When I press for information, what I learn is that either the person has never tried to make a pie crust and is afraid to, or the person had a bad experience making one and never tried to make another. There are a few reasons for this fear.

First, many people don't realize that pie crust dough is temperature-dependent. The flakiness in a pie crust is created by keeping the fat in the dough solid (i.e., cold) until it is put in the oven. When it's heated in the oven, the water in the fat and the dough creates steam that pushes up against the layers of dough, creating the flakiness. If the butter melts into the dough before the pie crust goes into the oven, the crust ends up tough and not flaky because no layers can be formed. Pie crust dough needs to be cold enough that the butter doesn't melt into the dough yet warm enough to roll properly. There is a small window of temperatures where this occurs.

Second, many gluten-intolerant folks can't eat dairy, so they use butter substitutes. I've found that butter substitutes don't work well in pie crust. Butter substitutes contain too much water and they melt at a much lower temperature than butter, lard, or shortening.

Thus, if you are dairy-free, try using shortening for your pie crust instead of a butter replacer (see page 29).

Third, to get a flaky pie crust, the baker needs to use as little liquid in the dough as possible. Using too much liquid results in a tough dough because the liquid glues the crust together.

Finally, rolling the crust worries folks because they think it won't come out well. Here's a tip: Roll the dough between two pieces of plastic wrap. This keeps the dough together.

It is important to prepare the dough in a cool environment. A kitchen that is 60° to 67°F [15° to 19°C] is ideal. A kitchen that is too warm will make preparing the pie crust more difficult, because it is more difficult to keep the dough at the optimal temperature. If you are making the dough on a day that is supposed to be very warm, start early in the morning and cool the dough in the refrigerator as often as is needed.

2½ cups [360 g] Jeanne's Gluten-Free All-Purpose Flour (page 39)

1 Tbsp granulated sugar

¼ tsp salt

1 cup [220 g] unsalted butter, cold and cut into pieces

1 Tbsp vinegar (optional; I use apple cider vinegar)

4 to 7 Tbsp ice-cold water (use as little as possible)

Tapioca flour for dusting

1. In a large bowl, mix together the all-purpose flour, sugar, and salt with a spoon. Add the butter and use your fingers or a pastry cutter to rub the butter into the dry ingredients. This will take a bit of time, so work as quickly as you can so that the butter doesn't get warm and start to melt into the dough. The mixture should look like wet sand mixed with pebbles of varying sizes. (I like to mix the butter in by hand to get a feel for the dough, but you could also pulse the ingredients in a food processor.)

2. Rub the vinegar (if using) into the mixture by hand. Add the water 1 Tbsp at a time, rubbing it into the mixture. Add just enough water to create a dough that holds together but isn't wet.

3. Divide the dough into two equal pieces, shape them into disks, and wrap each disk in plastic wrap. Refrigerate the disks for about 30 minutes, or until the disks are cool and nicely firm but not rock hard—65° to 67°F [18° to 19°C]. If the disks become rock hard, remove them from the refrigerator and leave them on a counter to warm up to 65° to 67°F [18° to 19°C] (but no warmer) before rolling.

4. Dust tapioca flour over a rolling surface and a rolling pin. Remove a disk of dough from the refrigerator and unwrap it. Place the dough on the rolling surface and sprinkle tapioca flour over the dough. The key to successfully rolling out gluten-free pie-crust dough is to go slow and use a light touch. If the dough starts cracking, slow down and don't press as hard with the rolling pin. Carefully and patiently roll out the dough into a round that is 12 in [30 cm] in diameter (it should be about 3 in [8 cm] larger than the pie pan). If the dough sticks to the rolling pin, sprinkle more tapioca flour over the top of the dough. While you're rolling the dough, it should be cool but not too cold. It should roll fairly easily and should not break while you're rolling it. If it does break a little bit, just smooth

the dough over the breaks. If the dough seems too cold, and it's hard to roll and breaking a lot, stop and let it warm up a little before you continue. Alternately, if the dough is floppy and seems to be sweating, then it's too warm and should be refrigerated for a while longer to cool it down. As I mentioned, you can also roll the dough between two sheets of plastic wrap.

5. Next, you are going to roll the dough around the rolling pin to transfer it to the pie pan. Sprinkle tapioca flour over the surface of the dough. Place the rolling pin on one edge of the dough and wrap the dough around the roller until you've gotten all the dough onto the rolling pin. If the dough is at the right temperature, it should roll easily around the pin without breaking. If the dough breaks a lot while you're rolling it around the pin, it's a bit too cold. Stop and let the dough warm up a bit before proceeding.

6. Place the rolling pin at the edge of the pie pan and unroll the dough onto the pie pan so that the pan is covered evenly. Carefully press the dough into place in the pan. Proceed slowly, starting in the middle of the pan and working out to the bottom corners and then up the sides. If the dough breaks, just use your fingers to smooth the dough back together.

7. When the dough reaches the rim of the pan, press it onto the rim. Finally, press down and carefully tear off any dough that hangs over the rim (set these scraps aside—you will use them later).

8. Place the pie pan in the refrigerator while you roll out the second disk of dough.

Store the dough-lined pan or disks of dough individually wrapped in plastic wrap in the refrigerator for up to 3 days. For long-term storage, use a metal pie pan, wrap the dough-lined pan well in plastic wrap, and freeze for up to 3 months.

PÂTE À CHOUX DOUGH

Pâte à choux is one of the most amazing doughs in the pastry world. It is easy to make and it creates pastries that are so light and airy that it almost seems like magic that they puff as much as they do. The secret to the puff is cooking the dough, which gelatinizes the starch in the flour and creates a stronger mesh to contain the steam created by cooking the eggs. And, to be more accurate, pâte à choux is not really a dough, it is a paste. Indeed, it is often called choux paste in the pastry world.

1 cup [240 ml] water

6 Tbsp [85 g] cold unsalted butter, cut into small pieces

½ tsp salt

1½ tsp granulated sugar

1¼ cups [180 g] Jeanne's Gluten-Free All-Purpose Flour (page 39)

4 extra-large eggs

1. In a medium heavy-bottomed pan over medium-high heat, bring the water, butter, salt, and sugar to a rolling boil. Turn the heat to medium-low and add the flour all at once. Stir vigorously with a wooden spoon for 3 minutes. The mixture will be sticky and hard to stir; stir as best you can, moving the dough around to make sure that all the dough hits the bottom of the pan. Starch will begin to cover the bottom of the pan—this is fine.

2. After 3 minutes, remove the pan from the heat. Dump the mixture into the bowl of a stand mixer fitted with the paddle attachment. Mix the dough on medium-high speed until the steam has been released from the dough, about 2 minutes.

3. Once all the steam has been released from the dough, add the eggs, one at a time, mixing on low speed between each addition. At this point the dough will look like a soupy mess. Don't worry—it's supposed to look this way. Mix the dough on medium speed until it stops looking soupy and starts looking like curdled cream (again, normal). Increase the speed to medium-high and beat for about 2½ minutes longer, until the dough moves into its final stage—smooth and satiny. A perfect pâte à choux dough looks like smooth cake frosting (even though it is a very sticky dough). I've found that sometimes a layer of starch ends up on the bottom of the mixing bowl. This is fine—just leave it in the bowl when you scrape out the dough.

Notes: Unshaped pâte à choux dough doesn't store well, because the leavening action is caused by the air bubbles that have been built up during the mixing and cooking process. Storing the dough collapses the air bubbles, creating a dough that doesn't perform well.

Pâte à choux dough is designed to be spooned or piped into shapes for baking or frying. With cream puffs, gougères, and beignets, you can use a table-spoon measure (or better, a 1-Tbsp scoop) to spoon out the dough onto baking sheets or into oil. But for other shapes, such as those used for éclairs, churros, and French crullers, the dough has to be piped out with a pastry bag fitted with a pastry tip. In each recipe, I recommend tip sizes, but as you become more experienced with the dough, you can use the sizes you prefer.

Pâte à choux dough that's been piped into shapes freezes beautifully. Just pipe the desired shape onto a baking sheet lined with parchment paper and place the baking sheet in the freezer. After 30 minutes, remove the baking sheet from the freezer, pop the pâte à choux shapes off the parchment paper, and place them in a zip-top bag. Place the bag in the freezer for up to 3 months. Defrost the shapes before baking.

SOURCES FOR INGREDIENTS AND EQUIPMENT

INGREDIENTS

Gluten-Free Flours and Gums

Authentic Foods *www.authenticfoods.com*

They carry all the flours in my all-purpose flour mix, as well as sorghum flour and xanthan gum. Their Multi-Blend Flour performs well as a substitute for my all-purpose flour mix.

Bob's Red Mill *www.bobsredmill.com*

They carry all the flours used in my all-purpose flour mix and in the sourdough starter, as well as xanthan gum and an aluminum-free double-acting baking powder.

California Rice Oil Company
www.californiariceoil.com

A good source for rice bran oil, a neutral-flavored oil that's perfect for deep-frying.

King Arthur Flour *www.kingarthurflour.com*

Their Gluten-Free Multipurpose Flour performs the closest to mine. It doesn't contain xanthan gum, so you'll need to add that separately (¼ tsp per 1 cup [160 g] of flour).

Maskal Teff *www.teffco.com*

Their teff flour is gluten-free and finely ground. It works well in the sourdough recipe.

Wholesome Sweeteners
www.wholesomesweeteners.com

They have a confectioners' sugar that uses tapioca starch instead of cornstarch.

Raw Quinoa Flakes *www.ancientharvest.com*

EQUIPMENT

King Arthur Flour *www.kingarthurflour.com*

They have a wonderful selection of heavy-duty baking pans and other baking tools that make baking easier. They also carry a hamburger bun pan (under the name "Individual Pie and Burger Bun Pan") and a hot dog bun pan (under the name "New England Hot Dog Bun Pan").

Williams-Sonoma *www.williams-sonoma.com*

Williams-Sonoma has a terrific selection of baking pans that won't warp, rust, or corrode. I like their Traditional Finish line.

Bundt Pans

Nordic Ware *www.buynordicware.com*

Nordic Ware's Bundt pans are heavy-duty and long-lasting, and they offer dozens of shapes and sizes.

Challah Pans

Kaiser Bakeware

Available in countless kitchenware stores and from online retailers.

Cookie Cutters

Ateco Brand

This company manufactures cookie-cutter sets that are quite handy. They are available in countless kitchenware stores and from online retailers.

Dough Rising Containers

Cambro *www.cambro.com*

They offer a selection of dough-rising containers. Some contain bisphenol A (BPA) and some don't. Because of the health problems associated with BPA, I recommend that you buy containers that are BPA-free.

Kitchen Scale

Escali *www.escali.com*

Escali makes a number of kitchen scales that measure in both grams and ounces.

Parchment Paper

www.ifyoucare.com

This brand manufactures parchment paper that is unbleached and coated with silicone and can be composted.

Pastry Bags, Pastry Tips, and Couplers

Ateco Brand

Available in countless kitchenware stores and from online retailers, including www.cakesuppliesdepot.com.

Waffle-Cone Iron

Chef's Choice *www.edgecraft.com*

I use the Waffle Cone Express 838, a stand-alone electric iron, for the ice-cream cone and *stroopwafel* recipes in the book.

INDEX

INDEX